The
Family Book
About
Sexuality

Other Books by the Authors

By Mary S. Calderone, M.D.:

Sexuality and Human Values *(editor)*
Manual of Family Planning and Contraceptive Practice *(editor)*
Release from Sexual Tensions
Abortion in the United States *(editor)*

By Eric W. Johnson:

How to Live Through Junior High School
Love and Sex in Plain Language
Love and Sex and Growing Up *(with Corinne B. Johnson)*
Sex: Telling It Straight
V.D.: Venereal Disease and What You Should Do About It
Guide to the Subject of Sex—For Teachers
How to Relate to Sex Education Programs: A Guide for Parents
How to Achieve Competence in English
Teaching School: Points Picked Up
An Introduction to Jesus of Nazareth

The Family Book About Sexuality

Mary S. Calderone, M.D., and Eric W. Johnson

Drawings by Vivien Cohen

HARPER & ROW, PUBLISHERS, New York
Cambridge, Hagerstown, Philadelphia, San Francisco
London, Mexico City, São Paulo, Sydney
1817

Published by arrangement with Bantam Books, Inc.

U.S. Library of Congress Cataloging in Publication Data

Calderone, Mary Steichen.
    The family book about sexuality.

    Includes index.
    1. Sex—Handbooks, manuals, etc. I. Johnson,
Eric W., joint author. II. Title.
[DNLM: 1. Sex. HQ21 C146f]
HQ21.C24   301.41   79-2592
ISBN 0–690–01910–6

---

81 82 83 84 85 10 9 8 7 6 5 4 3

To those of all ages who love life and each other

Contents

Acknowledgments

The following people have read either the manuscript or parts of it or given their expertise in special areas, or both, and their help was of great value to us: Lorna Brown, M.A., Lin Hodes, A.C.S.W., Gary F. Kelly, M.Ed., David Mace, Ph.D., Rob Roy MacGregor, M.D., Luigi Mastroianni, Jr., M.D., John Money, Ph.D., Wardell Pomeroy, Ph.D., Leah C. Schaefer, Ed.D., and Susan Fox Ziff, Sex Education Consultant for SIECUS.

None of the above, however, is responsible for our statements, attitudes, or errors, whether of omission or commission.

Neither are our wonderful editors, Jean Highland, formerly of Bantam Books, Beatrice Rosenfeld of Lippincott & Crowell, and Peg Cameron of Harper & Row, who are, however, definitely responsible for consistent support, enthusiasm and guidance, and gentle insistence on getting the thing done when sometimes we faltered.

Most of all we thank Marc Jaffe, as Editor-in-Chief and then President and Publisher of Bantam Books, who, when the first nebulous idea was laid before him, told us to march on with it.

Everyone interested in the book should, as we are, be appreciative of Leney LaRossa of Bantam, for her expertness as an unobtrusive but firm expediter, and of Peggy Hoover, for being a marvelous copy editor.

And we also acknowledge to each other the warmth and harmony that grew between us during the experience of working together on something important to both of us.

MARY S. CALDERONE, M.D.
ERIC W. JOHNSON

Spring 1981

About This Book

This book is about the nature and development of human sexuality. It tells everything that most members of any family will want to know about sex.

The main part of the book, Chapters 1–11, is written so that it can be read straight through. But people often want to find out about a specific matter quickly. That is what the Concise A–to–Z Encyclopedia (beginning on page 229) is for. In this Encyclopedia you can immediately find just about any item concerning sex and sexuality that you might have a question about. From there you may be referred to other items in the Encyclopedia. Thus the book gives you the best of both worlds: the world of making sense, and the world of quickly found facts.

The Concise A–to–Z Encyclopedia can also help you get even more out of the main part of this book. You may want to refer now and then to the Encyclopedia while reading Chapters 1–11. Also, the General Index at the back of the book will help you to locate discussions of any subject, whether in the main chapters or in the Encyclopedia.

Preface:
Is This Book for You?

This book is for anyone of any age who can read and who wants to find out more about the sexual parts of our lives. People from around age ten right on through old age will find interesting information in it from reliable scientific sources. Even younger children have many questions about sex. If they are free to dip into the book whenever they wish, they will find parts that are helpful and useful to them too, and it will help them take part in family discussions about sexual questions. Parts that they don't need to understand yet will slip right by them.

Why did we write this book? So that more and more people could begin to understand the important sexual parts of our lives, the roles that sex plays in all lives, the many new facts that are being learned from research about sex and sexuality. We also wanted to explain and put into perspective some new attitudes that scientific and religious leaders are developing about sex. These can help make sex less something to be afraid of or ashamed of and more understandable—and therefore easier to manage responsibly. Yet the sexual part of our lives can be just as mysterious, wonderful, and rewarding as it has ever been, or more so.

What is the book really about? It is about sexuality: all our experiences, our learnings, our knowledge, our dreams, our fantasies, our sexual experiences, and our relationships—the parts of our lives that have to do with our being male or female. The book explains the facts that can help us understand the great force of sexuality, so that we can learn how to use it better than before, in order to achieve joy and happiness in being men or women.

What is the book supposed to do? It is supposed to open windows of knowledge and give us insight into ourselves and others as the sexual beings that we all are right from birth. In this way each of us can develop our own sexuality in ways best suited to our individual selves, to our aspirations, and to our responsibilities to others and to ourselves.

We, the two authors, are old friends. We are also Friends: that is, we are members of the Religious Society of Friends, or Quakers. Quakers believe that all human beings have a right to all the information that can help them to arrive at rational and responsible decisions about the conduct of their lives. Quakers also have concerns about the rights of others, and so our concern as authors is to provide this information about sex. We describe rather than advocate. We try to explain all sides of a subject on which serious professionals in the field disagree; we do not advocate any specific position on an issue other than to indicate, when possible, where most workers, researchers, therapists, and religious counselors in the field of human sexuality tend to agree.

Sexuality is part of life from the moment of our birth to the end of our days. We know that two aspects of sex, pleasure and procreation, have often been used without a sense of responsibility for their consequences—present and future—for the individuals involved, for others not directly involved, and for society. Any irresponsible use of sex is likely to damage individuals and society; therefore such irresponsibility is, in the deepest sense, immoral.

Because of the work in which both of us have been involved over the past fifteen years, we share the conviction of countless others that sexuality is one of the two great human endowments, comparable to the mind in importance, and that pleasure and joy from the use of both these great human faculties is enhanced by sound knowledge about them, combined with the conviction of the infinite worth of each individual person.

We believe that a family is the best setting for learning how to develop and use one's sexuality. We are convinced that caring and trust are essential for the development of love within the family, and that love is essential to the development of true intimacy between all family members. Such intimacy within a family is what human beings need, seek, and long for from their earliest days to their last. But we recognize, too, that not all persons are able or willing—or, in some cases, do not choose—to develop this part of their lives.

We have spoken of trust. Trust has to be built on truth. If family members keep the truth from one another, they cannot learn to trust each other, no matter what their ages may be. The things we say in this book about sex and sexuality will be truths, as nearly as we can determine them. How our readers take and apply these truths in their own lives will depend very much on their own values. As Quakers, our moral values depend on our belief in the infinite worth of each human being and on our belief that as human beings we are obliged to deal with others as we would like others to deal with us—trustingly, caringly, and responsibly.

We believe that responsible people can accept these positive moral values no matter what their religious beliefs may be, or even if they do not consider themselves to be religious at all. These values relate to all of life, not just to sex and sexuality. We believe that sexuality as a part of life has no morality special to itself but that morality or immorality lies in the way each of us *uses* sexuality in our life relationships.

For all these reasons we have written this book for you and for your family to share together.

MSC
EWJ

The
Family Book
About
Sexuality

1
Understanding Ourselves as Sexual Persons

We believe this may be the most significant chapter in the book, for in it we try to bring you up-to-date on important facts science has discovered about how people develop into sexual persons and live their lives as sexual persons. Many of these facts have emerged from the research on human sexuality by scientists at major universities only over the past ten to fifteen years. Understanding the facts in this chapter, and understanding ourselves as sexual persons, can help us all to think through some of the things we have been taking for granted about the role of sex in our lives—things that really should not be taken for granted by anyone.

The assumptions upon which this book is based, and which this chapter is designed to clarify, are these: We are all sexual, all of our lives, each in our own unique way at any given moment. There are as many different ways of being sexual as there are people in the world. And for each of us individually, there are as many different ways of being sexual as there are days in our lives. Our sexuality may prove to be the second most important thing about us. Having been born with the mind and body of a human being is the first.

To begin with, let's establish how we are using the words *sex, sexuality,* and *sexual,* to avoid misunderstanding about their meanings.

The word *sex* today is most often used in two ways: (1) to label gender, that is, whether a person belongs to the male or the female gender or sex; and (2) to refer to the physical part of a relationship. People use the word in the second way when they say, "I had sex last night," meaning a physical, erotic, or genital relationship.

The word *sexuality* is today used to mean something much broader—the whole person, including his or her thoughts, experiences, learnings, ideas, values, and imaginings, as these have to do with his being male or her being female.

The word *sexual,* therefore, is used mostly in the same sense as sexuality. Your sexual self is your whole self as girl or boy or woman or man; your sexual feelings are feelings that have to do not just with the physical but also with your own male or female role in life, or the relationships you may be having with people of the opposite sex or your own sex, at whatever age. Very often these may have nothing at all to do with physical actions.

Sexual relationships need not, and most often do not, involve sex in its physical aspect: child and child, adolescent and adolescent, husband and wife, parent and parent, parents and children, friend and friend, man and woman, man and man, woman and woman, employer and employee, student and student, student and teacher, colleague and colleague—all these people are having sexual relationships in the sense that they are, in part, relating to each other as the male or the female each of them is at any given moment. While genital sexual activity is an important part of some of our human relationships, it takes up a very small part of waking time in a very small proportion of the people to whom we relate.

The Process of Sexualization

As children grow up, some of the most important things they learn have to do with their sense of a sexual self. Children are constantly learning, by observation, by being taught, or by experiencing, what their culture considers desirable for males or females to be or to do. We can call this aspect of growth and development as a male or a female the process of sexualization. This process, like other life processes such as acquiring knowledge and developing the mind, begins at birth and goes on throughout life. It is a dynamic process, one that is never still, never totally in balance.

At most times in the history of the world, certain societies have had fixed patterns by which they molded the natures and relationships of their boys and girls; every child was taught to do certain things at a given stage in his or her life and thus grew up knowing exactly what was expected of him as male or of her as female at every stage. But our society no longer has such fixed patterns. The process of sexualization for any one individual usually turns out to be quite different from the process experienced by any other individual.

The process of sexualization must be distinguished from the development of reproductivity, or the capacity to reproduce (see Chapter 3). Reproductivity simply means that the female can become pregnant and the male can make her pregnant—that they have reached puberty. Children usually reach this stage sometime in the early teens, sometimes even earlier. Puberty does not mean that the boy is now a man and the girl is now a woman. It also does not mean that either of them is sexually mature, in the full sense of the word *sexual*. It merely means that they are capable of reproducing. Actually, the girl can become pregnant before she has developed any capacity for sex feelings at all. This is not true of the boy, however, for until he can ejaculate he cannot impregnate, and he cannot ejaculate without experiencing strong sex feelings.

Let us go step-by-step through the process by which sexuality is developed.

Prenatal Sexual Development

Conception is the very beginning of sexual development. In Chapter 3 you'll read how the sperm from the father fertilizes an egg from the mother so that conception occurs. At the instant of fertilization the gender of the future baby is determined by the sex chromosome carried by the sperm. Sperm are of two kinds: (1) those carrying an X, or female-producing, chromosome; and (2) those carrying a Y, or male-producing, chromosome. The sex chromosome in the egg is *always* X, so if the sperm that fertilizes it also carries an X chromosome, the baby-to-be will be XX, or female. If the fertilizing sperm has a Y sex chromosome, however, then the baby-to-be will be an XY, or male. This determination is the only function of the sex chromosome—conveying the genetic signal, X or Y, to a certain tiny group of cells in the new life that will cause those cells eventually to become ovaries (XX) or testicles (XY).

These cells receiving the message of the sex chromosome themselves then take over the program for developing a male or a female according to the code. If they receive a code XX message to become ovaries, they will eventually manufacture the female hormone estro-

gen. Even without it the uterus, fallopian tubes, the ovaries themselves, the vagina, clitoris, and labia (see Figures 6 and 8, pp. 42, 44)
would still develop, because the mother's own ovaries manufacture
estrogen that circulates in her blood and passes to the baby through
the placenta. On the other hand, if the message is for that group of
cells to develop into testicles, these cells begin to manufacture male
hormone (testosterone), which will not only cause the development
of the male genital organs—penis, scrotum, testicles, prostate, ducts,
seminal vesicles, etc. (see Figure 2, p. 36)—but will also suppress the
development of the female organs. All these things begin to happen
between six and twelve weeks after fertilization.

The effects of the sex hormones manufactured according to the
code message are also felt in a certain area of the brain. Researchers
now believe that a predisposition toward eventual male or female
sexual behavior may be communicated to the sex center while the
baby is still developing in its mother's uterus, but more research is
needed to find out exactly how and when.

The Process of Birth

Birth has always been looked upon as an important event in the life
of the mother—and indeed it is. But it is also a most powerful event
in the life of the baby itself. Consider what actually happens to a baby
during the process of birth. For nine months it has been floating
peacefully in a warm space, without being touched, without light,
almost without sound, with an even temperature, and cushioned from
all shocks by the fluid in which it floats. Now, as the birth process
proceeds, the powerful muscles of the uterus keep thrusting the baby
downward against the resisting tissues of the birth canal, through a
quite tight opening (the neck of the womb, or cervix), then ever more
powerfully downward through the stretching vagina between the
bones of the mother's pelvis, and finally out into the cool air and the
light. The mother's abdominal muscles help to push the baby as well,
but the fluid in which the baby had been floating has drained out of
the birth passage and no longer cushions it. As the baby is thrust into
the world it is generally to the accompaniment of very bright light and
the noise of human voices—sights and sounds never experienced
before. It feels air on its skin for the first time, and this is not only drier

but considerably cooler than the warm liquid in which it had been floating. All these experiences together usually take some hours, but if the birth process is short, they can be compressed into a few minutes.

We are used to thinking of a baby as tender and delicate, but it must be quite tough to withstand all this. Imagine how you would feel or react if you were to experience the same pushing process for several hours. It is now believed that the more quiet and peaceful we can make the first hours and days of the baby's life, the more easily and gently it can adapt to the new circumstances. It is also thought now that what the baby experiences during and immediately after birth may be one of many influences on the kind of person she or he becomes.

Acquiring Gender Identity

The very first announcement made about the baby is "It's a boy" or "It's a girl." It is especially important that this announcement be correct and accurate, for if the baby were to be identified at birth as of the gender other than its real one, some serious psychological problems could later arise that might be difficult or impossible to correct. Incorrect gender identification can occur on rare occasions when the genitals of a baby are not clearly identifiable as belonging specifically to one or the other of the two sexes.

During the first two years the parents and others, without realizing it, spend a great deal of time giving the baby cues about which gender it belongs to. For instance, mothers may tend to dress their girl babies in pink and their boy babies in blue (in France, just the opposite!). They talk to the baby, even when it is very tiny—"What a fine big boy!" or "What a lovely little girl!" Studies show that parents tend to hold and touch a girl baby quite differently from the way they hold and touch a boy baby. Both parents may give the baby toys, or play games with it, that specifically identify it as male or female. They make definite statements that tell the toddler to which sex it belongs: "When you go to the toilet we put the seat back and you stand up just like Daddy," or, to a girl, "Girls don't stand up to the toilet like Daddy but sit on the seat the way Mommy does." There are plenty of cues all the time that identify girls with females, boys with males. In any case, by the age of three at the very latest, boys and girls should be and usually are firmly fixed in their separate gender identities. They have learned that "I'm a boy" or "I'm a girl," and they feel quite sure about it.

Learning Gender Role Behavior

Through childhood and well into adolescence, the child becomes increasingly aware of the kinds of behavior that parents or other adults consider appropriate for a boy or a girl. For instance, it used to be that no boy would be interested in learning how to cook; that was his sister's role. Then about twenty years ago the idea of the backyard barbecue began to take hold; here it was Daddy who usually played the role of cook, for friends as well as for the family. Little boys grew up with this, and it is not surprising that as this barrier went down others did also. Boys began to experiment with various kinds of cooking, even cooking in the kitchen, and they did not feel they were going to become professional chefs or that they were sissies. Today men find great pleasure in cooking for their wives, children, and friends, perhaps some meals during the week, perhaps alternating with a working wife, sometimes even all the meals. This is a good example of how gender role behavior adapts itself to changing times (more about that in Chapter 2). Another example of learning gender role behavior is found in Scotland, where there are many men who enjoy knitting.

We could cite more examples. But the important thing to remember is that possession of male chromosomes and organs or of female chromosomes and organs is not what determines how people feel about their masculinity or femininity as related to certain forms of behavior. Rather, what determines this is how those people were brought up to feel about themselves and their lives. Such attitudes and feelings are learned from the attitudes of the people around them.

Reaching Puberty

Puberty is no mysterious thing. It is that period, usually in the early teens, when there is a sudden spurt of bodily development as the sex glands (ovaries or testicles) increase their production of sex hormones

sufficiently to begin to turn the boy into a man or the girl into a woman. These hormones determine both the reproductivity and the bodily characteristics that go with being an adult female or adult male. Dr. John Money of the Gender Identity Center at Johns Hopkins University has said, "It is also the moment when the revelation of the identity and orientation that were already programmed occurs." The child suddenly realizes "I am almost a man!" or "I am almost a woman!" The belief of most adults that puberty is also the time when the erotic or sex drive begins is one that has caused a great deal of misunderstanding and anguish. There is no basis in fact for this belief; the sex drive, the drive to experience erotic sexual feelings, is normally present from birth.

The Importance of Touching and Skin Contact

Touching and skin contact have been found to be very important for the healthy development of a child's sexual system and also for a child's well-being and sense of itself as a good person.

The skin is an important organ in itself, with a number of functions. One is to protect everything inside the body from dirt or germs. Another is to keep the temperature of the inner part of the body at a constant level: On a hot day the blood vessels in the skin dilate to keep the body cool; on a cold day the blood vessels contract to keep body heat from escaping. The skin also functions as a warning system, telling the body about such dangerous things as burning or freezing temperatures, bruises, or other outside factors to be avoided.

But one of the most important functions of the skin is its part in the sense of touch. Tiny babies and small children need to feel their parents' skin against their own. Such intimate closeness gives them a sense of comfort, of safety, and of the peacefulness of being cared for and helped and loved. And this is true not only for babies and small children but also for adults, most of whom never lose the need for this kind of touching. Throughout our lives most of us need it, want it, should have it— and we should feel free to give it to others who are near and dear to us.

It has been found that babies who don't have sufficient skin-to-skin caressing in early life fail to develop a sense of well-being. When babies whose mothers have died or cannot take care of them are left for too long with caretakers who do not fondle them enough, they do

not do well, even when well fed, but tend to grow and develop slowly and sometimes even to sicken and die. This is because in some hospitals or other institutions the adults who are looking after the babies may not have the time—or the knowledge and caring, for that matter —to provide this vital life-affirming physical contact and the handling and rocking that go with it.

The need of babies for this kind of closeness is related to another function of the skin. It is an organ by which we express love, eventually including erotic, sexual love. Just as the baby perceives the mother's love when the mother tenderly strokes its body, so later in life that same child can perceive the love felt for it by another person, when that person's hands and fingers express love and caring by the way they smooth and stroke and caress the skin.

The skin, therefore, is a most important part of the sexual system. The more the child has had an opportunity to experience gentleness, caring, and trust as the parents care for its body, and the more the child is allowed by the parent to like, enjoy, and become master of its own body, the better able it will be, after it grows up, to experience closeness and warmth and trusting with another person.

How Parents Affect Sexualization

By now it may be clear that sex education begins in the very first years of a child's life and is of highest importance in the formation of the child's personality and later capacity for a healthy sexual life. Parents are apt to think of sex education only in terms of the information— mostly about reproduction—that they may or may not choose consciously to give. But far more important are the attitudes that parents unconsciously convey about sex, about themselves or each other, as male or female.

For instance, the father may come into the room while the mother is holding the baby. If the relationship between the mother and father is happy and comfortable, the child will sense this—the mother's muscles remain relaxed, her voice as she speaks to the father is warm and welcoming. But if the father and mother have been having trouble relating to each other, her muscles may tense up as he enters the room, her voice may become sharp and defensive, or even angry and unfriendly, and his may too.

Even a tiny baby will sense these attitudes, so this is early sex education. The mother's and father's self-images, their role behaviors and attitudes, their fear of or comfort with the erotic aspects of sex in their own lives—all these become, through them, important factors in the sexualization process of their child. During this process the child can develop happy, comfortable attitudes about itself as male or female, or negative and uncomfortable ones.

So if parents don't feel comfortable about each other—as mates, as parents, or in their sex roles—what then? Could this adversely affect their children in some way, far in the future, in their own marriage relationships? Yes. So we should bear in mind that parents in reality bring up not just their own child but also someone's probable future husband or wife, and probably a parent of their own grandchildren.

Other Factors in Sexualization

As children grow, they come in contact with others who affect their development—brothers and sisters, relatives, friends, teachers and professionals, even strangers. Any one of us who comes in contact with children and young people provides a kind of role model for them, a model of a certain kind of man, a certain kind of woman. Children or young people, perhaps without realizing it, will absorb many things about a person and may react unconsciously with "I would like to be like that person" or "I do not want to be like that person." The whole society today, especially as revealed in the media, is a factor in the process of sexualization. Right now many of the role models provided by TV, movies, magazines, and newspapers are people we would *not* like our children to grow up to be like.

We should all be thinking about what can be done to provide good role models for our children and young people: What is it, what does it mean, to be a man, to be a woman? What kinds of men and women does the society need today in order to survive, to get better? These are some important questions for everyone to think about and for families to talk about together, at the dinner table, in the evening after homework, on weekends. In this way children and parents can get closer together, because they can learn to talk freely with each other about all sorts of things that need to be discussed but that are best talked about between people who love and trust one another.

We can also gain understanding of ourselves and our sexuality by looking at the successes and failures of other groups of people. For instance, among the Pilagá Indians in Argentina, children are given great sexual freedom right from infancy. The sex play of boys together and of girls together is accepted until the age of five; after that, sex play between boys and girls together is also accepted, until adolescence. Yet sexual problems that are common in our society and other Western societies (see Chapter 9) do not exist among the Pilagá Indians; rape and incest are unknown, and so are sexual problems requiring therapy. In societies like that of the Pilagás, of course, factors other than sexual freedom must also play a part in accounting for their lack of the sexual problems that plague our society. For example, the Pilagás don't have television; they don't have written historical or religious traditions; their social roles are simpler to learn; they have fewer rules; and there is a good deal of self-discipline on the part of the adults, so that each one is aware of his or her other responsibilities in the society.

It would certainly be naïve to suppose that merely to arrange for one family, or even a group of families, to develop more relaxed attitudes regarding their children would alone decrease the sexual problems these children might experience in later adult life. There are too many other factors outside the family to be taken into account. Not the least of these are problems the children who are brought up differently might run into in later relationships with peers who were brought up in a more traditional manner. The Pilagá Indian children are brought up in more or less the same way and with similar values. Our children, and their parents, must adjust to a society with many different values and standards of behavior—each one considered to be the "right" one, all others "wrong." That kind of society is difficult to grow up in.

But our society is not staying the same as it was even only ten years ago. One important reason for this is that women are evolving greatly from their role as inferiors of men to a new role as partners. Women today are freer to do or become what they wish. Some choose to stay at home and bring up their children, others choose to combine mothering and homemaking with job or career, others choose to delay childbearing until their thirties or perhaps to forego it permanently. This increase in freedom for women also gives men more freedom— to choose to be homemakers, for instance. It will be about twenty years before the effects of these new factors can be judged. Even then it will be important to remember that everything that has happened between now and then cannot be laid at the door of the present changing attitudes about women and sexuality. Such simple answers are never appropriate for complex questions.

In summary, by the time a child enters kindergarten it has already had the most important and long-lasting sex education it can ever have. For good or for ill, the parents have been the primary educators, both in terms of information and even more in terms of their attitudes about themselves as male or female, about each other as man and woman, and about sex, both as erotic experience and as relationship.

Much ongoing scientific research is helping to develop new concepts and knowledge about expanded sex roles and relationships for women and men as society changes. Today's young parents have moved away from their own parents' understanding of sexuality. They do not want the sexual ignorance, discomforts, anxieties, distastes, fears, and shame that they may have experienced to continue to be passed on from generation to generation. They want to help their own children to progress rather than regress in sexual knowledge and attitudes—to become healthier and happier sexually than many of them are. One main purpose of this book is to provide some of that help.

2
The Human Sexual Response Systems:
How They Develop and How They Work

Every human being is born with the capacity to experience sexual pleasure and responsiveness. The pioneer work of William H. Masters and Virginia E. Johnson in the last fifteen years has greatly increased our understanding of this sexual response system. But we still have far to go in our scientific understanding of it as a body system more or less distinct from the reproductive system; there are still mysteries about how the sexual response system functions.

The major difference between functioning of the reproductive system and the sexual response systems in the male and in the female is this: After puberty, reproductive and sexual functioning are the same in the male but not in the female. In the male, reproductive functioning is attained automatically with the achievement of ejaculation at puberty, and by the age of eighteen practically 100 percent of males have experienced ejaculation. Actually the male could not play his part in reproduction unless he experienced the sexual pleasure that results in ejaculation. But in the female it is different. Even though she too attains reproductive maturity at puberty, it is entirely possible, and often happens, that she becomes pregnant without experiencing sexual pleasure then or sometimes ever.

This difference between the two sexes is basic, and it is important to understand. The process of reproduction in the female is automatic, and the brain areas that control it do not operate consciously. But, independently of the reproductive system, her sexual response system, which is capable of functioning from the moment of birth up to the end of life, does not always function automatically. The brain areas that control it operate at *both* the conscious level and the unconscious level, and things can happen in childhood that may interfere with her sexual response functioning in adult life.

Compare Figure 6 (on p. 42), showing the female reproductive system, with Figure 8, the sexual response system. In the *reproductive* functioning, Figure 6, the organs principally involved are the ovaries, the fallopian tubes, and the uterus, with the vagina involved only passively—at the very beginning of the reproductive process, when it is the passageway by which the sperm move toward the egg, and at the very end, when it is the passageway through which the baby enters the world.

In the diagram of the female sexual response system, Figure 4, notice that the organs principally involved in *sexual pleasure* are the clitoris, as the main source of pleasure; the internal and external lips of the vulva; and the muscular tissues that surround the vagina within the pelvis, at both its outer and deeper areas. It is these muscles that provide the pleasurable contractions of orgasm. The mouth, the lips, the breasts, the skin, and the anus are secondary sex organs.

Different women may give the primary and secondary sex organs different weights of importance for sexual pleasure, not only according to their individual experiences and preferences but also at different moments in their lives. Most women also give different weights to different sources of stimulation. It is well known that whereas most men find intercourse the most desirable form of stimulation, many women do not, but may find more pleasure and a higher degree of stimulation arising out of mouth or finger contact. Masters and Johnson found very consistently that women appeared to be more highly aroused in sexual self-pleasuring than in sexual intercourse, and many found it easier to experience orgasm following masturbation than during intercourse. But most of the women studied enjoyed and *desired* most the orgasm resulting from sexual intercourse, even though orgasm following masturbation might be more intense.

The capacity of females for orgasm differs from individual to individual more than it does in males. Some never experience orgasm in their lives; some experience it as babies, even before conscious memory, and continue to experience it throughout their lives; some never experience more than one orgasm for each episode; some experience single orgasms for some time before they discover that they have a capacity for multiple orgasms; and some experience multiple orgasms throughout their lives. The range is great. Many of the differences depend on circumstances; others are independent of circumstances. Many explanations have been offered as to why at least one third of all women have difficulty in experiencing orgasm during intercourse, but without shedding much light on the problem. However, one valid explanation is that during the most common position in intercourse (man on top), the penis does not stimulate the clitoris, and clitoral stimulation is often necessary for a woman to have an orgasm.

The Sexual Response Cycle

Basically, what is called the sexual response cycle works about the same way for those men and women who experience arousal. Whether in self-pleasuring or in pleasuring each other, whether heterosexually or homosexually, there are four stages, each one leading to the next.

1. *The excitement stage.* In the excitement stage the body begins to respond to sexual stimulation, such as from thoughts, imaginings, dreams, sights, sounds, body odors, and body touch. The excitement begins with erection in the male and with lubrication of the vagina in the female. Various movements provide stimulation and, if stimulation is continued, excitement increases and the plateau stage is reached.

2. *The plateau stage.* Depending upon the intensity of reaction and the desire of the people involved, the plateau stage can be quite short or very prolonged. It is called "plateau" because it can be continued for variable lengths of time, until the sense of tension and pleasure increase to that moment when orgasm is felt by one partner or both as inevitable. During the plateau stage the blood trapped in the sex organs of both males and females causes pleasurable swelling, and this leads into the orgasmic stage.

3. *The orgasmic stage.* Once a certain pitch of tension has been reached in the plateau stage, orgasm is triggered. In both male and female it consists of a series of muscular contractions, according to the research of Masters and Johnson numbering from perhaps six to fifteen—each contraction lasting a little less than one second. In the male, the focus of orgasm concentrates in the mind, which perceives it as taking place in the penis, the prostate gland, and the seminal vesicles. In the female the focus of orgasm also concentrates in the mind, which perceives it as taking place in the muscles and tissues around and deep in the vagina. In both male and female, the whole

body is often involved in muscle tension and even spasmodic contractions of limbs, fingers, toes, or the face; this is especially so in the female. Those women who are multi-orgasmic may experience several orgasms before satisfaction.

4. *The resolution stage.* For males, immediately after orgasm comes the resolution stage, during which tensions relax and pulse, breathing, and blood pressure return to their usual rates. Then there follows a period during which the man cannot respond to new stimulation, the refractory period. In some men this period is very brief—minutes or hours. In others, especially in older men, it can last several hours or days, depending on age, vigor, and interest. In women, the resolution stage is immediate and short. Her refractory period is variable, but lengthens as she gets older.

The Development of Sexuality

Examination of the wide range of differences in the sexual responses of women, compared to the much narrower range of differences in the responses of men, has led to a search for explanations. The variations may result from childhood experiences. During childhood, natural erotic tendencies begin to be expressed. The widely differing ways in which adults react to such expression may well have an effect on sexual response once the child is grown up. To understand the sexuality of women and of men, it is helpful to understand the sexuality that is characteristic of all children.

The Sexuality of Infancy

Most people don't think of babies and young children as sexual, or if they observe some behavior that might be interpreted as sexual, they resist this thought as something frightening or bad and try to stop that behavior. Here is how it is now understood that sexuality in the normal child develops if not interfered with:

Newborn babies begin life with breathing, and their first cry is eagerly listened for because it means that the breathing or respiratory system is functioning properly. Signs of the functioning of other systems of the body are also watched for: the first bowel movement shows that the intestinal tract is working; the first feedings, not vomited, prove the same thing about the digestive system; the heart is listened to; testing for reflexes, like tapping the knee or the heel with a rubber hammer or seeing how the pupils of the eye react to light, shows how well the brain and nervous system are working, and so forth.

Soon after birth, two signs serve as indicators that the sexual response system is working normally: a boy baby has one of a lifelong series of erections of his penis, and a girl baby every few hours shows signs of fluid in her vagina, similar to the lubricating fluid that will be produced later whenever she is sexually aroused. That normal babies are sexual creatures is a surprise to many people, but it is a fact.

It is just as automatic for the sexual response system to function thus at this time in the baby's life as it will later be automatic for the reproductive system to function in early puberty. You would think, then, that the sexual response system would continue working smoothly throughout life as a natural, normal thing, and that we would not see so many people who experience difficulties in one way or another with their sexual-erotic functioning. Unfortunately, however, things happen on the way to adult life that can in the end interfere with the success of sexual response functioning.

A comparison can be made with the digestive system, at the lower end of which, for instance, trouble can begin with too early insistence on bowel training. This can lead to poor attitudes about going to the toilet or even to constipation or other disturbances in later life. In the same way, mothers who insist on feeding children a certain amount of food in a certain way, and who force their wishes on the child, often end up with a child whose natural appetite has been distorted and who has problems with eating. We have had to learn how to avoid these problems by teaching mothers to let their young children eat what they choose of the right foods, keeping wrong foods from them, and not feeding them again until the next meal—but never forcing them to eat.

In the same way, parents with the best intentions in the world have tended to interfere with the natural evolution of their children's sexuality. For one thing, not enough American babies receive the close body contact with their parents, particularly their mothers, that they need. It is good to see more and more young mothers today nursing their babies and carrying them around close to their bodies with a carrying sling. It is good to know, too, that an increasing number of young parents enjoy holding their babies against their bare skin and gently stroking or massaging the baby's body.

Meeting the other needs of the baby is also important. When the baby cries, it is simply telling you of its needs or wants, and the job of a parent is to learn to interpret what these might be at that moment. By having its needs and wants met, the baby very early learns that it can trust the world around it and so becomes more and more able to bear frustration and meet the world confidently rather than in fear, loneliness, or anger.

The very first contact of mother and baby may be the most vital of all. The first hour or two, even the first few minutes, are those in which it is easiest and most rewarding for both to form their first bond. The baby should be given to the mother at once, before it is clothed or even bathed, so that with her own fingers she can touch it all over to make sure it is all right—and to give it its first sensation of direct relation to another person.

New mothers have been observed to touch the feet and hands first, then the body, and then the baby's face, after which the hands return to the body, to smooth and massage it. Meanwhile, the mother is looking intently at the baby, looking straight into its eyes, and, wonderfully, the baby is usually looking straight back at her. These two human beings so important to each other are saying many things without words that lay the foundation for a strong relationship together. As long as the baby is breathing well, all this should happen even before the baby has eye-drops or is examined by the doctor, for something much more important and long-lasting is happening.

Studies show that those babies whose mothers had been helped to have this experience with their brand-new infants thrived and gained weight better, and that the mothers were more likely to be successful at nursing them, as compared with other mothers and babies who had not been given this opportunity.

As soon after birth as possible, the baby's father should have the same experience offered to him; this will be important for him and for the baby, and for exactly the same reasons. Thereafter, both mother and father will find it always more rewarding to continue this strong, close-touching relationship with their baby, and the baby will thrive on it.

Just as important later are the attitudes of the parents about the baby's own good bodily feelings. The baby's fingers will eventually explore its body, discover the various fascinating things such as its nose, its ears, its hair, its belly button, its toes. These discoveries delight parents. But when it comes to discoveries in the area between the belly button and the knees—that is too often a different story. When the baby boy's fingers find his penis while the mother is bathing or diapering him, she usually begins her interference right then, afraid her child may break the taboo on the pleasure of sex "too early." She is thinking of sex in the adult sense, of course, but only because no one has helped her understand that childhood sex feelings are quite different from those of an adult and that they occur naturally as part of the pleasure of touch. The reactions of mothers may vary. One might simply remove the baby's hand from his genital area; another might cover the baby quickly with the diaper; another might slap the baby's hand and speak harshly.

If the baby is a girl, the mother's panic may be greater and her reaction stronger. If the father is standing by, the mother may be terribly embarrassed and upset; she might be even more upset if one of the baby's grandmothers is also watching. She wants to prevent any activity that they could interpret as abnormal.

No one has ever reassured the mother that not only is it normal for a baby to find pleasure in its own body, but it is also an important part of the baby's growth and development and should not be interfered with. She may have heard a neighbor tell tales of the supposed harms and evils of masturbation. She has no way of knowing that these are myths and untruths handed down from the dark ages. Neither does she know that masturbation for release of tension and to experience pleasure occurs throughout the lives of most people, with only positive effects—unless they are made to feel anxious or guilty about it.

When a baby discovers its genital organs, it is actually initiating the active functioning of the sexual response system which, years later, will be physiologically ready enough to permit normal sexual functioning accompanied by a sense of competence, fulfillment, and pleasure. Each system of the body—the heart, the respiratory system, the digestive system, the nervous system, and so forth—has a specific purpose in life, a specific way of functioning. The sexual response system is no exception. But unlike the other body systems, the functioning of this system is not a life-or-death matter; many people live satisfying and creative lives even if they choose to ignore or repress their sexual functioning. The possibility of such repressions, however, should not be forced upon children. The choice need be considered only by mature adults who have all the facts in their possession and who elect not to exercise their erotic powers.

Sex Roles and the Sexuality of Childhood

The young child will also be learning what its nongenital sex role should be in life. Here again the principal teachers are the parents, who by their words or their attitudes give answers to these questions: What should little girls do? What should little boys do? What may both girls and boys, women and men do? Each parent, each family unit, and each society usually has quite specific convictions about the "correct" answers to these important social questions; there will be marked differences in these answers in various parts of the world or even in parts of the same country. The convictions based on the answers will be conveyed to the child both directly and indirectly day after day by the parents, and they will affect the child's eventual patterns of sexual beliefs and behavior. In the United States, these beliefs are not uniform and they are changing. Men and women and boys and girls can today do and be many more of the same things in everyday life than they were permitted even a decade or two ago.

Some people worry about what is sometimes called "unisex." They worry that children will grow up confused about their gender roles. Children might get confused about changing gender roles today if the adults around them get confused. But if the child grows up knowing that the primary difference between males and females has to do with their reproductive function—men produce sperm, and women produce eggs that can be fertilized by the sperm and carried until birth—and if children can be taught to name and take pride in their own special organs that will perform those functions, then the wage-earning occupations of men and women are of less importance in distinguishing between them. Mothers can be bus drivers and fathers can be cooks and still be looked upon as mothers and fathers, real women and real men.

If parents are aware that their child has been born with the same natural capacities for erotic feelings that every other child has, they will find it easier to learn the attitudes of calm and noninterfering acceptance of this part of life. This, in turn, will assure the child that its body does indeed belong to him or her and to no one else. Naturally, parents' efforts must be exercised in relation to what is acceptable social behavior. For example, the child must understand early that today most people believe one's sex life should be private and enjoyed in privacy. There is no need for furtiveness, but there is a need to respect the feelings of others.

The Lessons of Nudity

One question that comes up in almost every family concerns nudity: Should parents and children see each others' bodies in the nude? If so, when and where?

Unless the idea of nudity is entirely comfortable for parents, if they are going to try it at all they should try it gradually, not suddenly. Older children cannot easily learn to take nudity for granted if it has not been a part of family life during their early years. But with very young children accustomed from the beginning to nudity in themselves and their parents, a great deal is taken for granted, and it doesn't seem to be much of a thing to them. What nudity does is make it easy for children to become absolutely certain about just how men and women are made. This knowledge is of great importance in assuring the child of its own correct gender. The differences in body states and sizes—and in body organs themselves—can then be taken for granted and will provide an accurate image of how they themselves, or the opposite sex, will look when grown up. Children whose parents feel at ease in such natural events as stepping out of the shower, toweling, and walking back to their room to dress are fortunate.

As children get older, they may copy their age-mates and become more comfortable if nudity is *not* practiced, even though they grew up with it. They will demonstrate this by choosing to be clothed or covered where before they were happy to prance around with nothing on. Parents can read these signs and be sensitive to them without necessarily changing their own preferred patterns. Privacy must always be respected, by grown-ups and children alike.

Increased Interest in Sex

Extreme curiosity or repeated questions about sex should be carefully analyzed: Why is the child so curious? Why is she or he not satisfied with simple answers? What basic needs for information or reassurance do the questions indicate? Studies have shown that most parents tend

to be convinced their children are less capable (by about two years) of absorbing knowledge about sexual matters than they are about other things, but this is not so.

It may be helpful for parents to know that many of the anxieties young children have that result in their heightened interest in the area of sex or greater activity in masturbation may not be related to sex at all but may spring from quite different causes: a recent severe illness or a death in the family, loss of a job or heavy pressures on the job in one or both parents, the arrival of a new brother or sister, heavy academic demands at school, a bullying child on the block, recent hospitalization, and so on. Such anxieties can cause a sense of being overwhelmed, with the child coming to feel as if the illness or death or loss of job was really in some way his or her responsibility. Such pressures can add greatly to the other factors that may already be upsetting the child, even though he or she may be too young to talk about it. The child may turn to the familiar self-touching that is pleasurable, to relieve these anxieties and find comfort.

Sometimes parents get upset when they think their children show too much interest in sex when they play. Children do a lot of what scientists have come to call "rehearsal play": "I'll be the mommy and you be the daddy. I'll cook and you read the paper." They go through the motions of identification with the grown-up world, which enjoys and encourages this. Early grade school rooms have housekeeping areas where rehearsal play can be carried out by both boys and girls.

But suppose the children's rehearsal play is about heterosexual activities, and they pretend to go through *those* motions? "I'll be the daddy and put the seed in you." "And I'll be the mommy and push the baby out of my belly button." To many parents that's not cute, it's disgusting or frightening. For the children, however, such play does not have the sexual meanings it does for the parents. And actually, this kind of play may help children to grow up solidly sure of how their sex roles are differentiated from one another's: primarily by the eventual functions of their own sex organs—the boy's penis to release sperm and the girl's vagina to convey them to the egg that can be fertilized by a sperm, so that she can carry a baby in her body until it is born. This sure knowledge, and their satisfaction in it, is part of the development of a sense of security that children need about their own gender roles in life.

Sex rehearsal play takes place because of the need of young children to confirm any kind of important knowledge, not once but many times in many ways. Harm occurs when there are outcries or punishment by adults. Gentle but firm supervision and calm handling will make it easier to meet with positive and creative attitudes the many other sexual situations that will be inevitable with children growing up, particularly in today's open and sex-saturated society. In general, the balance between "What will the neighbors say?" and the evolution of one's own sexually healthy child must be tipped in favor of the child, not the other way around.

When confronted by sexual situations like sex rehearsal play in their young children, parents can say such things as: "Bodies are made to feel good in many different ways. Cool water on your skin, good smells, lovely tastes—all these experiences of your body are good. But touching is special—so special you will probably feel that having your body touched should come only from yourself. Special places in your body that feel good when they are touched are your sexual places, and that should be a private thing, just for you alone, for now."

Masturbation

The development of the sexual response system needs to continue smoothly throughout infancy, childhood, and adolescence. One of its most important functions is its role in developing a strong sense of the self. An increasing number of sexologists and sex therapists now agree that masturbation has a specific role to play in the sexual evolution and total life cycle of the human being. They recognize also that great numbers of adults, well into old age, utilize self-stimulation as a form of release and pleasure, sometimes in painful situations such as illness of the partner, or separation by long periods of travel, death, or divorce, but usually as part of ordinary life.

Masturbation can also be looked upon as rehearsal for mature sex. Just as adolescents are constantly trying all sorts of new ways to test their bodies—in sports, in activities like driving a car, in going without food or sleep—so too they need to find out how their bodies perform sexually. Masturbation is a safe way to do this, because it does not involve another person. In a sense, too, the young person learns how to relate to himself or herself sexually, and this helps prepare for eventually relating to another person. Getting to know yourself intimately is good rehearsal for getting to know another person intimately.

While professional people and researchers do not consider masturbation to be a problem itself, society makes it one in looking upon it as somehow harmful, mentally unhealthy, sinful, or, at best, immature behavior that mature people should outgrow.

According to the most careful studies we have, in the United States and Canada well over 95 percent of males and 75 percent of females do masturbate at one or more periods in their lives, and the amount of masturbation and the ages of it are unrelated to religious affiliation or frequency of church attendance. Also, we know of no studies showing that masturbation causes or is evidence of disorder. However, the fact that many people who do masturbate are also aware of strong statements against it, especially by churches, can cause them needless suffering, guilt, and worry. We can say today that one of the main sources of failure to achieve sexual satisfaction in adult life is interference by parents early in life with the child's discovery of its own body as a source of pleasure.

Parents as Role Models

Children who have loving parents—loving with each other and with their children—will find it easy to accept the good examples set by their parents. They follow bad examples too. Mothers and fathers are usually not aware of how closely and constantly their children watch them and copy them. In this way, children learn how men and women deal with each other—honestly, trustingly and kindly, or sharply and hurtfully, playing games against each other.

We have said that parents are bringing up not just their child but probably the future husband or wife of some other person, who also will bring to the marriage the effects of the role-modeling of his or her parents. How will the two sets of parents be reflected, years later, in the lives of the family that may include their own future grandchildren?

The relationship of a mother and a father, and how they themselves feel about each other and about erotic sex, is inevitably an important influence on every child. One of the difficulties that children face today in growing up is the wide variety of attitudes parents have about sex and how their children should learn and feel about it:

Some parents have fine sex lives but don't want to talk to or teach their children about sex.

Some parents believe that sex is a bad thing, to be repressed or enjoyed seldom, even in marriage.

Some parents would like to have better, warmer sex lives, but their own upbringing has made letting go with enjoyment almost impossible for them.

Some parents look upon sex as a piece of cake—to be had and enjoyed with almost anyone.

Some parents regard sex as a joking matter.

Some parents experience practically no sex feelings and don't understand what all the fuss is about.

Some parents hedge sex around with so many rules and restrictions and ceremonies that it is never a spontaneous and free experience for them.

Some parents have been taught by life experiences to link sex with violence and anger.

Some parents have found it impossible to enjoy sex except under unusual circumstances, and so they seek out these circumstances constantly.

And many parents, of course, have joyous, rewarding sexual lives and are living examples of love and consideration for their children.

Some parents who read this may feel that something very important is missing from their lives, deeply concerned that they do not fall into the last group. These couples, if they wish, can get help from accredited marriage or sex counselors (see Sources of Help, p. 315).

Learning Sexual Techniques

There really are no recipes for concocting a perfect sexual relationship. Two unique individuals get together and develop a relationship which they may eventually decide will involve sexual intercourse. From then on they are probably largely on their own as they find out what pleases, satisfies, and fulfills them as individuals and as a couple.

There certainly are books that can help, particularly those which describe or illustrate various positions and techniques. Provided the couple is flexible about trying things, these can help them to develop the kind of spontaneous and free experimentation between them that remains, for many, the best way for discovering the most satisfying ways of sexual pleasuring. Furthermore, just as one does not try to take a course in calculus before one has learned simple arithmetic, so there is a natural progression from the earlier and simpler elements of sexual loving to the more sophisticated, and this enjoyable progression can continue for many years.

What is most important is not time but how both people feel about themselves and about each other, what the motives are in their exploration, and how well they are able to talk together by words and body language about their emotions and bodily feelings. Obviously, if one of a couple finds certain sexual activities pleasurable and acceptable but the other does not, then the one should not force these on the other. However, the one who is moving more slowly into sexual experience can try to be open to learning new ways of expressing physical pleasure, so that in the end a harmonious balance can be achieved between the desires and sexual capacities of the two.

In the Victorian age it was not considered proper for married people even to talk about their sexual preferences and habits. In the 1920s there was more openness, but at the same time books began to be published that indicated there were only certain ways to experience sexual relationships if one wanted to get the most satisfaction out of them. People believed them and began to measure themselves against what the books said. This had very poor results, because competitiveness in sexual matters never helps enjoyment or performance but, rather, impedes both. In this period there was always the difficulty, too, that a Victorian-minded man could marry a woman with freer and more spontaneous approaches to sex life, or the other way around; this difference in attitude often resulted in great difficulties in adjustment between them.

Gradually in the past few years a more open and simpler attitude has been adopted by an increasing number of people: do what you enjoy, don't force yourself for the other person, let your imagination be your guide, but *communicate,* so that each can know what the other is feeling. Above all, don't strive grimly and compulsively for orgasm every time. Grimness, compulsiveness, speed, and competitiveness are death blows to sexual enjoyment. Spontaneousness, warmth, freedom, communication, time, and laughter—these are its life breath. Sexologists recommend that enjoyment be enhanced by mutural pleasuring, with no exclusive concern as to whether or not an orgasm occurs. Given these kinds of attitudes, orgasms do happen and many relational difficulties do resolve themselves. All the above applies equally to heterosexual or homosexual relationships.

Special Needs in Sexual Response

We referred earlier to the fact that childhood events can affect sexual response later in the adult. For example, some adults cannot achieve sexual satisfaction except under very special sets of circumstances. In one case, a man needed his partner to wear shiny black patent leather shoes during sexual intercourse. After working with a psychotherapist for some time, this shoe fetishism, as it is called, was traced back to when he was a boy of six or seven. He had been hiding under the sofa from his mother because he was masturbating and knew she would be angry. She apparently guessed where he was and approached the sofa, calling to him to come out. At the very moment that he finished his masturbation, her shiny black patent leather shoes near the sofa were right there in front of his eyes. As a result, his fear and his sexual excitement came to be bound up with the sight of these shoes, and in his adult life this caused a compulsion to include shoes in his lovemaking that disturbed his marital relationship.

In another case, a woman found she could not enjoy sex unless some kind of physical striking or punishment accompanied it. A psychotherapist helped her trace this back to something that happened when she was three or four. She had misbehaved, and her father laid her across his knees and spanked her. He happened to be wearing his pajamas, and at the moment of the spanking she saw his penis through the open fly. As a result, as an adult the woman had come to associate physical spanking with experiencing sexual pleasure.

These are two relatively uncommon examples of a kind of early sexual conditioning, but they point up how events in early life can influence sexual functioning when people reach adulthood.

Sexual Dysfunctions

A sexual dysfunction is a part of the sexual process that doesn't work right. Some sexual dysfunctions in the male are inability to achieve ejaculation or erection (called impotence), and ejaculation too soon, usually almost before intercourse has really begun (called premature ejaculation). Some sexual dysfunctions in the female are inability to experience orgasm (often called frigidity), uncontrollable tightening of the muscles around the entrance of the vagina which prevents the penis from entering the vagina (vaginismus), and painful intercourse (dyspareunia). Masters and Johnson identified these dysfunctions clearly and indicated successful ways of treating them. As a result, the science of sex therapy has developed to include a wide range of treatments that can result in resolving the sexual problems that can trouble relationships. The science of sex therapy is in its early days, but it is developing rapidly throughout the world.

Achieving Intimacy

One of the most important factors in the successful expression of sexuality between two people is communication—the ability to talk with the other person about sex in simple but honest language. This ability is closely related to the capacity the two people involved have for intimacy.

What is intimacy? It comes from the wish—the decision—of two people to form a strong, long-lasting, close relationship. One can certainly have an intimate relationship without ever having, or even thinking about having, sex as part of it. But it is hard to think of the reverse, that is, of any sexual relationship that will be long-lasting without the balance and support that true intimacy can give it. What then is intimacy? It is closeness. It comes from a Latin word meaning the highest degree of within-ness.

Intimacy is the most important quality in a major life relationship. Most people cannot achieve true intimacy with more than a small number of people, for intimacy requires *time,* a good amount of time, as its first ingredient. Intimacy doesn't happen over a cup of tea, or overnight. The second ingredient for intimacy must be *mutuality,* that is, the desire of each person for intimacy with the other. The third factor is *reciprocity,* which has to do with exchange and commitment. Eventually both must want intimacy with each other equally.

And true intimacy cannot be achieved without *trust*, a most delicate and vital factor. Two individuals take many steps toward trust in each other, every step almost inevitably involving small revealments as each one opens his or her innermost self to the other and tests the safety of that opening. Virginia Johnson, of the famous Masters and Johnson team, has called this process "the exchange of vulnerabilities," meaning that by revealing themselves to each other the two partners are opening themselves up to the real possibility of being hurt, scorned, or rejected by the other. Successive experiences of openness safely engaged in serve to build up the trust to its ultimate expression, which is open and free delight one in the other. And this, to us, has to be the ultimate meaning of the word *intimacy,* for when two people delight each other, and delight in each other, in an atmosphere of security based on mutuality, reciprocity, and total trust each in the other, whatever their age or sex or relationship, this is surely the kind of relationship that every human being seeks, even if it does not involve physical sex.

We hope this chapter has helped you to a better understanding of highly varied aspects of human sexuality called erotic sex and the way it can fit into a relationship. Understanding it, in ourselves first and then in our children, can help all of us to accept and learn how to use it responsibly, appropriately, and with fulfillment in our lives, and to put our children on the road to doing the same thing. Ignoring it, repressing it, punishing it, fearing it—these negative attitudes do just the opposite by imprisoning us in walls of frustration, despair, and aloneness. We should not be afraid of erotic sex in ourselves or in our children, but instead learn how to treat it with dignity, honor, and responsibility—as well as with joy.

3
How Human Beings Have Children:
The Human Reproductive Systems

At this point we would like to come back to the distinction made in Chapter 2 between two systems in human beings, the *reproductive system* and the *sexual response system*. This distinction may surprise you, for it is not commonly made. Most people think, simply, "Sex—yes, that has to do with having children. Oh, and it also involves a lot of feelings." Of course, the reproductive and and the sexual systems are closely related to each other in the working of our bodies, minds, and feelings, but they are not the same.

As we grow up, our reproductive system—the system that enables us to become mothers or fathers—generally does not begin to function until somewhere in our teens. Assuming we have led relatively healthy lives, it develops almost automatically. Its schedule of development, although different for each of us, is quite straightforward and very little affected by what we think, learn, or do. We automatically become capable of reproducing.

The Reproductive Systems

Human life results almost always from sexual intercourse between a male and a female. During intercourse, or coitus, the male ejaculates millions of sperm cells from his penis into the upper part of the vagina of the female. These sperm travel up the reproductive tract of the female. If they meet an egg cell, which has been released from one of the female's two ovaries, several sperm immediately surround the egg cell, the *ovum,* trying to penetrate its wall. One sperm, and only one, enters the egg, and this results in an instantaneous chemical reaction so that the cell wall shuts out all other sperm. About 266 days later, if all goes normally, the two joined cells have multiplied, by division, into some 200 billion cells, and a baby is born.

That, in simplest terms, is the story of how human beings beget children. But the full story is much more complex and very interesting.

The major basic difference between male and female, between the two *genders,* is that the male can ejaculate and can impregnate the female, while the female is the one who can be impregnated. Four other things the female can do that the male cannot are: menstruate, gestate (develop a life inside her), give birth, and lactate (give milk). Aside from these differences, males and females are capable of sharing each other's tasks and functions and feelings and exchanging roles freely—if they wish to and if society, that is, other people, allows them to.

The Male Reproductive Organs

The reproductive organs of a male consist of a remarkable and intricate system of glands, tubes, containers, valves, and muscles that work together to produce sperm, to store it until needed, and then to deliver it into the female's body. A man's most obvious reproductive organ—which is also his sexual organ—is his *penis.* Another word for penis is *phallus,* from the Greek. When limp (or flaccid) a grown man's penis is about the length of a finger but somewhat thicker. When erect, the penis increases greatly in size and somewhat in diameter and stands stiffly up and out from the body. An erect penis is usually six inches or more in length. When it becomes erect, a small limp penis increases proportionately more in size than a large limp penis, so that erection is, to use the phrase of sex researchers Masters and Johnson, the great equalizer of penis size. Except for obvious and rare abnormalities, penises of any size work perfectly well in performing their reproductive function. And there is no relationship between the size of the penis and body build, race, or reproductive power.

The penis is composed mostly of spongy tissue containing many small blood vessels and nerves. (It contains no bone as do the penises of some other male mammals, such as dogs.) A small tube, the *urethra,* runs the length of the penis and functions as a passageway to empty urine from the bladder and as a passageway for the ejaculation of

Fig. 1. Male figure

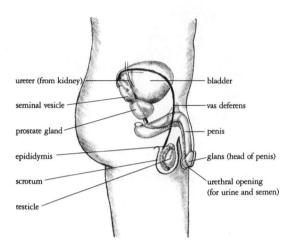

ureter (from kidney)
seminal vesicle
prostate gland
epididymis
scrotum
testicle

bladder
vas deferens
penis
glans (head of penis)
urethral opening
(for urine and semen)

Fig. 2. Male genito-urinary system

semen. Urine and semen cannot use this passage at the same time—
they cannot get mixed together—because when a man is about to
ejaculate, a valve automatically closes off the connection with the
bladder. Also, two small glands (Cowper's glands) secrete a special
substance just before ejaculation that neutralizes any acid (which
would kill the sperm) that might remain from previous passage of
urine through the urethra.

At the end of the penis is the head, or *glans,* which is its most
sensitive part because it is supplied with many nerves. The glans is
covered by a loose sheath of skin, the *foreskin.* When the penis
becomes erect, the foreskin is retracted, exposing the glans. The
foreskin can be pushed back from the glans, making it possible to clean
underneath it. It is necessary to clean underneath the foreskin because
small glands near the end of the penis produce a cheesy substance
called *smegma.* No one knows what smegma is for, but it has a certain
odor that can be unpleasant when too much is allowed to collect under
the foreskin. (Similar glands in females also produce smegma around
the clitoris, the corresponding female organ for sexual pleasure).

In the United States, many male infants have this foreskin

Fig. 3. *Left,* circumcised penis; *right,* uncircumcised penis

removed in the hospital on the second day after birth by means of a surgical operation called *circumcision* (cutting around). The doctor pulls the foreskin out in front of the penis and neatly cuts off part of it with a special device. Those who advocate circumcision say that it promotes cleanliness. Opponents are against the pain endured by the baby and the occasional accidents related to circumcision. Despite various beliefs to the contrary, there is no evidence that circumcised males are any more or any less responsive sexually than uncircumcised ones, or that circumcision affects reproduction.

Under a man's penis hangs a sac of loose, crinkly skin called the *scrotum.* The scrotum is divided into two compartments, each of which contains a *testicle,* an *epididymis,* and the lower part of the *vas deferens,* all of which we shall explain below. The scrotal covering also contains muscles that contract when cold, thus pulling the testicles up nearer the body. These muscles work involuntarily and operate like a sort of thermostat to keep the testicles at just the right temperature—lower than that inside the body, but not too much lower—for the manufacture of sperm. Generally, a man's left testicle hangs down slightly lower than his right, although both are the same size.

Fig. 4. The penis when limp and when erect

The two *testicles*—also called *testes* (*testis* being the singular), and a number of less formal terms—are the sperm-makers. They are oval-shaped and approximately 1½ to 2 inches long in a grown man, about the size of a plum. Each testicle contains perhaps 270 yards—over one eighth of a mile—of threadlike, coiled-up tubules (tiny tubes) in which sperm are continuously made after a boy has reached puberty. These sperm pass into the *epididymis,* another collection of tubules, in which they mature as they pass through and on into the *vas deferens.*

Sperm are the male reproductive cells. The scientific words for them are *spermatozoon* (singular) and *spermatozoa* (plural). Sperm are invisible to the human eye, except under a microscope, a single sperm being about as long as two thirds the thickness of an average human hair. A sperm is shaped somewhat like a tadpole, with a tail that lashes about and enables it to swim along. If one could line up sperm head to tail, it would take five hundred of them to make an inch. Yet, small as they are, each sperm contains all that is needed to unite with an egg in a woman and start a baby.

We now come to that part of the male reproductive system which might be called "storage and delivery." Once manufactured and matured, the sperm pass along the vas deferens and are stored there near the openings of the *seminal vesicles*, two small pouches well inside the man's body (see Figure 2). Here they remain quite inactive until they are ejaculated (see p. 57), when the seminal vesicles release a fluid which activates the sperm. At the time of ejaculation, a thick, milky fluid secreted by the *prostate gland* is also added. This mixture of sperm and fluid is then called *semen*, and it nourishes the sperm and keeps them alive while in the vagina until a number of them find their way from the vagina into the cervix and then upward toward an ovum.

The *prostate gland*, which lies just below the bladder, is a most important part of the delivery system for the sperm. It manufactures the milky part of the semen, of which the sperm form only a minute portion of the volume. When a man becomes sexually excited, and his erect penis is ready for *orgasm* (see pp. 16 and 271), the muscles of the prostate and other muscles near it contract in a series of quick spasms that propel the semen down the urethra and *ejaculate* it out of the opening at the tip of the penis. These spasms of ejaculation—that is, when the male has an orgasm, or "comes"—are highly pleasurable. The desire for this pleasure is the principal reason why men want to have intercourse—that, or to create a child.

The Female Reproductive Organs

We said that the man's most obvious reproductive organ is his penis. The organ of the female that most nearly corresponds to the penis is the *clitoris*, which, although small, contains a concentration of sensitive nerves almost exactly like those in the head of the penis. However, the clitoris is not concerned with the process of reproduction and is not, therefore, considered a part of the female reproductive system. It is, however, as we have said, a very important part of a female's sexual response system.

A woman's primary reproductive organs are her *ovaries*, which correspond to the testicles in the man. The two ovaries, each the shape of a flattened oval and about 1½ to 2 inches long, lie inside the lower part of the abdomen, one on each side (see Figure 6). When a girl is born, her ovaries already contain about 400,000 immature eggs, or *ova*. The ovaries do not manufacture ova, but rather store them ready to bring to maturity after *puberty* (see pp. 49 and 279). That's when the ova start maturing, usually one ovum each month, roughly halfway

Fig. 5. Female figure

between two menstrual periods. However, the time intervals differ with different women, ranging from twenty-one to thirty-eight days. They may also vary in an individual woman, depending upon particular circumstances in her life.

The ovum matures within a little saclike bubble on the surface of the ovary. The wall of this sac gradually becomes thinner, and the sac contains an increasing amount of fluid surrounding the ovum. During the process called *ovulation,* an opening is created in the sac, so that the ovum and fluid are expelled. Some women can feel a slight twinge about the time this happens, although the twinge (called *Mittelschmerz,* German for "middle pain") may occur as long as one day before or one day after the actual ovulation, or may never be felt at all. It is therefore not a reliable indicator of the moment of ovulation. When the egg is released, it is transported along with its fluid and surrounding cells into the opening at the end of the fallopian tube, assisted in its journey by the motion of waving fingerlike threads *(fimbriae)* at the opening of the tube. As the ovum is thus picked up, it is moved down the tube toward the uterus, propelled by the action of minute hairlike *cilia* which wave downward toward the uterus. Whether it is fertilized or not, the ovum is retained within the fallopian tube for approximately three days, after which it is delivered into the uterus. If the ovum has not been fertilized, it begins to disintegrate in the uterus and soon disappears. (The human ovum is much smaller than the period at the end of this sentence. It would take two hundred eggs side by side to cover an inch. However, compared to a sperm, the egg is a giant (see Figure 7).

In preparation for the possible arrival of a fertilized egg—called a *zygote*—the uterus has been developing, over a period of about two weeks, a thick, soft, velvety lining, the *endometrium,* which is made up mostly of blood vessels. In this lining the zygote can be imbedded and continue its growth. If no egg is fertilized, the uterus sheds its lining in the process called *menstruation.*

If an egg encounters sperm in the tube, it probably will be fertilized. Then it continues down the fallopian tube, its cells dividing rapidly all the while, so that by the time it has been floated down and into the *uterus* (or *womb*) it has divided several times and contains between eight and sixteen cells. The uterus is an amazing organ about the size and shape of a small pear, some 3 inches long in a woman who has not had children. It is strongly muscular, yet stretchable. In the lining of the uterus the fertilized egg becomes implanted and will

Fig. 6. Female reproductive system

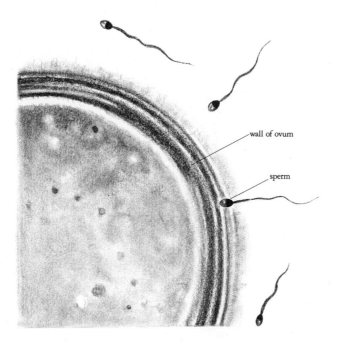

wall of ovum

sperm

Fig. 7. Moment of fertilization

grow into a baby. As the baby grows, so will the uterus to accommodate it within its strong muscular walls. These muscles, aided by the
muscles of the abdomen, will not only protect the baby but will later
do the work—the labor—of pushing the baby out through the birth
canal (vagina) and into the world.

The vagina actually belongs to both the reproductive system and
the sexual response system. It is the place where the penis deposits the
sperm during sexual intercourse; it is the main passage through which
the baby passes when it is born; and it is the passage for the menstrual
flow. The outer opening of the vagina is not a visible hole and can be
seen only when the lips of the vulva are parted. The entrance to the
vagina of a woman before she has had intercourse is usually partly
closed by a membrane called the *hymen.* No one knows of any particular use for the hymen. In most women it is quite delicate, in a few it
is rather tough. In some cases the hymen has only a small opening,
which permits the exit of the menstrual flow; in other cases there are
a number of openings, either large or small; in still others there is no

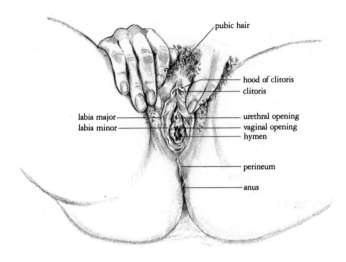

Fig. 8. Female genital area

hymen at all (see Figure 9). Many people mistakenly believe it is possible to tell whether or not a woman is a virgin (one who has not had sexual intercourse) by whether her hymen is unbroken or broken. If it is unbroken, yes, she is a virgin, but if it is broken, no one can say (except the woman herself), for in many girls an ample opening develops quite naturally, or the hymen may even have been almost entirely absent at birth. Also, using a tampon during menstruation may enlarge to some degree the opening in the hymen of a woman who is a virgin, although the largest tampons are smaller than an erect penis. With the help of a hand mirror and a flashlight, girls and women can easily examine and identify for themselves all the external organs we have mentioned, and it is helpful for them to become acquainted with their bodies in this way.

The vagina most of the time is a soft, muscular tube about 3 or 4 inches long that, except when it is being used as a passageway, is rather like a collapsed balloon. Its inner lining is soft and moist, much like the lining of a person's mouth. Most of its length it is not sensitive

Fig. 9. Different types of hymen

to touch, but the outer end—the area surrounding the opening—is sensitive and excitable. When a woman is sexually aroused, the walls of her vagina produce a slippery fluid that makes it easy for an erect penis to enter.

At the upper end of the vagina is the *cervix,* or neck of the uterus, the passage into the uterus. This passage is not much larger than the lead of a pencil and is called the *cervical canal.* It is large enough for thousands of sperm to pass through at each ejaculation.

Menstruation

If, as is usually the case, no egg has been fertilized and become implanted in the lining of the wall of the uterus (the endometrium), that lining is no longer needed and is shed, or discarded. This process is called menstruation. Many women, when they menstruate, say they are "having their period." The menstrual flow lasts from three to six

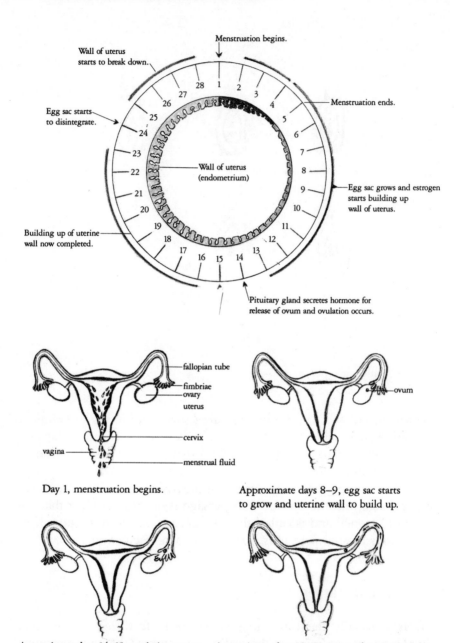

Day 1, menstruation begins.

Approximate days 8–9, egg sac starts to grow and uterine wall to build up.

Approximate days 14–15, ovulation occurs.

Approximate days 19–20, ovum about to enter uterus, building of uterine wall now completed.

Fig. 10. *Above,* scheme of typical menstrual cycle by days; *below,* menstrual cycle days. It is not bleeding in the ordinary sense of the word, although the flow is red and contains blood and tissue, including minute blood vessels. Ordinarily, menstruation does not weaken a woman, for it merely discards material that her body has already supplied but that is no longer needed. Menstruation usually occurs at four-week intervals, but this can vary from three to five weeks or more.

For menstruation a woman needs to wear some disposable absorbent material to collect the menstrual flow. One such device is a pad or napkin (such as Kotex, Modess, or Stay-Free) that is held in place against the opening of the vagina by an elastic panty, a belt, or a sticky backing that makes it cling to a panty. Another menstrual aid is a tampon or insert (such as Tampax or Playtex) made of absorbent material shaped into a small roll that can be easily inserted into the vagina to absorb the flow. The use of tampons was linked in 1980 to a rare disease, toxic shock syndrome. It appears, however, that any possible risk of this may be reduced by off-and-on use—for example, using a pad at night and a tampon during the day. (See Figure 11.) Women may wish to consult their doctors about it.

Some women find the few days before and during menstruation somewhat uncomfortable. Part of the discomfort may be caused by congestion of the blood vessels in and around the uterus before the flow begins; part by the contraction of the uterine muscles to discard the lining, which may be felt as pains or aches in the lower back; part by a tendency in some women to accumulate fluids in the tissues, which gives a heavy feeling to the body; and part by the chemical changes in the woman's body as the glands of her ovaries secrete less of the hormones that prepared her uterus for a possible pregnancy and may also have given her a feeling of well-being. Thus, during her period a woman may feel edgy and may tire more readily than usual. Some women may feel low during these days if they have a negative attitude toward the whole process of menstruation; some women may still be calling it "the curse." If a woman experiences nausea, vomiting, or severe cramps, or if she feels very depressed during menstruation, she should consult her doctor.

Today's girls and women lead their usual lives during their periods. With the modern methods of protection against the flow now available, there is no reason why they should not participate in all sports and other activities, including swimming.

thin beltless
panty shield

beltless pad to adhere
to underpants

typical tampon

menstrual pad

bladder
uterus
tampon
vagina
anus
tampon string

Fig. 11. Menstrual aids

When a woman menstruates, it is a clear sign that she is not pregnant. On the other hand, if she does not menstruate within a week or two of her usual time, and if she has been having sexual intercourse, this is a sign that she may be pregnant, and she will want to check with a doctor or clinic to find out for sure. (Other signs of possible pregnancy are discussed later in this chapter.)

The Puberty Timetable

How can a girl know when she is about to have her first menstrual period, or a boy when he will have his first ejaculation of semen? When will they reach *puberty,* as it is called? Usually, girls and boys are very much interested in knowing this, and some are quite worried about it. Parents ought to be aware of this concern and anticipate it by providing full information.

Perhaps the most important point to make is that there is tremendous variation in the ages at which people reach puberty; there is no single "right" or "proper" age. Further, there is no relationship between people's ability to respond sexually and the age at which they first menstruate or ejaculate. Also, it's interesting to note that in the United States over the past hundred years the average age for reaching puberty has decreased by about four years—or four months for each decade. That means the average age for reaching puberty in the 1870s was probably seventeen, in contrast to today's average age in the early teens.

Boys

In general, boys have their first ejaculation quite some time before they appear to be "men." This first ejaculation announces that a boy has arrived at puberty, that he is capable of making a female pregnant. Although, in general, boys' physical development comes about two years later than that of girls, the average age of first ejaculation is only about six months to a year later than that for first menstruation in girls. However, the general impression one gets, based on body shape and size, is that boys are about two years behind girls in reaching full physical maturity, even though, in fact, they are much less far behind in their capacity to reproduce.

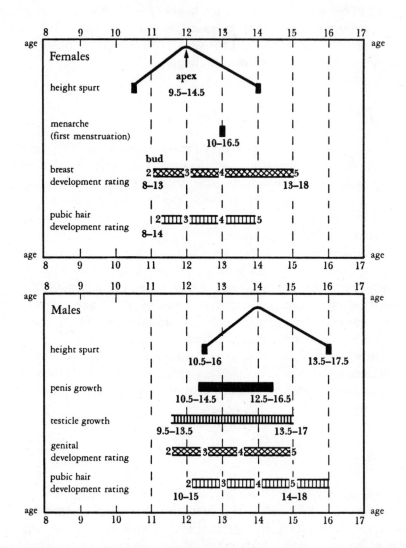

Chart 1. Sequence of Physical Events In Adolescent Development. The average age is represented. The age range within which each event may begin and end is given by the figures directly below the start and finish of the bar or graph (except for the female height spurt, for which the age range of apex is given).

Usually the first stirrings of puberty and the beginnings of adolescence are marked by the start of a spurt in growth. Chart 1 shows that the average male begins his growth spurt at about age 12½ and finishes it at age 16, with the fastest rate of growth coming, on the average, around age 14. However, note that the age *range* for the *start* of the growth spurt is from 10½ to 16, while the age range for its completion is 13½ to 17½. Many perfectly healthy individuals fall outside these typical ranges, so that some boys actually complete their growth spurts before others have even begun theirs. In a single year of his growth spurt, a boy may become 2½ to 5 inches taller. The upper-age figures of the growth spurt do not indicate that a boy has reached his full height at these ages, only that his period of extra-rapid growth has ended. Usually, he will continue to grow for from two to four more years.

A boy may have been masturbating and experiencing orgasm for a number of years, even though his first ejaculation of semen will not occur until his growth spurt, and he cannot predict exactly when that will be. On the average—but remember the great variation—it comes about a year after his penis and testicles have noticeably started to grow (see "genital development rating" in Chart 1) and at about the time that his growth spurt peaks. A fairly reliable sign of approaching ejaculation is the appearance, just above the penis, of pubic hair, at first downy but gradually becoming darker and coarser. Usually somewhat later, hair begins to grow under the arms (axillary hair). About three to four months after the first *curly* pubic hair appears, the first seminal ejaculation will probably happen—perhaps in a wet dream (nocturnal emission), perhaps in masturbation; there are great variations. The change of voice in early adolescence generally begins to be noticeable a few months *after* the first ejaculation. This change, a part of the growth spurt, is caused by a rather rapid growth in the size of the larynx (voice box).

Two sources of embarrassment to many boys during their adolescence are *acne* and *gynecomastia.* Acne is a skin condition, especially of the face, that causes pimples, often rather deep ones, to form when the skin begins to secrete increased amounts of an oily substance which clogs the pores. (Acne occurs in some girls, too, but usually not nearly so severely as in boys.) Gynecomastia (not nearly as bad as it sounds!) is the name doctors give to the temporary enlargement of the breasts which occurs in about 80 percent of boys during puberty. It is probably caused by very small amount of female sex hormones

Fig. 12. Three males: *left to right,* prepuberty, early puberty, postpuberty

Fig. 13. Three adolescent males of the same age but at different stages of growth

normally produced by the testicles, and it soon disappears as the body adjusts to the changes of adolescence.

It is perfectly normal for a boy to reach puberty as early as age 10 or 11 or as late as 15 or 16. The drawings in Figure 13 illustrate the differences in normal development.

Girls

Girls also experience an adolescent growth spurt, usually—but not always—about two years before boys. A look back at Chart 1 will show that on the average it begins at age 10½ and ends at age 14. Generally, a girl's first menstruation (called *menarche*) comes about three quarters of the way through her growth spurt, not, as in boys, at its apex. There is an age range of three to five years in the time girls reach the apex, and, as with boys, some girls will have completed their spurt before others have started theirs. The drawings in Figure 14 illustrate how great the physical differences are and how misleading it is to make generalizations about the rate and stages of adolescent physical development.

On the average—and remember that few people are exactly at the average—a girl's breasts begin to bud about three to four years before menarche and become noticeable two to three years before. About one and a half to two and a half years before, pubic hair appears above her genitals, and underarm hair appears about six months before.

A girl's first menstruation is the sign that she has arrived at puberty, that she might be capable of being impregnated. Even though in many girls there is a gap of several months to more than a year between first menstruation and first ovulation, it is impossible to tell which girls have this gap. In fact, some girls may first ovulate even *before* they menstruate, so that it is entirely possible for a sexually active girl to become pregnant before her first menstruation. Once a girl has ovulated she is thereafter fertile.

The Reproductive Act

A new human life can be started by the joining of a fertile male and a fertile female in *sexual intercourse.* Another standard word for this act is *coitus.* In animals it is called copulation—mounting or covering, in

Fig. 14. Three females: *left to right*, prepuberty, early puberty, postpuberty

Fig. 15. Four adolescent females of the same age but at different stages of growth

farm language. In sexual intercourse, the erect penis of the man enters the vagina of the woman and, after a variable period of time involving various movements, generally pleasurable to both, the man ejaculates semen into the upper end of the vagina. One ejaculation usually contains about a teaspoonful of semen including some 150 million to 600 million sperm, which are only a minute proportion of the volume of the semen.

Some of these millions of sperm enter the cervical canal and the uterus. The notion many people have that sperm have a sense of purpose and swim steadily toward their goal, the unfertilized egg, is a false one. Once sperm are ejaculated, their swimming motion is quite random, but it is somewhat guided by tubelike formations in the cervical mucus and by muscular contractions of the uterus. When some of the sperm reach the entrance to the fallopian tubes, they enter and move through the tubes, on out the other end, and into the abdominal cavity. Their movement up the tubes is caused partly by their own swimming action, partly by the direction given by the mucus, and partly by contracting movements of the tubes themselves (called peristalsis). Sperm have been detected in the fallopian tubes within five minutes after ejaculation, and generally, from that point on, several sperm are passing through the tubes at any given time, over a period of two to three days, in some cases as many as five, ready to fertilize an egg that may be on its way down. The whole matter of how the egg is moved down the tube and how sperm pass into and up through the tubes is a complicated one, not entirely understood. But it works. An egg gets fertilized and begins the process of multiplying and dividing which, if nothing interferes with it, will eventually result in a baby.

Of course, there is much more to sexual intercourse than we have described here, as you saw in Chapter 2 on the sexual response systems. Just remember what Dr. Wardell Pomeroy says: "Penises and vaginas do not love each other; only people can do that."

Pregnancy

Once an egg is fertilized, the woman is pregnant and the lining of her uterus is needed; therefore she does not menstruate again until the pregnancy is over. Missing her "period" is one of the early signs that she can expect a baby, although one missed period is not a totally sure sign, for some women occasionally skip a period without being pregnant. However, ten days to two weeks after her usual time for menstruation has passed, a woman will want to know for sure if she is pregnant, and a doctor or technician can tell by any one of several tests of her blood or urine. Other early signs of pregnancy that the woman herself can notice are enlargement and tenderness of the breasts; "morning sickness," a feeling of nausea or aversion to food that some women experience during the first six weeks, most often in the morning; the need to urinate more frequently than usual; and a sense of fatigue and a need to sleep more than usual.

Sexual Intercourse During Pregnancy

While she is pregnant, a woman's ovaries produce no more mature eggs. Thus, when she has sexual intercourse there is no chance of starting another baby. But under normal circumstances, both man and woman can certainly enjoy intercourse during her pregnancy. The feelings of closeness and pleasure that sexual intercourse provides are just as important—perhaps even more so—during pregnancy as at other times. It is not true that the motions of intercourse or of orgasm will harm the developing baby or cause a miscarriage. However, because of recent research possibly linking infections with intercourse in the last month of pregnancy, sexual relations toward the end of the period of gestation should be discussed with the obstetrician. Of course, if a woman should ever experience pain or bleeding during pregnancy she should consult her doctor at once. Intercourse may be resumed very soon after childbirth whenever all bleeding has ceased and if it does not cause the mother discomfort, usually after four to six weeks.

Care During Pregnancy

When a woman realizes she is pregnant, or thinks she may be pregnant, she should be in touch with a doctor regularly to be sure that everything is going all right and to get advice on such matters as diet.

In general, whatever makes a pregnant woman healthy is likely to improve the health of her baby, and whatever is damaging to her health may endanger the baby. That is why it is important for a pregnant woman to be constantly under the care of a doctor and to tell him or her everything about her food and drug or medication habits. Even when the pregnant woman suffers from poor health, however, in the vast majority of cases her baby is born healthy.

More and more women are participating in classes and groups to help them enjoy their pregnancies and to prepare themselves for childbirth. Husbands often join the classes so that the pregnancy and birth can become a closely shared experience for the couple.

Tobacco, Drugs, and Alcohol During Pregnancy

Whatever a pregnant woman takes into her system will have some effect on the life growing within her. The food she eats nourishes both her and, through the exchange across the placental-endometrial barrier, the baby. There is much study now under way to determine the effects of substances other than food taken into the expectant mother's system.

It has been observed that when a mother smokes, the fetus becomes more active and its heartbeat speeds up. Mothers who smoke give birth, on the average, to somewhat smaller babies than those who do not, and the babies' chances of survival are slightly decreased. Marijuana has a temporary effect on the fetus, but as yet no known harmful one. Heavy drugs, especially heroin, are very injurious to the baby. If the mother is addicted, the baby will be born an addict and suffer the same severe withdrawal symptoms that an adult addict suffers when suddenly taken off the drug. Other drugs—even those that are commonly obtained without a prescription—can also have major effects. No pregnant woman should use any drug or medicine at all without the advice of her doctor.

As for alcohol, when the mother drinks very moderately the baby's movements inside the uterus are slowed down while the alcohol is in the mother's bloodstream, but if the mother drinks more than just a moderate amount, the chances of her having a severely defective baby are much higher than normal.

From Fertilization to Birth

The average length of time from fertilization until birth is about 266 days, a little less than nine months. The length of time from the last menstrual period is 280 days, a bit over nine months. In general, we divide the period of pregnancy into three *trimesters,* each about three months long.

From the beginning of pregnancy until its eighth week, the future baby is known as an *embryo,* after which it is called a *fetus.* It gets its nourishment through a thick, disk-shaped collection of very fine blood vessels and tissue, the *placenta,* to which it is connected by a long, ropelike cord, the *umbilical cord.* The minute blood vessels of the placenta grow outward to lie alongside those of the mother's uterine lining, her *endometrium.* Through the very thin walls of both sets of blood vessels, an exchange occurs of nutritional elements and oxygen, which pass from the bloodstream of the mother to the bloodstream of the growing baby; waste materials from the baby pass the other way, from baby to mother, whose kidneys then excrete them. Food and oxygen are carried to the baby, and waste is carried from the baby, through the umbilical blood vessels. The embryo makes its own blood, which never mixes with the blood of the mother and may be of a different blood type.

The First Trimester (About Weeks 1–13)

At first, the human embryo resembles the embryos of other animals. For a short time it has what look like the beginnings of gills, as in fish embryos, and later what appears to be a tail. But these are not real gills or a real tail, and they turn into real parts of the baby. Even later its body is covered with fine, downy hair, which it soon loses.

At *four weeks* the embryo is about ¼ inch long. It has lost its "gills" but still has its "tail," and an ordinary observer would not be able to distinguish it from the embryo of a fish, turtle, chicken, cat, rabbit, or dog. At as early as six weeks, brain waves have been recorded in a human embryo.

At *nine weeks* the fetus has grown to 1½ inches in length and weighs only about 1/20 of an ounce. To reach an average birth weight only seven months later, it will have to grow about 2,400 times heavier. As you can see from Figure 16, the fetus has a large head, and fingers and toes are starting to appear. The head contains the beginnings of eyes, ears, nose, and mouth, and the heart is pumping blood through the tiny body. The umbilical cord is connected to the placenta, which has grown into the muscular wall of the uterus. The reproductive system of the fetus has now been developing for about three or four weeks. By the ninth week, if one were able to examine the fetus with a microscope, it would be possible to tell whether these beginnings would turn out to be testicles or ovaries.

At *twelve weeks* the fetus has made a great spurt of growth and is now about 4 inches long but weighs only 1/3 ounce—about 1/50 pound. The beginnings of the testicles or ovaries have now grown larger and have moved lower in the body of the fetus, but not to their final positions. The penis of a male fetus and the clitoris of a female fetus are not distinguishable; they look very much alike at this stage.

The Second Trimester (About Weeks 14–25)

By *sixteen to seventeen* weeks the fetus has grown to be 7 or 8 inches long and weighs 1/3 pound. Its bones have begun to develop, and its arms and legs can move. The mother may now be able to feel the first faint flutter of activity inside her womb, called "quickening," although the fetus has been moving, unfelt, for some weeks prior to this. Figure 16 shows a picture of a five-month-old fetus, umbilically attached to its placenta and floating in fluid inside the *amniotic sac,* to cushion it from bumps. Notice that by now it looks more like a skinny baby with fairly well developed hands and feet and an oversized head.

At *twenty-one weeks* the fetus would be about 10 inches long if its curled-up legs were stretched out straight. It weighs about ¾ pound and is covered with downy hair. (No one knows why it develops body hair at this stage, only to lose it about a month later.)

At *twenty-five weeks,* the fetus is 12 inches long and weighs about 1¼ pounds—still quite thin, not yet having begun to store up body fat. (It is losing its body hair, which stays floating around in the amniotic fluid until expelled during the birth process.)

If the fetus should be born, or delivered, at the end of the second trimester, it would have only a slight chance (perhaps 5 to 10 percent) of survival, if given heroic care for many weeks by doctors and nurses. By weeks 29 or 30, the chances will have risen to 50 percent. As the fetus develops through the third trimester, its chances of surviving increase steadily. Medical technology has, over the years, been able to lower the age of viability—the age at which a fetus is likely to be born alive. For it just to be born alive, however, does not always at nine weeks   at five months

Fig. 16. Actual size of fetus at two stages

mean that it will stay alive or have all its systems functioning normally.

A baby born weighing less than 5½ pounds is called *premature.* One of the main facilities for the care of a premature baby is an incubator, a small, heated, enclosed, boxlike bed that keeps it warm and protected and allows it to be handled as little as possible while being fed and cared for.

The Third Trimester (About Weeks 26–38)

At *twenty-nine weeks* the fetus is about 14 inches long and probably weighs over 2 pounds. The body hair is gone. In the next two months it will have to increase its weight three or four times to reach the average birth weight. Around this time the testicles of the male fetus have, in almost every case, descended into the scrotum, and the penis is having periodic erections.

During weeks *thirty to thirty-eight,* the eighth and ninth months, the fetus grows rapidly to an average weight of 7½ pounds and, at the end of the 266-day gestation period, perhaps a few days earlier, perhaps a few days later, it is full-term and ready to be born. In the United States its chances of survival after birth are just over 98 percent. (Several countries have even better survival rates.)

In the last trimester of pregnancy things get a bit crowded inside the mother's abdomen as the baby and the uterus expand and press upon the other organs (see Figure 17). This is when an expectant mother urinates more often than usual and may want to eat smaller, more frequent meals.

Childbirth

For most of the hundreds of thousands of years that human beings have been reproducing their kind, childbirth was looked upon as a natural phenomenon, experienced without special help, except for that given by other women. Often it was a quite casual event, with only a brief interruption of the mother's daily life. But during this long period of prehistory and history, the numbers of infants dying at birth or shortly afterward (the infant mortality rate) was very high.

Until about 150 years ago, babies in the Western world were usually born at home, often with the help of a specially trained woman called a *midwife*. While certainly not a physician, the midwife knew how to help a mother have a delivery that was more comfortable and safe than if no experienced person were present. Since the early eighteenth century and until very recently, the conduct of childbirth has been more and more taken over by male doctors and surgeons. It has become more of a medical process than a natural one, with women having their babies in hospitals rather than at home, and with emphasis on anesthetics, surgical instruments such as forceps, and a team of medical technicians assisting. Husbands were rarely allowed to be present.

The development of the specialty of *obstetrics* (an *obstetrician* is a doctor who specializes in childbirth), with its highly developed procedures and its emphasis on sterile conditions and anesthetics, rapidly reduced the infant and maternal mortality rates. But it also took childbirth out of the home and out of the context of the family, and it may have encouraged the notion that pregnancy and giving birth were more medical problems to be dealt with by doctors than natural parts of ongoing family life. Mothers tended to become isolated from the process of birth (during it they were often made unconscious, or nearly so, by anesthesia) and were physically separated from their babies during their stay at the hospital, except for nursing time. As for fathers, they were considered to have done their part nine months earlier and were not welcome either as observers or as participants in the process of birth; fathers were often not even permitted to hold their babies in the hospital.

Today, however, there is a growing conviction on the part of mothers, fathers, and many doctors and nurses—and the midwives who have again become part of the birth team—that childbirth can and should be made less clinical and more natural; that, if they wish, mothers should be awake and aware during childbirth; that fathers (again, if they wish) be in on the preparation for childbirth and with their wives, helping them during the birth itself; and that babies should room in with their mothers much of the time they are in the hospital, rather than being whisked off to the hospital nursery for most of the time. Some parents are now even deciding to have their babies born at home, with a midwife attending. If that is their choice, they should make sure that medical help will be available in case of complications. As of now, the American College of Obstetricians and Gynecologists opposes home births because of the possible risks involved.

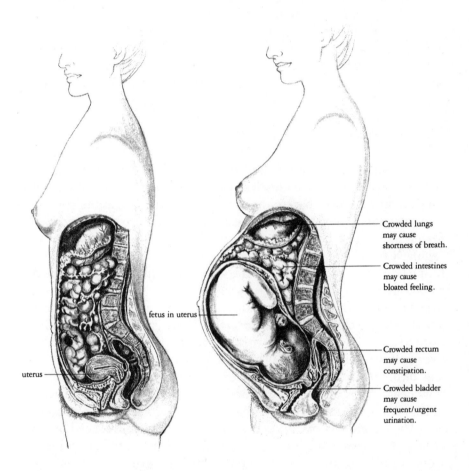

Fig. 17. Effect of pregnancy on body organs: *left*, normal position; *right*, at ninth month of pregnancy

Preparation for childbirth according to a "natural" way involves teaching a prospective mother and father exactly how childbirth works, what the mother's body will be doing during the birth, and how she can relax and cooperate with the actual processes of labor and delivery and in fact enjoy the whole experience, the hard work, and especially the product from the very instant of its birth. People who are interested in training for this kind of childbirth experience can obtain more information about it by writing to any of the several organizations listed under Sources of Help in the back of the book.

The Process of Childbirth

The mother's first signal that her time has come is usually the start of contractions of the strong muscles of the uterus, accompanied by a dull ache across the lower back or a sensation of tightening as the contractions increase in power. At first these contractions are spaced perhaps fifteen minutes to half an hour apart, but when they begin to come regularly every five to ten minutes, the mother should be taken to the hospital, or the doctor or midwife who will help her with the birth should be called in.

The muscular contractions are called *labor,* and a woman who is about to bear a child is said to be *in labor.* There is no doubt that giving birth to a child is usually hard work. It can also be very uncomfortable over a short period of time, but much of the discomfort in a normal birth can be avoided by the expectant mother who has conditioned her body for childbirth and who understands so well what is happening during the birth that she can help guide the process.

The normal discomfort of a woman in childbirth is caused by the aching of the powerful muscles that work to push out the baby. Many women prefer to have an anesthetic, which relieves the discomfort. Other women would rather be fully conscious while bearing a child, with only a mild anesthetic or none at all. But understanding what the experience of childbirth involves tends to relieve fear and anxiety, and it is this that helps to relax the muscles around the vagina, and particularly the cervix, which must dilate, or stretch, to permit passage of the baby. Understanding the process and learning how to cooperate in it can make the mother more relaxed, which increases the ease of the birth and may help speed the arrival of the baby.

Labor in childbirth is divided into three stages. The *first stage* extends from the time when contractions become regular until the cervix is well opened—dilated—about 4 inches. The first stage of labor is the longest, lasting on the average about fifteen hours for a first pregnancy, perhaps four to eight hours or even less in subsequent ones. There is a great variation in the duration of labor, some babies taking a full day or more to be born, others coming in a few hours or even minutes.

The *second stage* of labor extends from the time of full dilation of the cervix until the baby is born. It lasts anywhere from a few minutes to a few hours. Usually, early in active labor, the covering membranes that enclosed the baby break by themselves, and the amniotic fluid they contained, which had acted as a cushion for the baby, flows out through the vagina and helps to lubricate it. Sometimes labor is progressing well into the second stage but the membranes haven't broken by themselves. In such cases the doctor may use a device that painlessly pinches an opening in the membranes so that the fluid will come out and the period of labor be shortened. After this "rush of waters," as it is called, and once the baby's head has passed the cervix, the baby is fairly quickly pushed down through the vagina and out into the world by a series of hard contractions of the uterus and of the mother's abdominal muscles. The head generally comes first; it is usually a tight fit, but the bones of the head are compressible enough to be undamaged. The head serves well as a kind of wedge to open the way for the rest of the body. The doctor or midwife is waiting to guide the head gently as it emerges and to help the baby come out easily as the birth is completed. The birth attendant then lays the baby on the mother's abdomen where she can see it and, after a minute or so, ties and cuts the umbilical cord about 2 inches from where it is attached on the baby's belly. This is painless, since the cord contains no nerves. (A person's navel, or belly button, is the small scar that shows where the cord was attached.)

The *third stage* of labor, which is usually over within fifteen minutes, follows the birth. The uterus goes on contracting, but less vigorously, as the placenta slowly separates from the wall of the uterus where it has been attached and is passed out. After the doctor has examined this *afterbirth,* it is disposed of.

In about one birth in ten, the baby's head may be too large to pass through the mother's pelvic opening, or the baby may be in such a position that a normal birth would be difficult or dangerous. In such cases, the baby is delivered by what is called a *cesarean section* (named

1.Birth process begins.

2.Cervix is dilating; baby is moving down.

3.Baby's head enters pelvic outlet.

4.Baby pushes upward out of vaginal canal.

5.Birth nearly completed.

6.Contractions squeeze placenta making it fall away from lining of uterus and it is expelled.

Fig. 18a. Childbirth, internal view

1. Top of baby's head appears ("crowns").

2. Head emerging.

3. Head has emerged.

4. Head turns.

5a. Upper shoulder emerges.
5b. Lower shoulder emerges.

6. Birth is completed;
father and mother look at baby.

Fig. 18b. Childbirth, as seen from outside

for Julius Caesar, who was supposed to have been born this way). The doctor makes a surgical incision in the abdominal wall and the uterus, lifts the baby out, and carefully sews up the opening. Some mothers have several children by cesarean, and their babies are just as healthy as those born in the usual way. It is especially important for the mother-infant bonding to let her have time with her baby as soon as possible after delivery (see Chapter 1) in the case of cesarean birth.

Newborn Babies

At birth, the baby is on its own for the first time, and its first task is to start breathing—something it did not need to and could not do floating in amniotic fluid inside the uterus (although fetuses do perform breathing actions even when they are thus immersed). Usually the doctor or midwife suctions out the baby's nose and throat with a rubber bulb syringe or suction machine, to clear out any fluid or mucus that might interfere with the start of breathing. After its first breath or two, the baby is likely to utter a small, high cry, which is a delightful sound to the mother and all others present.

Many people, having seen babies a few weeks old or more and knowing how cute and pretty they look, are a bit disappointed and even shocked when they see a new one. A newborn baby is usually not at all beautiful or even cute. It is wrinkly, splotchy, and often quite red. The face may be swollen and look troubled, stupid, or even worn out. In general, the baby doesn't appear to be much of an addition to the world. One must remember that the process of getting born can sometimes be quite hard on a baby, which has been subjected to some strong pushing around. Its color will soon become normal, however, and its skin will look better before long. In less than a month it will be a cute and desirable-looking baby; every day after birth seems to work wonders.

A newborn can see enough to tell light from dark, but things are blurry to it at first, until its eyes learn to focus. The baby can taste, and it can feel pain and pressure. It does not like loud noises or the sensation of falling. It quickly learns that the way to get what it needs is to cry. Many babies do a lot of crying during the first month, whether they need something or not.

One activity the newborn does very well is sucking. It has very strong sucking muscles and a little pad of fat in each cheek to help it.

Fig. 19. Baby nursing from mother; *inset,* diagram of breast

It will turn its head to suck on anything that touches its face near its mouth. Its mother has just the right equipment for it to suck on: at the tip of each breast is a nipple, and within the breasts are the glands that manufacture milk, and a network of small tubes that bring the milk to the nipple whenever the baby sucks.

For the first day or two after the birth, the fluid from the mother's breasts, called colostrum, is slight in amount, yellowish, and watery. Even though it contains little nourishment, it is important to the baby's health because it contains special and important substances that give the baby temporary protection from infections to which it may now be exposed—at least until its own immunity system develops. The baby's sucking stimulates the breast glands to make the mother's milk. Milk from the mother's breast is a perfect food for the human baby because it is clean, safe, at no cost, and digestible, always just the right temperature and always available, with just the right proportions of protein, fats, carbohydrates, minerals, and vitamins.

One of the most important things in people's lives, especially when they are infants, is being held close by those who love them. It makes them feel warm and secure and helps build a foundation of emotional strength. (We talked in Chapter 1 about this formation of mother-baby bonding as an early form of "education" in sexuality.) Many mothers get great pleasure from the experience of nursing their babies, just because of the close link it gives them with their child. Many mothers also find that it can be somewhat sexually arousing, and they may feel frightened of and even guilty about this. Being aroused in this way by nursing is a quite normal reaction of pleasure, and there is no need for fright or guilt.

Many mothers do not wish to, or are not able to, nurse their babies. There is no reason for them to feel distressed about this, even though they are missing what might be a great joy. Babies fed from a bottle and rubber nipple with the modern formulas that are very similar to breast milk grow to be as sturdy and healthy as breast-fed babies. But the mother and father of the bottle-fed baby must be especially aware of the importance of body contact during the first year and hold the baby in their arms lovingly while the child has its bottle, taking plenty of time and allowing bare-skin contact and gentle stroking of the baby's body.

Twins and Other Multiple Births

One birth in every ninety or so produces twins, and one in seven or eight thousand produces triplets. Multiple births come about in one of two ways. In the first, a single egg is fertilized by a single sperm in the usual manner; then the zygote splits into two or three parts, each of which forms an embryo that develops independently. Babies formed this way are termed *identical twins* or *triplets,* and since a single sperm with either an X or a Y chromosome fertilized the egg, they are always of the same sex. They share one placenta and, with exactly the same genetic inheritance, they usually look almost exactly alike.

In the second way that multiple births occur, two or more eggs are ovulated at about the same time, whether from one or both ovaries, and each is fertilized by a different sperm. These babies are called *fraternal* (the word means like brothers or sisters), and are no more likely to resemble each other than any other brothers or sisters in a family, except, of course, they are born at one time. They may be of the same sex or different sexes.

Identical twins get their nourishment from a single placenta, but each fraternal twin has its own placenta. Twins are likely to weigh less than single babies but are not necessarily premature in birth weights.

Triplets, quadruplets, and quintuplets—the latter two being very rare—usually develop from more than one egg. They can be combinations of identical and fraternal or all fraternal babies. Even more rarely do they come as a result of one fertilized egg splitting apart a number of times. (Recently there has been an increase in the number of multiple pregnancies as a result of the use of certain fertility drugs by women who are otherwise unable to become pregnant. These drugs can occasionally cause the release of several ova, and the babies born are always fraternal siblings, not identical ones.)

Menopause

Usually between the ages of forty-five and fifty-five a woman stops menstruating. This is not a single, sudden event but a process lasting several months or years, called *menopause* (sometimes "change of life"). At the end of the process, a woman's ovaries will no longer

placenta

amniotic fluid

placenta

amniotic fluid

placenta

Fig. 20. The two types of twins: *left*, fraternal, from two eggs, having two placentas—sexes may differ; *right*, identical, from one egg, having single placenta—same sex discharge eggs and she can no longer become pregnant. This can, but need not, be a difficult time for a woman, involving as it does a number of hormonal and psychological changes and adjustments. But it does not mean that her sexual response system has stopped functioning, only her reproductive system. Her sexual life can and should remain just the same after menopause as before—and often even better, since there are no more worries about an unwanted pregnancy.

Many women fear menopause because they have heard tales from their mothers' or grandmothers' generations about hot flashes, weakness, and so forth. Generally speaking, attitudes today about menopause are different, so that psychologically a woman understands that it is not to be feared but simply dealt with matter-of-factly. Her periods have stopped. If they had been profuse she may have been anemic, but after menopause she will not be. And she no longer has to deal with menstruation; if she and her husband go on an extended trip she can leave sanitary napkins or tampons and contraceptive measures at home, never to be needed again. For many women this brings on feelings of well-being and a renewed sense of vitality and, often, romance and capacity for sexual enjoyment.

Some women may not be so fortunate. If the physical symptoms are bothersome, their gynecologists may prescribe estrogen replacement therapy for a shorter or longer time, depending on the need and the physician's opinion regarding it. Some women who have wanted children and had none, or not as many as they would have liked, may feel depressed at being confronted by the end of any prospect of having babies. Here again a physician can be helpful by providing mild antidepressants; the family and the husband can also be helpful by not belittling her feelings but by showing her extra tender concern and affection. Change of pace such as a trip is very often helpful, as can be the arrival of grandchildren. In any case, the woman should always bear in mind that whatever sexual life she enjoyed previously, she can enjoy undiminished, or even enhanced, for the rest of her life.

With men there is no similar phenomenon physically. Some men reach a certain age around fifty, however, and begin to reassess their lives and perhaps find them wanting. This is a psychological depression that can be recognized and, again, helped by a loving family, and sometimes by a physician.

A Word About Heredity

The subject of human heredity, by which each of us inherits traits and characteristics from both parents, is too complicated to discuss fully in this book. But everyone should know that in each human egg cell and each human sperm cell are twenty-three minute bodies called *chromosomes,* which determine the heredity of the life that is begun when egg and sperm unite. These forty-six chromosomes (twenty-three pairs) transmit an extremely detailed and complicated code of instructions, called *genes* (from which word comes the adjective *genetic,* meaning "having to do with inherited characteristics"). Among the thousands of traits programmed by the chromosomes in the developing embryo are the color of the skin, eyes, and hair; the shape of the face and the other parts of the body; eventual height and body build; and the potential intelligence—all the inborn things that make each individual different from any other. All people carry traits inherited from their mother and father and through them from previous generations on both sides.

Gender and Heredity

One important factor is not inherited: *gender*—whether a baby is male or female. This is determined by the sex chromosome in the sperm. There are two types of sperm, those that carry a Y chromosome which, when it unites with the X chromosome of an ovum, will produce a male (XY), and those that carry an X chromosome, which will produce a female (XX). The sex, or gender, of a child is determined by the sperm at the moment of fertilization, and nothing that happens after that instant can change it.

Nature and Nurture

Although a person's gender is determined at the moment of fertilization, how people *feel* about their gender depends on how they are treated after birth. Let us look more closely at what else besides gender comes to us inherently at birth (we'll call this our *nature*) and also at the experiences and treatment we receive after birth (we'll call this our *nurture*). We must begin with conception.

When the egg and the sperm fuse at the moment of fertilization, they mingle their chromosomal materials, and the single cell formed by the fusion immediately begins the division that will take the rapidly multiplying cells through a number of complex processes and end 266 or so days later in the birth of a baby. The new human being just formed is alive and growing, but it is not yet the entity it will appear to be perhaps ten weeks later in the pregnancy, and it will not be capable of independent life outside the mother until, at the earliest, about the twenty-fourth week. Even if born at the end of the usual nine months, it is far from being able to live independently. It will for some time need a very complex support and nurture system called a mother!

Fertilization marks the beginning of an individual who will be born unique. This means that no other human being has ever existed, or can ever exist, who will have *exactly* that particular combination of forty-six chromosomes, each one bearing a thousand or more genes in all their particular myriads of combinations, complexities, and possibilities for interaction. So one of the most difficult and yet fascinating questions that scientists have had to grapple with since the development of our knowledge about how heredity works is: How much weight should be given to the many various forces acting upon the individual after birth? The nature vs. nurture question is one that has engaged the attention and motivated the research of scientists for some time, both scientists in the field of genetics (the study of inherited characteristics) and scientists in the somewhat newer field of human behavior (sociologists, psychologists, anthropologists). Right now, there seems to be a tentative meeting of minds that can be stated like this: There is no way known at present to alter the heredity of individuals. There are, however, many ways in which the nurture (environment) of individuals acts upon their particular combination of inherited traits and brings about specific results. For example:

A child is born to parents who are of average intelligence. One parent is quick to feel things—to be angry, to be irritated, to pass judgment, to make decisions, to accept new ideas, to move into action. The other parent is deliberate, thoughtful, considered, slow to accept ideas but persistent once action has been initiated. What effect will these two different people have upon the child born to them? Here are some special factors that might play a role:

1. The father had wanted a boy, the mother a girl; or—
   The father had wanted a girl, the mother a boy.
2. Both parents had wanted the same thing and got it; or—
   Both parents had wanted the same thing and were disappointed.
3. There was at least one child of the same sex already in the family,
   but none of the other sex; or—
   There was no child of the same sex already in the family,
   but one or more of the other sex.
4. The father's occupation was such that he was at home daily for
   breakfast, dinner, and weekends; or—
   The father's occupation was such that he was away for extended
   periods of time.
5. The mother knew nothing about the father's business or profession,
   so that he would not talk about it at home; or—
   The mother knew enough about it that the father's work was the
   most common topic of conversation at home.
6. The mother had never worked outside the home and did not expect
   to; or—
   The mother had worked outside the home and expected to do so
   again.
7. There was a fairly large group of immediate family members
   (grandparents, aunts, uncles, cousins) not too far away, and the
   child's parents got along well with them; or—
   One of the child's parents did not get along well with them; or—
   Neither of the child's parents got along well with them.
8. The child's parents had no family members living, or there were
   none geographically close enough to see them more than once
   a year, and then only hurriedly.
9. The child's parents belonged to a strongly religious sect and followed its teachings strictly; or—
   One of the parents belonged to such a sect, but the other was hostile
   to the beliefs; or—
   Both parents were aggressively antireligious.
10. The family was white or black or Spanish-American or Asian-
    American or of some other racial or national group.

You can see the infinite and bewildering number of possibilities that just these ordinary but often conflicting elements of *nurture* open up for influencing the *nature* of the child. How can we tell what might have been if one or more of the factors we have listed had been different? For example, would Hitler have grown up to be the cruel, ruthless dictator we knew if he had had a loving, caring father in his early life? Would Albert Einstein have been the scientist we knew if he had had parents who pushed and nagged him to finish his education —which he never did?

We can never know the answers. Some studies of identical twins (who always have exactly the same hereditary genes) who were separated very early and brought up quite differently without contact with each other seem to show how important *both* nature and nurture are for eventual outcomes. Right now, we have to accept nature as it comes, but nurture is so important that we can and must do something about making the child's upbringing as warm and beneficial as possible from birth onward. Providing factual information about sex and reproduction is only one of the important acts of nurture that parents can perform for their children. In chapters 1 and 2 we mentioned others.

4
Family Planning

If a woman had her first child at age sixteen and gave birth each year until she reached menopause at, say, age forty-six, she would have produced thirty children—more if some of the births had been of twins or triplets. Although having thirty children is possible, from every point of view it would be a disaster: for the mother, for the father or fathers, for the children, for the society, and for the world. If most women had thirty children, or even ten—in other words, if the birth rate were very high—the earth would quickly become so densely populated that poverty, overcrowding, misery, disease, starvation, and early death would become the normal expectation for almost everyone. This has actually been the case for some time in a number of countries.

During humankind's previous history, there have been no reliable means of *contraception,* that is, ways to prevent pregnancy. World population was kept low by very high death rates. Many babies died in infancy, and most other people died young because there was no sanitation of water and milk and no effective medical science to cure diseases or to control plagues and epidemics. It was only after the beginning of this century that the world as a whole came to have a population problem, even though local areas might have suffered from overpopulation. However, in those countries in which modern medicine developed, and especially in those countries which enjoyed sanitation of waste disposal and of water and milk supplies, the death rates were sharply lowered, people lived longer, and a population explosion began. We will say more about the complicated question of population control toward the end of this chapter, the central point being that, having learned to control most deadly diseases and thus drastically to lower death rates, almost all countries must now learn to lower, equally drastically, their birth rates.

Family Planning for Health Reasons

It is not only because of population difficulties that family planning must become a vital part of the health habits of every sexually active couple. One fact that many people ignore is the high risk that accompanies pregnancy in a woman under eighteen. The risk is not only to her health—and even to her life—but equally to the health of her baby after it is born.

The main cause for the higher health risk in this age-group is that the typical unmarried pregnant teenager in our society does not, for a number of reasons, receive medical attention, nutritional advice, and general support equivalent to those given a typical, married pregnant woman. Many unmarried pregnant teenage girls hide their pregnancies for too long, and both they and their babies suffer. The babies are more likely to be born prematurely, and this results in a higher-than-normal rate of mental retardation, so that such babies are likely to be dependent for the rest of their lives either on the mother and her family or on the state. But if a teenage woman is given good prenatal care, nutrition, and attention, her chances of having a healthy baby are as good as any other woman's.

There is another risk: teenage girls are known to have a suicide rate much higher than the rate of suicide in women over eighteen, and teenage girls who are pregnant show an even higher suicide rate—the second major cause (after accidents) of death in teenagers.

Another fact is that the health risks to the mother and baby rise slightly in pregnancies after the age of forty. We should remember, also, that a mother who is dragged out with too many births too close together finds it difficult to be a good, nurturing mother to her children. When there are too many to feed, clothe, and be patient with, other troubles such as malnutrition, a higher rate of childhood and respiratory diseases, decreased ability to learn, and child abuse arise. Thus the need to have some kind of family planning for the sake of the health of the mother and the baby is vital for every couple to understand and for society to support.

A Couple's Decisions and Actions

Many people believe that the primary responsibility for family planning and for decisions about contraception and what method to use is the woman's. This is erroneous. The most successful users of family planning are those couples who decide together what method to use, and who practice it together. For instance, if the decision is for a condom, the couple can make its use a part of their lovemaking foreplay, with the woman taking responsibility for applying it as a loving and care-taking gesture on behalf of both. In the use of the diaphragm, as will be seen later, if intercourse takes place more than once in the six-hour period following ejaculation the diaphragm must not be removed. Instead, with the diaphragm still in place, an injection of spermicidal cream or jelly should be made. Here again the couple can share in this responsibility, for the wife can load the applicator and leave it beside the bed, and the husband can inject it when it is needed.

But of all the decisions that must be made regarding family planning, none is more important than the choice of method. A well-trained family-planning physician or a family-planning service in a good center will describe each method thoroughly for every couple, showing all the various chemicals and devices that are available for them to choose from. After this, the couple can have the time to discuss which method will best suit their particular needs. They can always begin with one method and, if it does not suit them, shift to another, until they find the method that they prefer. When people find the method they will use with the greatest degree of consistency, that is how the best rate of control of pregnancy can be achieved.

Methods of Contraception

Contraception, or birth control, is important not only from the point of view of world population but also from that of the individual family, whose future well-being may depend upon the ability of the parents to plan and have the number of children they want, when and how far apart they wish to have them. In fact, contraception is vitally important for everyone who is having sexual intercourse but does not wish to have a child as a result.

In general, we can say that today our knowledge of methods of birth control is adequate to keep the world's birth rate, the population of the world, and the number of children in any family, community, or group within desired limits and to protect those who wish to have intercourse without risk of pregnancy. What is not known as yet is how to get that knowledge to people who need to use these methods in such a way that they will be motivated to use them consistently.

The essential thing in preventing the conception of a child is to keep a live sperm cell from meeting a live egg cell and joining with and fertilizing it. Here are the principal methods of contraception.

Methods That Do Not Require a Doctor's Help

ABSTINENCE

Abstinence means abstaining from—that is, not having—sexual intercourse. It is a widely used and totally effective method of birth control, for couples who are willing to forgo sexual intercourse. Periodic abstinence is an essential part of the natural family planning method, which is explained below.

CONDOMS

A condom (also called a rubber, prophylactic, safety, or sheath) is a thin rubber device shaped like the finger of a glove. It is placed over the penis after erection but before sexual intercourse, and it prevents the ejaculated semen from entering the vagina. Condoms are by far the most commonly used contraceptive device in the United States and can be bought by anyone at any drugstore without prescription. Condoms come in packages rolled and ready for use. Some contain a small amount of lubricant to make them easier to put on. There are a number of "ifs" to their successful use: if the condom is a new one, without pinholes; if the couple makes certain that the woman's vagina is not dry but is lubricated before insertion; if, when the condom is put on, a small space is left at the end to receive the semen; if the man carefully holds the condom in place with his fingers as he withdraws his penis *before* he loses his erection completely, so that no semen will spill out; and if there is no continuation of intercourse after the first ejaculation without changing condoms—then it is a highly effective method of contraception. If condoms are used hastily or inexpertly,

diaphragm

preparation of diaphragm

insertion of diaphragm

diaphragm in place

foam, jelly, and tablet or suppository

insertion of foam or jelly

contraceptive tablet or suppository

various brands of birth control pills

condom

rolled-up condom

condom unrolled

condom with receptacle for sperm

condom unrolled onto erect penis

Lippes loop

copper 7

copper T

Saf-T-Coil

IUD

ovary
tube
uterus
vagina

types of IUD

Space is left between end of penis and end of condom to contain semen.

Fig. 21. Contraceptives

or if they have been kept a long time so the rubber has deteriorated (or even a short time in the hot glove compartment of a car), they are not reliable. (The practice of using plastic sheeting like Saran Wrap as a sort of condom may be better than using nothing at all, but such sheeting is very unreliable, since it tears or comes off easily.)

Condoms are also very effective in reducing the likelihood of transmitting venereal disease during sexual intercourse, provided there has been no contact between the uncovered penis and the woman's genitals prior to penetration.

FOAMS, CREAMS, JELLIES

Sperm-killing chemicals can be bought without prescription at the drugstore and are available in various kinds of foams, creams, and jellies that the woman can place in her vagina before each act of intercourse. The foam is probably the most effective, but it is not as effective as the condom, the pill, the IUD, or the diaphragm. Users should follow directions on the package exactly but also be skeptical of claims for effectiveness, which can be exaggerated.

WITHDRAWAL

One of the oldest methods of birth control, and still frequently used, is withdrawal. (The technical term is *coitus interruptus.*) This requires the man, just before he ejaculates, to withdraw his penis from the woman's vagina and to ejaculate well away from the vaginal opening. Although the method is far more effective than using no method at all, it is not effective enough, because (1) many men, at the height of sexual excitement and pleasure just before ejaculation, do not have the self-control to withdraw; (2) the pleasure of ejaculation is considerably reduced when ejaculation occurs outside the vagina; and (3) many men, before ejaculation, secrete a small amount of fluid containing enough sperm to cause pregnancy.

COMBINED METHODS

A combination of two methods has, in practice, been found to have a higher effectiveness rate than either method used alone. Such a combination is possible in two ways: the use of the condom or of withdrawal, each with the addition of the vaginal foam. In the case of withdrawal, the chances of pregnancy are greatly reduced if the woman has, previous to intercourse, inserted a contraceptive foam, in case semen leaks before ejaculation or the man does not withdraw in time. The use of foam with the condom provides an even higher degree of freedom from pregnancy—probably as high as the pill or the IUD.

What must be remembered is that, as with all other methods, effectiveness depends very specifically on consistency of use. *If a hundred couples use the same method for a year, omission of the method, no matter how good it is, even once by five or ten couples, can result in several pregnancies among the hundred in the course of that year.*

Methods That Do Require a Doctor's Help

THE PILL

First put on the market in 1960 and steadily improved ever since, the birth control pill is the second most commonly used method of contraception in the Western world. The pill is taken by mouth and contains synthetic chemicals that resemble closely the two hormones (progesterone and estrogen) that prevent a pregnant woman from ovulating. With their use, no egg is released to be fertilized. Thus they induce a kind of chemical imitation of pregnancy.

Different brands and types of pills use different amounts and kinds of chemicals, and for each the directions are specific and should be followed *exactly.* In most cases, beginning on the fifth day after menstruation starts, the woman takes one pill a day for three weeks and then stops for a week, during which a vaginal flow very much like menstruation occurs. Taking a pill for one day or a few days is useless. If a woman forgets to take her pill for a single day, she should take the forgotten pill along with the scheduled one the very next day. If she forgets two or three days in succession, she definitely risks pregnancy and should immediately use a substitute method of contraception until a new pill cycle is begun—diaphragm and foam, or condom and foam, are suggested. Generally, the pills are sold in dispensers that make it as easy as possible to remember to take one each day; some dispensers contain seven placebo pills (pills containing no chemicals) for the fourth week, so that a woman does not break the habit of taking a pill every day of her life, even during the week when her flow is occurring. When used properly, the pill is an almost 100 percent effective means of contraception.

Birth control pills are available only by prescription, and the prescribing doctor should explain all the possible side effects, such as nausea, weight gain, headaches, and increased vaginal discharge. Generally, these effects tend to disappear as women adjust after two or three months of use. Women with a history of blood clots may be advised by their physician against the pill, even though the increased danger of death by blood clot is slight—only one eighteenth that of the danger of death from labor and childbirth.

In general, it is believed today that the pill should not be taken by women over the age of forty, because of possible increased rate of heart attacks; or by pregnant women or those who think they may be pregnant, because of possible injury to the embryo or fetus (this is why they are always started at the end of a normal menstrual period); or by very young women, because of questions about the number of years it can safely be used. Smaller and smaller doses of the hormones in each pill are now being used, and a woman should ask her doctor all the questions that occur to her and follow his or her advice scrupulously.

There have recently been a considerable number of fears voiced concerning the connection between use of the pill and increased incidence of cancer. The facts are that the pill was introduced on an experimental basis in 1954 and for the succeeding six years was used on large numbers of women in clinical trials both in the United States and abroad. Since then, it has been used by millions of women. Thus far, in spite of careful scrutiny, no relationship between cancer and the pill has been established. There does, however, seem to be a relationship between age, the pill, and smoking. Women over forty who smoke do exhibit an increased rate of coronary disease and stroke when on the pill. It is likely that tobacco and the pill in some way reinforce each other's effects, whereas either alone has only a slight effect on the incidence of heart disease and stroke. This is also undoubtedly the case even in young women who smoke.

INTRAUTERINE DEVICE (IUD)

It has been known for centuries that placing a foreign object in the uterus of a female tends to prevent pregnancy. Arabs would prevent female camels used in desert caravans from becoming pregnant by placing a stone inside the uterus.

In recent years, copper-containing plastic devices (the Copper T or Copper 7) and plastic devices shaped as rings, coils, and loops have been developed. They are called intrauterine devices—IUDs—and are inserted by a doctor into the flat, triangular cavity of the uterus, where, by a process not fully understood, they seem to interfere in some way with implantation of the fertilized egg in the uterine lining or with the development of the embryo. A commonly used IUD is the Lippes double-S Loop. To insert it the doctor straightens it in a plastic tube like a soda straw, which is then passed through the cervical canal of the uterus. The loop is then pushed out of the tube upward into the uterus, where it resumes its built-in double-S curved shape. From the lower end of the device a thin plastic thread extends through the cervix into the vagina, where the woman can feel it with her finger and make sure it is still in place. If it has been expelled (which is more likely to happen in women who have never had a child and whose uterine cavity is therefore smaller), it should be replaced at once or another means of contraception used.

The advantages of the IUD are that it is a quite effective means of contraception, that it is inexpensive and long-lasting, and that it requires little attention once inserted. Its disadvantages are that in some instances, especially in women who have never been pregnant, it can cause bleeding, uterine cramps, or pelvic pain; that it causes an increased incidence of tubal pregnancy; and that it may cause pelvic inflammation (often without noticeable symptoms) and even blocking of the fallopian tubes, and thus infertility. Therefore, many doctors are coming to feel that it is inadvisable for women who have never been pregnant to use an IUD. In any case, IUDs must be inserted with trained skill and care, so that infection of or damage to the uterus does not occur.

THE DIAPHRAGM

A diaphragm is a round rubber cap, between 2 to 3 inches in diameter, which a woman places in the upper part of her vagina so as to wall off the cervix from the lower part, thus preventing sperm from entering. It is obtained by prescription only because it must be specially fitted for size and shape by a doctor, who will then show the woman exactly how to place it correctly. It should always be used with a spermicidal cream or jelly, which creates a barrier that keeps sperm from the cervix and which kills any sperm that might migrate around the edge of the diaphragm and thus reach the cervix. For the cream or jelly to be effective, the diaphragm should be in place not more than six hours before intercourse and should be left in place for at least six hours after the last ejaculation, but not for more than sixteen.

From time to time, a woman should have her doctor check the fit of her diaphragm. This is essential after she has given birth or if she has had a significant loss or gain of weight, for both events are likely to change the size of her vaginal canal and make refitting necessary. Especially vigorous intercourse, or intercourse positions resulting in especially deep penetration, are possible causes for displacement of the diaphragm—making use of the cream or jelly even more essential. The diaphragm is a very effective means of birth control if used with consistency and care.

NATURAL FAMILY PLANNING METHOD

The natural family planning (NFP) method of birth control has evolved out of what was formerly called the "rhythm method." It is based on the regular, or rhythmical, nature of the menstrual cycle of most women most of the time. It involves *periodic abstinence,* that is, abstaining from sexual intercourse during the two or three days *after* ovulation, when there may be one or more live eggs in the fallopian tubes, and for two or three days *before* ovulation, since sperm can remain alive in the tubes or uterus and fertilize an egg on its way down.

The NFP method requires teaching women *fertility awareness,* that is, recognizing various signs and symptoms that indicate the days on which they may become pregnant. Learning this awareness is not nearly so simple as learning to use the pill, a diaphragm, or (for the man) a condom, but those who have developed the method report that in recent years a relatively high level of reliability can be attained if the teaching is skillful and the couple using the method does so with care and consistency. Although no drugs or devices are needed, it is important that a couple (especially the woman) considering using NFP be taught by a qualified specialist, either a doctor or a person or couple trained by doctors and experts and experienced in its successful use. (See p. 315 for sources of information and instruction.)

There are four methods a woman may use to determine which days in her cycle are fertile and which are "safe." Probably she will use two or more methods in combination.

The calendar method. This method, though still the one most widely used in natural family planning, is not the most satisfactory. It requires the woman to keep a continuous record of the length of her menstrual cycles over a period of six to nine months and then follow a formula to calculate her fertile days and her "safe" days. Here is the formula: subtract 18 from the number of days in the shortest menstrual cycle in the previous six to nine months (this represents the *earliest* day for the start of her fertile time) and 11 from the number of days in the longest menstrual cycle (this represents the *latest* day for the finish of her fertile time). For example, if, in the previous six to nine months her shortest menstrual cycle was 25 days and her longest was 30, the figures would be 7 (25 minus 18 equals 7) and 19 (30 minus 11 equals 19), which would indicate that, always considering Day 1 as the day she began to menstruate, she might be fertile from Day 7 until Day 19 and infertile from Days 1 to 6 and Day 20 on. Thus, she should consider Day 1 through Day 6 as "safe," then avoid intercourse between Days 7 and 19, and then consider Day 20 through to Day 6 of the *next* menstruation to be her "safe" days.

The basal body temperature method. This method is based on the woman's taking her temperature every morning *before* she has gotten out of bed. She may do this rectally, vaginally, or orally, but always in the same way. This basal body temperature (BBT) is usually very slightly below normal during the week before ovulation but rises to very slightly above normal just before ovulation. When the temperature has remained relatively higher for three consecutive days, the safe days may have been considered to have begun. Convenient charts and instructions for taking and recording the BBT are available from most family-planning clinics.

The cervical mucus method. This method is based on the fact that just before ovulation most women show noticeable changes in the mucus discharged through the opening of the cervix (the *os*) and thence from the vagina. Usually the mucus is yellowish and rather thick, and the vagina quite dry (except when the woman is sexually aroused), but around the time of ovulation the mucus changes and becomes clearer and thinner, more like the white of a raw egg. Women can be taught to evaluate their vaginal discharge daily and thus to tell when ovulation is likely to occur.

The cervical os method. This method is based on changes in the position and texture of the opening (os) of a woman's cervix. Just before ovulation, the os retreats somewhat farther from the external opening of the vagina so that it is harder to reach, and at the same time it softens so that its texture is somewhat like that of the upper lip, whereas at other times the texture is more like that of the tip of the nose. By noticing these changes, the woman can tell when ovulation is about to occur.

When used together, the BBT, the mucus evaluation, and the cervical os methods are called the *sympto-thermic method,* and a woman who uses all three may achieve a fairly high rate of fertility control. However, the results of several studies of the effectiveness rates of NFP methods do not agree, ranging widely from 1.5 observed pregnancies per hundred woman-years to the very high rate of 33.

The NFP methods are considered to be "natural" and thus acceptable to those Roman Catholics whose beliefs do not permit them to use medical methods of conception control. Supporters of NFP, many of them not Catholics, point out that it avoids any possible dangers or discomforts that might result from chemicals or devices, that it "puts a woman in touch with her own body" in a way that is satisfying to her, that the periods of abstinence required increase the opportunities for better communication about sexual matters between partners, and that periodic abstinence may actually serve to.enhance the pleasure of intercourse during the safe days. Those who do not support the method point out the complexity of the procedures involved and the low rate of reliability according to many studies, and maintain that with many couples the required period of abstinence may prove frustrating to the expression of sexual desire natural to intimate living.

STERILIZATION

An increasing number of men and women who are certain they want no (or no more) children choose to have themselves sterilized. There are two methods of sterilization.

Vasectomy for the man. Vasectomy involves removing a short section from each of the man's two vas deferens tubes (vasa deferentia) and tying the remaining ends. This is done in the doctor's office and requires only a local anesthetic and two tiny incisions in the scrotum. The sperm are thus prevented from reaching the seminal vesicles and so the semen ejaculated contains none. (Viable sperm may remain in the man's reproductive system for two or three months after the operation, however; therefore the couple should use another means of contraception during that time.) There is no noticeable reduction in the volume of semen ejaculated, since sperm make up such an infinitesimal proportion of the total amount. The blocked sperm are simply absorbed into the man's body and disappear. A vasectomy should be considered permanent, although modern microsurgical techniques sometimes succeed in reopening the vasa deferentia.

Tubal ligation for the woman. The tubal ligation method (commonly called "having your tubes tied") involves removing a short section of each fallopian tube so that egg cells cannot reach the uterus from the ovaries or be reached by sperm cells. A tubal ligation is now almost as simple an operation as a vasectomy, although it must be done in a hospital or a special clinic. A small incision is made in the navel (so that the scar will not be noticeable) and an instrument called a laparoscope is inserted. It enables the doctor to see the tubes by means of a miniature light and telescope and to cauterize (burn out) a small section of each tube and seal off the ends. In most centers, laparoscopy is carried out under general anesthetic, although only a local anesthetic may be used in places where general anesthetic is unavailable. Like the vasectomy, this operation should be considered permanent, for the possibilities for successfully reopening and rejoining the tubes are slim. Culdoscopy—using a similar instrument through the vagina —can also be used, but it requires special training and thus is not as easily available.

Neither a vasectomy nor a tubal ligation interferes with sexual pleasure, unless for some reason a person has some negative emotional reaction to the operation. Since sterilization makes it unnecessary to worry about pregnancy or planning for contraception, it can in effect increase the pleasure a couple experiences in intercourse.

"MORNING-AFTER" CONTRACEPTION

When a woman has had unprotected sexual intercourse and then realizes that she may become pregnant and does not wish to do so, she has two possibilities: one is to have an IUD inserted within two or three days; the other is to take a pill containing a synthetic estrogen. The latter method may cause nausea, vomiting, headache, and other symptoms. Although its success rate is very high, if it should not happen to succeed the chances are greatly increased that if the baby born is a girl she may develop cancer of the vagina when she is grown. Therefore, before a woman is given a "morning-after" pill she should make certain that she is not already carrying a baby and that she is ready to accept a termination of her pregnancy in case the pill should fail.

Methods Not Recommended at All

DOUCHING

Douching as a contraceptive method involves squirting water or other liquid into the vagina immediately after the man ejaculates, the idea being to kill or wash away the sperm. Even if the woman runs from bed to bathroom, a douche is quite ineffective because sperm, when ejaculated, begin at once to move up the cervical canal and out of harm's way. There are a number of douching fluids sold in stores for which claims of contraceptive effectiveness are made or assumed by the user. But none of the douches works as a contraceptive. This method is therefore strongly advised against.

URINATION AFTER INTERCOURSE

A method that some women use to attempt to kill the sperm is urination right after sexual intercourse. This is of no use whatsoever, because the vagina, into which the sperm are ejaculated, and the urethra, through which the urine passes, are entirely separate, even though their external openings are close to each other.

SUPPOSITORIES

Many suppositories are advertised as contraceptives but are not effective at all because body heat melts them into a liquid that runs out before or during intercourse.

Comparing the Effectiveness of Contraceptive Methods

Doctors and scientists are constantly working on improving methods and discovering new ways of preventing unwanted pregnancy. Some developments not yet perfected are birth control pills for males that would stop the production of sperm; small capsules that can be implanted under a woman's skin to release small doses of chemicals into her bloodstream and prevent pregnancy for periods of a year or longer; methods for reversing sterilization operations in both men and women, so that a person could be sterilized and then de-sterilized. If ever perfected, some of the new methods may turn out to be more effective, more convenient and pleasant to use, less expensive, and less likely to have undesirable side effects than many of the methods now available.

In addition to new methods, the old ones are being worked on steadily, and sometimes ways are found to make them more effective. Thus, the rates of effectiveness are likely to change from year to year. Before giving the latest figures available, we should point out that it is much easier to ask "How effective is my birth control method?" than it is to give the answer. Much depends on how carefully, competently, and consistently the method is used. For example, *theoretically* the pill is almost 100 percent effective, but *actually* from 4 to 10 women out of 100 using the pill for a year will become pregnant. Why? Because of human error. The women forget to take their pill, despite forget-proof packaging. Table 1 gives the effectiveness rate actually observed for each method of contraception.The figures emphasize again how important it is to use all methods of contraception exactly according to directions and with care and consistency. Over a number of years of sexual activity, careless or occasional forgetting is likely to result in pregnancy.

We also want to emphasize that much wrong information about birth control methods is passed around, and many women get pregnant because they used a method that does not work or used a good method incorrectly. People planning to use a contraceptive method should make certain that it is approved by the medical profession and that the specific product used is approved for birth control by the United States Food and Drug Administration.

Getting Advice About Contraception

Any person of any age, married or unmarried, if he or she expects to have sexual intercourse and does not wish to cause pregnancy or become pregnant, should get the best possible advice about methods of contraception. Especially at the beginning of sexual activity, but also as a person becomes more experienced, it is very helpful to seek

Table 1
Number of pregnancies expected in 100 sexually active women during the first year of use of various methods of contraception, arranged in order from least to most effective method*

	Pregnancies Observed in Actual Experience
No contraceptive at all	90
Douche	40
Withdrawal	20–25
Spermicidal foam	22
Natural family planning (calendar method only; see page 89)	21
Diaphragm (with spermicidal cream or jelly)	17
Condom (alone)	10
The pill (depending on type)	4–10
Condom plus foam	5
IUD	5
Vasectomy	0.15
Tubal ligation	0.04

*Adapted from *Contraceptive Technology, 1980–81, 10th Revised Edition,* by Robert A. Hatcher, M.D., et al., published by Irvington Publishers, 551 Fifth Avenue, New York, N.Y. 10017.

advice (preferably together with one's partner) from a well-informed professional person and to get answers to such questions as:

What method of contraception is best for me, in my circumstances?
What method is best for my partner?
Are there reasons that I should not be sexually active?
Are there reasons that I should not use contraception?
What are the advantages and disadvantages of the method that I may choose?
What must I do to be sure that I use the method in the most effective way?
Are there dangers to the health of my partner or me in using the

method of contraception I am considering? If so, what are they and how can we avoid them?

What are the names of the products that will be best for me to use, and what is the best source of supply? If I need a prescription, where can I get it?

If I am a minor, should I discuss with my parents my intention of becoming sexually active? Or that I am already sexually active? What is the best way to go about this discussion?

Should I include my sexual partner in this or a later discussion?

We believe that it is best for children and their parents to be open with each other about matters of sexual information. Therefore, we hope that sharing this book will encourage parents and children, as well as husbands and wives and sexual partners, to talk openly together as each feels ready to do so. But like it or not, it is a fact that many children do not want to or cannot bring themselves to talk with their parents about their sexual feelings, plans, or, in some cases, even the simple facts. Some parents are not available for such discussion, and many parents find it difficult—or impossible—to talk about such things with their children. We recognize these realities and we also recognize the strong need many people feel, even within the family (sometimes especially within the family) to have their privacy protected.

Thus, although we strongly favor family discussion, we are glad that there are organizations that have professionals available to whom young people can go to discuss sexual matters and from whom they can obtain information and needed products. These organizations, though they may strongly advise family discussion, will protect the privacy of those who come. It is legal in all states for such discussions to be kept private and for contraceptive information and materials, including whatever prescriptions are required, to be given to minors without the knowledge or consent of their parents.

There are many who feel that such discussion and provision of contraceptive materials to minors without the consent of parents is a threat to the strength and solidarity of the family. We know, however, that even among the members of many warm, loving families, in which there is generally a readiness to share and talk things over, the area of sex seems special and is particularly difficult to discuss. Therefore, parents or children should try not to feel threatened by discussions outside the family.

Some of the professionals and organizations available for confidential discussion and advice about contraception and all related questions are:

The family doctor. It should be remembered that many doctors have not yet been trained to discuss sexual questions with their patients, although an increasing number of medical schools and other medical organizations are now providing training in this field. Also, some doctors feel obligated to share with parents the matters that young people discuss with them.

Planned Parenthood. This organization has centers throughout the United States and the world where counseling is available, either individually or in groups, and where contraceptive materials and devices are obtainable and doctors on hand to give prescriptions, advice, and instruction (see Sources of Help p. 315).

Family-planning clinics connected with hospitals. Here contraceptive information, services, and products are available.

Family-planning clinics of city, county, and state health departments. Here, too, contraceptive information, advice, services, and products are available. Look up the clinics in the telephone directory under "Health" or "Public Health" under the name of the city, county, or state.

Natural Family Planning. For Catholics and others who wish instruction in the natural family planning method, many dioceses of the Roman Catholic Church maintain a Family Life Bureau. Look it up under "Diocese," "Archdiocese," or "Catholic Church," subheading "Family Life Bureau" (or see Sources of Help, p. 315).

The family minister, priest, or rabbi. Increasing numbers of religious workers are receiving training in counseling on questions of sexual behavior. A minister, priest, or rabbi may be helpful in discussing with you the moral aspects of the choices you are making, but he or she is not qualified to give medical advice.

When Contraception Fails

It is a sad fact that for a variety of reasons—carelessness, ignorance, use of unreliable methods of contraception, or allowing one's reason and planning to be overcome by the feelings and emotions of the moment—millions of women of all ages, including very young girls, become pregnant each year and wish they had not. These women have a number of choices. One is to marry (this choice is rarely advised because almost all such marriages have been shown to end in divorce); one is to carry their pregnancy through to term, have their baby, and keep it as a single parent; another is to have the baby and, if single, give it up for adoption; and yet another is to terminate the pregnancy by means of an abortion.

Keeping the Baby

For a woman who becomes pregnant when she did not choose to, the decision to give birth to the baby and keep it may be a hard one to make. She may feel unready for the responsibilities of parenthood; the father may not wish to help her, or, even if he does, if they are not committed to each other, she may not wish him to do so; her plans for education and career may be interrupted or even permanently changed; she may not be able to afford the costs of childbirth and, later, child care if she wishes or needs to go to work. Much, of course, depends on how much support she can count on from others, her family, the neighborhood, her friends, and various family-service agencies. Yet, despite the problems, many women choose to bear and keep their babies, and when they look back on the decision later, many but not all are glad, or cannot imagine having decided otherwise. Certainly, most women who find themselves pregnant not by choice will want to talk over their situation, and the future welfare of their prospective child, with other people whose opinion and experience they respect—with their family, possibly with an adviser from their church or synagogue, and probably with a professional counselor or social worker.

Giving the Baby Up for Adoption

Painful as it may be for a mother who has just given birth to a baby to which, during the nine months of pregnancy, she has usually become emotionally attached, adoption is often the best solution for both mother and child. In most cases, the baby is given up almost immediately after birth, before mother and child develop an even stronger attachment to each other. It will be helpful for the mother, after the adoption, to talk over her feelings with a counselor.

When children are adopted, they have full legal rights as members of their adoptive family. Many children are adopted by relatives of their natural parents, such as an uncle and aunt, or grandparents. Most adoptions in the United States are arranged through licensed agencies, although quite a few others are worked out by physicians or lawyers. In most states, when the child is not already known by them, neither the adoptive parents nor the adopted child are permitted to know the identity of the natural parents, and the natural parents may not know who adopted their child. This is in order to avoid the stress and confusion that occur if a natural parent undergoes a change of mind and seeks to have the child returned.

In general, it can be said that adopted children have just about the same kind of chance of being brought up to lead happy, satisfying lives as do children brought up by their natural parents. Thus a mother can give up her child in the confidence that it will have a good future, most likely a better one than it would have had with her if she was not well prepared to care for it until it had grown up.

Abortion

There are two kinds of abortion: spontaneous and induced. A *spontaneous abortion,* commonly called a miscarriage, occurs when the pregnant woman's uterus spontaneously (by itself) expels the embryo or fetus. About 10 to 15 percent of all pregnancies end in this way, most of them before the eleventh or twelfth week. About half the miscarried embryos are found to have one or more major defects. The signs of miscarriage are vaginal bleeding and pelvic cramps. If these occur and then the signs of pregnancy disappear, a woman can assume she has had a miscarriage. (Remember, an eight-week-old embryo is only an inch long and weighs about two grams—or three one-hundredths of an ounce, about one third the weight of a dime—so that the actual event of miscarriage is usually not very noticeable.) Some women believe that they can bring on a miscarriage by such activities as jumping up and down vigorously or falling downstairs, but all they are likely to do is hurt themselves, leaving the pregnancy undisturbed.

An *induced abortion* is one that is brought about intentionally. There are several methods for inducing abortion. Abortions performed during the first trimester of pregnancy (the first three months) are much simpler and safer than those performed later, although any abortion done by a qualified doctor in a well-equipped facility is quite safe, with a lower problem rate than childbirth itself. Two methods are commonly used during the first three months of a pregnancy: the vacuum aspiration method and the D & C.

Vacuum aspiration method. About 85 percent of all legal abortions performed in the United States today are done by the vacuum aspiration method, often called the suction method. First, in most cases, some dilatation (enlarging) of the cervical opening is done, under local anesthesia and with only slight discomfort. Then the doctor uses a suction curette, which is a small plastic tube attached by a rubber tube to a suction machine. The tip of the plastic tube is inserted through the cervical canal into the uterus and, working somewhat like a miniature vacuum cleaner, sucks out the embryo and other products of conception. The whole process usually takes only a few minutes, is quite inexpensive, and can be done in a clinic or hospital on an outpatient basis, so that after a short rest the woman can go home. If performed before the eighth week of pregnancy it is almost painless. Complications and aftereffects are rare if the procedure is competently done.

Dilatation and curettage (D & C) method. Before the development of the vacuum method, the D & C method was very common. It involves dilating the cervical opening by passing into it a series of dilators of larger and larger thickness, and then inserting a curette (which is simply a blunt scraper) with which the doctor scrapes out the contents of the uterus. The D & C can also be performed on an outpatient basis. It takes somewhat longer than the suction method, involves considerably more discomfort, and must be done with care to avoid causing excessive bleeding of the uterus.

Saline injection method. After twelve weeks of pregnancy, neither the vacuum aspiration method nor the D & C can be performed safely. During the second trimester of pregnancy the most common method of performing abortions today is the saline injection. Under local anesthetic, a needle is inserted through the woman's abdomen into her uterus and about a cupful of amniotic fluid is removed; this fluid is replaced by an equal amount of a 20-percent salt solution. From twenty-four to forty-eight hours later, the uterus begins contracting and the woman miscarries spontaneously. Some doctors keep the patient in the hospital until the fetus is delivered; others permit her to go home, not to return until contractions have begun. The saline injection method does involve some dangers, such as hemorrhaging and infection. Therefore, close follow-up is important after the procedure is completed.

Prostaglandins method. The above methods all involve surgical procedures and cannot be done unless good equipment is available. But there is now being developed a nonsurgical method that involves the use of prostaglandins. Many years ago it was observed that the injection of human semen into the uterus caused strong contractions of the uterine muscles. Later research showed that the chemical causing the contractions is produced by the prostate gland (hence the name), and techniques have now been developed to put fluid containing prostaglandins into the body of the pregnant woman, either by a catheter into her uterus, by a suppository placed in the vagina, where it is absorbed, or by intravenous injection. After a number of hours the woman aborts the fetus. Although the method has some uncomfortable side effects, it is approved by the Food and Drug Administration for use in second-trimester abortions. (It is thought that eventually prostaglandins may make possible the development of an abortion "pill.")

Abortions, especially when performed early in pregnancy, are quite safe, simple, and inexpensive. (The death rate for legal abortions in the United States is about 1 in 20,000 abortions, a rate much lower than that from childbirth, which in itself is by no means a risky procedure even under modern conditions.) But any woman considering an abortion should go only to a hospital or clinic registered for performing them, and the abortion should be performed only by a doctor. The doctor will know which method is the best one to use, given the circumstances of the woman and the stage of the pregnancy. Information about where to go and how (and whether) to proceed can be obtained from Planned Parenthood, a city, county, or state public health clinic, or any hospital.

It is important that the woman considering an abortion be given ample opportunity to talk with a counselor about her situation and the choices she has. If the woman decides to proceed with an abortion, the counselor should explain exactly what it will involve. For many women, an abortion is a minor event, both physically and psychologically; for others it may have deeper effects than they expect, especially on their emotions, if they believe that their decision means they are responsible for terminating a human life and feel guilty about this. It is therefore important that a woman also have a chance to talk about her feelings *after* the abortion has been performed. Of course, she should return to the hospital or clinic if she has any abnormal symptoms such as pain, fever, nausea, or bleeding following an abortion, or for further counseling.

Abortion and the Law

Before 1973 (before 1970 in New York State), performing an abortion was illegal in the United States except in cases where the life or health (or, in some situations, the welfare) of the mother was in jeopardy. And yet millions of abortions were performed illegally, often under very dangerous "back-alley" conditions, in which the life or future health of the mother was in great danger. Each year thousands of women died or were severely injured. When a procedure is illegal, it is of course impossible to regulate it by law, so people who are unscrupulous and unskilled often take over the business. Before legalized abortion, many women attempted to perform abortions on themselves by inserting a foreign object through the cervix into the uterus. Much suffering and many deaths were caused by such efforts, but those women who felt that, for whatever reason, they could not endure giving birth to and caring for a baby were apparently willing to risk their health and lives to avoid this. It has been pointed out by the medical and legal professions that, if abortion should be made illegal again, or very difficult or expensive to obtain, undoubtedly illegal "abortion mills" will again become common, with the same undesirable results as before.

In 1973 the United States Supreme Court ruled that no state could limit the right of a woman to have an abortion during the first trimester of her pregnancy. The court said that during the second trimester states might regulate medical practices (such as the licensing of physicians and the certification of hospitals and clinics to perform abortions), but that the right of a woman to have an abortion might not itself be limited. During the third trimester, the court said, states may prohibit abortions under conditions the states may determine, but they may not prohibit them if the health of the mother is endangered. The Supreme Court itself did not prohibit third-trimester abortions. The 1973 decision meant that it was now legal anywhere in the United States for a woman to have an abortion. She did not need the consent of her husband, nor did a girl need the consent of her parents.

Since the Supreme Court decision, there have been major efforts by groups (often calling themselves "Pro-Life" or "Right to Life") to have the United States Constitution amended to prohibit abortion entirely and to affirm the right to life and protection under the law for the embryo from the moment of conception. (The Supreme Court decision stated that it was not competent to say when life begins and that thus a person's life should be considered as beginning at the moment of birth.) Opponents of abortion are also attempting to get Congress and various states to pass laws prohibiting the spending of public funds to perform abortions, although free medical care is, in other respects, available at low or no cost to people of limited means. Such laws would have the effect of making abortions available only to those able to pay for them.

Abortion Pro and Con

Many people have very strong opinions about the rightness or wrongness of abortion. In the Soviet Union, the countries of Eastern Europe, and Japan, abortion is probably the most common method of birth control. In these countries there are more abortions each year than there are live births. In Western European countries and North and South America, where the influence of the Christian religions and especially of the Catholic church is strong, there has always been vigorous opposition to abortion. Public-opinion polls differ on how widespread the opposition is; much depends on how the question is put.

Here is a summary of the views of those who oppose a woman's right to choose an abortion:

From the moment of conception, the fertilized egg is an individual human life. The embryo as an individual life no more "belongs" to its mother or father than does a born child. It has its own unique genetic inheritance, and from the moment of conception its mother merely provides it with nourishment and a place to grow.

Furthermore, this individual human life is harmless and innocent. We have no right to kill it; to do so is murder. The baby growing inside the mother has a right to life as much as any other innocent human being, and it deserves the protection of the law. If we permit the killing of the most harmless human life with the greatest potential, there is nothing to stop us from taking other human lives—say, of unwanted children or of old people, or even of groups without whom we feel the world would be better off. If we oppose the killing of innocent human beings (which category does not necessarily include convicted criminals or enemies in war), we should oppose the killing of human life through abortion.

Those who favor a woman's right to choose an abortion express their views this way:

> Every woman, as a matter of her right to the enjoyment of life, liberty, and privacy, should be free to determine whether and when to bear children. It is far better to end an unwanted pregnancy than to encourage the evils resulting from forced pregnancy and childbirth. Therefore, no matter what her age, a woman should, with the medical advice of a doctor, have the right to secure an abortion and to do so without being required to consult with or secure the permission of any other person. To require her to bear a child she does not want is not only unfair to her but may also work hardships on her family. Furthermore, it is unfair to the prospective child for it to be born unwanted, more likely than a wanted child to experience hardships, deprivation, and often even abuse after it is born. Every child should have the right to be born into circumstances in which it is likely to receive the physical and emotional support and love it will need for a healthy, happy life.
>
> The argument that permitting the termination of pregnancy is murder or disrespectful of human life is unsound. An embryo or fetus is only an organism growing toward being a person, very different from a conscious, existing individual, born and actually living out in the world.
>
> Certainly, no woman should be *required* to have an abortion, and the moral convictions of people opposing abortion should be respected. But it is also wrong for opponents of abortion to force their convictions on others by encouraging the passage of laws restricting the right of a woman to choose whether or not to have a baby. However, abortion should not be considered a primary means of birth control, only a back-up method, when other means of birth control fail or are not used.

Major organizations of physicians, usually after much debate, have adopted positions on abortion. Here are the statements of three of them:

> *The American Psychiatric Association* [*December 1969*]: A decision to perform an abortion should be regarded as strictly a medical responsibility. It should be removed entirely from the jurisdiction of criminal law. Criminal penalties should be reserved for persons who perform abor-

tions without medical license or qualification to do so. A medical decision to perform an abortion is based on the careful and informed judgments of the physician and the patient. Among other factors to be considered in arriving at the decision is the motivation of the patient. Often psychiatric consultation can help clarify motivational problems and thereby contribute to the patient's welfare.

The American Medical Association [June 1970]: Whereas, Abortion, like any other medical procedure, should not be performed when contrary to the best interests of the patient since good medical practice requires due consideration for the patient's welfare and not mere acquiescence to the patient's demands; and

Whereas, The standards of sound clinical judgment together with informed patient consent should be determinative according to the merits of each individual case; therefore be it

Resolved, That abortion is a medical procedure and should be performed only by a duly licensed physician and surgeon in an accredited hospital acting only in conformance with standards of good medical practice and after consultation with two other physicians chosen because of their professional competence and within the Medical Practice Act of his State; and be it further

Resolved, That no physician or other professional personnel should be compelled to perform any act which violates his good medical judgment. Neither physician, hospital, nor hospital personnel shall be required to perform any act violative of personally held moral principles. In these circumstances good medical practice requires only that the physician or other professional personnel withdraw from the case so long as the withdrawal is consistent with good medical practice.

The American College of Obstetricians and Gynecologists [February 1973]: Abortion is a surgical procedure. For its performance, adequate facilities, equipment, and personnel are required to assure the highest standards of patient care. . . .

It is recognized that abortion may be performed at a patient's request or upon a physician's recommendation. No physician should be required to perform, nor should any patient be forced to accept, an abortion.

The usual informed consent, including operative permit, should be obtained. The same indications for consultation should apply to abortions as to other medical-surgical procedures.

[June 1974]: The American College of Obstetricians and Gynecologists affirms its support of unhindered access by women to safe abortion services, consistent with the conscientious beliefs of the women and physicians involved.

It is interesting to note that after the court decisions permitting abortions were made, a good many physicians and nurses found themselves more deeply affected by what they came to see as the termination of human life than they had expected to be. In other words, they found that abortion was not a matter to be taken as lightly as some pro-abortion advocates seemed to think; hence, for example, the last paragraph in the statement of the American Medical Association. Most doctors, however, feel that even though they themselves do not wish to perform abortions, they have an obligation to refer women desiring one to other physicians who will.

The Problem of Overpopulation

As we said at the beginning of this chapter, one of the difficulties with the male and female reproductive systems is that in the world today they are working only too well. If human reproduction is not soon drastically reduced, our earth will contain more people than its space and resources can possibly support. Even now, overpopulation is a fact —a fact in some families, a fact among some age-groups, a fact in some areas of some countries, and a fact as far as the resources of the entire world are concerned. Human fertility must somehow be reduced. If it is not, disaster is inevitable. Indeed, disaster quietly exists now in many places, with malnutrition perhaps the most common cause of death, and most of the world's people never have known what it is like regularly to have enough to eat.

Here are some interesting facts about population that will help you understand the situation the world today faces:

• It took hundreds of thousands of years from the beginning of humankind's existence on earth until 1830 for the world population to reach 1 billion. But then it took only one hundred years more to double and reach 2 billion in 1930. Improvements in medicine led to far fewer deaths than ever before, and it took only forty-five years for the next doubling: in 1975 the population was 4 billion. At the present growth rate (2 percent per year) the world population will have reached 8 billion by the year 2010, a doubling interval of only thirty-five years. At present, the world population increases each year by about 85 million people.

• In general, in the economically prosperous countries of the world the birth rates and death rates are low, whereas in the countries where poverty is the rule both rates are high. Also, in the rich countries, the difference between the birth rate and death rate tends to be small, whereas in poor countries it tends to be large because births outnumber deaths. In other words, the poorer countries tend to be the ones in which the population is increasing most rapidly.

• Certain world resources are strictly limited, for example, fossil fuels (oil, coal), other minerals, arable land, water, and air. Americans should know that because of their way of life and standard of living, the average American baby born can expect to consume thirty to fifty times more of the world's resources than the average baby born in India.

• People who are poor tend to have much higher birth rates than those who are prosperous. In the United States, for example, females who have their first three children before eighteen tend to end up, on the average, with eight children in all and very often on welfare. Health services, including family planning, are less available to the poor than to others.

• In general, people who have hope for the future and who expect their children and themselves to have a good life are people who plan to limit the number of children they have. They realize that the economic cost of a good life will be too great if the family income has to be shared by many children. And it is the poor people who have little hope for a better future, who have known only poverty for themselves and are resigned to poverty for their children, who tend not to plan (for planning never seems to make a difference in their lives) and not to limit family size. Thus those who can least afford large families are the ones who have them. It is generally the middle- and upper-class people who have the smaller families. The difficult problem that the world—and the United States—faces is how to give more people a sense of hope for the future, which may result in their having smaller families.

• One way to reduce family size and the rate of population growth would be to persuade young people to postpone the age at which they have their first child. The great majority of the over 1,000,000 pregnancies that occur each year in the United States in women who are 19 and under are unwanted, and the high rate of adolescent fertility (which need not be the same thing as adolescent sexual activity) is a major national problem today. If through education, persuasion, and providing both the means of family planning and the possibilities for a future filled with hope, we could delay the age of first childbirth so that the number of generations each hundred years would average three rather than five, population problems would be much nearer to solution.

Human Beings as Decision-Making Animals

In this chapter we have been talking about control of the human reproductive system. In this connection, it is important to point out that while in other, "lower," animals, sexual activity and reproductive activity are inseparable, in human beings they are merely closely related. The reproductive lives of other animals are governed by factors over which they have no control: the seasons of the year, the cycles of their glands and organs, the state of their nutrition, and so forth.

Female animals will copulate only when they are in heat; that is, when they are ovulating and are ready to be fertilized. During the period of heat, female animals give forth certain scents and signs (such as a slight bloody discharge from the uterus) that inform the male they are ready. The male then becomes sexually aroused (he "ruts" or becomes "rutty"), and mating takes place. Only when the female is in heat is the male interested in her sexually. Any farm boy or girl, or any owner or observer of a female dog when she is in heat, will have a vivid idea of how automatic, compulsive, and cyclical the reproductive lives of animals are. Animals have no choices to make and take no responsibility for their sexual actions, and the same species behave the same way the world over. (There are exceptions, such as rabbits, which have no heat periods; they copulate first and *then* the female ovulates.)

In human females there is no such thing as "heat." As we have explained, most women do not know when they are ovulating, and certainly a man cannot tell. Women do feel a greater desire for sexual activity at some times than at others, but not necessarily at the time when they are most likely to conceive. In the human male, there is no definite season when he is "rutty," although he too may feel more sexy at some times than at others.

Thus human beings are unique among animals in being able to make decisions about their sexual and reproductive behaviors. They have been endowed with the capacity to remember, to plan ahead, to make choices, and to learn from past experience in ways that will affect their futures, both sexually and reproductively. Human beings are responsible for how they will behave: they are taught, and they can learn.

5
Living Our Sexual Lives:
Influences and Patterns
During the Life Cycle

Human sexuality infuses, and in turn is infused by, every aspect of our lives. Each person's sexuality at any given moment is based on the genetic endowment with which he or she entered the world, plus the effects upon it of learning—or of lack of opportunity to learn—from life experiences.

Just as we accept responsibility for developing the minds of our children, so should we also accept responsibility for the development of their sexuality. This means that we must be open to examining and reexamining our ideas of what sexuality might and should be.

Sexual Programming Before Birth

In Chapter 1 we described how the sex chromosome of the sperm (X or Y) joins the sex chromosome of the egg (always X) to make the male (XY) or female (XX) embryo, the beginning of a new human life. The sole function of the sex chromosome of the sperm is then completed. Its genetic code message—this is to be a female or this is to be a male—has been delivered during the fertilization process to an already developing group of cells that are thereby destined to become gonads, or sex glands: testes in the case of an XY male, ovaries in the case of an XX female. This chain of events takes place during the first six weeks of the embryo's existence. The gonadal cells eventually produce either testosterone (male hormone in a male) or estrogen (female hormone in a female), which in turn assures the development of the various sex and reproductive organs. The chain of events also extends to the development of those nerves that will be needed for the functioning of the sex organs. For example, if the penis later on is to be capable of erection and ejaculation, there must also develop a network of connecting nerves from the penis, up the spinal cord, finally reaching the nerve cells in the sex center of the brain. This long connection will carry the sensation of pleasure in erection and orgasm to the consciousness of the male, for without this consciousness there would be no sexual desire, no erection and ejaculation, and therefore no procreation, no continuation of the human species. In exactly the same way, nerve pathways and sex-center brain connection are developed in the female. However, as we pointed out earlier, she need not experience pleasure in order to conceive.

Thus, the sex hormones assure that the right numbers and kinds of complex nerve circuits will be built between the end organs of sex and the brain. Whether the hormones sensitize the male brain sex centers to function later in certain male ways, or the female brain sex centers to function in certain female ways, is probable but not yet absolutely certain. Many scientists now believe so.

Sexual Programming After Birth

Does the development of male or female anatomy and nerve pathways and brain sex centers before birth guarantee development of matching male or female gender identity and behavior after birth and during growing up? Not necessarily. What it does guarantee is that the sexual system of either gender will have been so developed and sensitized by the sex hormones that it can accept the process of sexualization that will begin at the moment of birth (see Chapter 1). This process must take place in the right way if a child is to reach the critical age, usually twenty-four to thirty-six months, with an accurate and sure knowledge that it is male or female. By five years of age the child will also be well on the way to understanding the kinds of behaviors and attitudes that go with being female or male in his or her society. In Chapter 1 we pointed out that parents or their substitutes play the major role in this process of sexualization in the years before the child reaches kindergarten. By then it is clear that the most important sex education of its whole life will already have taken place and quite permanently, though not always successfully.

Helping or Hindering Sexualization

So the baby, whether boy or girl, can be said to come into the world with many of its sexual pages blank, so to speak, ready to be written on by its learning experiences. At birth the baby's anatomy has announced its gender, and the sex pathways to and from its brain are receptive to messages that relate to that gender and resistant to messages that relate to the opposite gender. There are always two kinds of messages that the growing child receives from grown-ups. For a boy there are not only positive messages that convey "You are a boy" but also negative messages saying "You are not a girl." These are continually being reinforced by other kinds of messages, not only "You are a boy and must act like one" but also, phrased negatively, "You are not a girl and so must not act like one." The negative message can actually imply that being a girl is a pretty poor thing to be.

For example, parents will praise a boy who is vigorous and assertive and who resists crying when he is hurt or upset. Or they may indicate that behaving in the opposite fashion—being gentle or sensitive, having a tendency to tears when feelings are hurt or physical injury occurs—is "too much like a girl, a sissy." Likewise, in the period before girls wore slacks or pants, mothers would keep telling their daughters to sit with their knees close together "like a little lady" and not to be boisterous or noisy or "bossy" or sit with their knees apart "like a man."

Or a mother trying to explain how babies are conceived and born might convey a dislike for sex and the reproductive processes and unconsciously appear to be saying of the child's father, "It was *his* fault we had you." This message would tend to confuse a child not only about his or her own value but also about the relative values of males and females, and a daughter might grow up to feel superior to males. The daughter might be more confused if a parent let her know that he or she had been wishing for a boy baby before her birth. This in turn might tend to decrease the daughter's feelings of self-worth, and this would be difficult for her to harmonize with the feeling of being superior to males. And all this would be a form of sex education.

In another case, a mother might convey her joy and satisfaction with sex and reproduction, and with her relationship with her husband, and might show that she loved having a baby, whether it was a boy or a girl. Such a positive attitude on the part of parents makes it more likely that their children will have good feelings about themselves and about their parents.

Parents also need to be aware that no matter how hard they try to love all their children and treat them alike, it is unrealistic to ignore the many factors that make equality of upbringing unlikely. Being born into a family of two is bound to be different from being born into a family of three, four, or more.

What Is "Normal"?

There are so many factors in life that must and do vary that it is almost impossible correctly to apply the word *normal* to sexuality. What does it mean? Usual? Natural? Ordinary? As it *ought* to be? Or as someone who claims to be an expert says it should be? Actually, in regard to sex, most people tend to call "normal" everything that they themselves do or feel or think, and to look upon as "abnormal" what someone else does or feels or thinks about sex that is different; they may even think of what someone else does sexually as a "deviation" or "perversion."

In its objective search for knowledge, science does not make judgments this way, for even in science the meaning of the word *normal* can vary. For example, normal body temperature generally means 98.6 degrees F (37 degrees C). If we took the temperatures of one hundred people, most would probably show this to be their "norm," but there would always be a few whose temperatures might usually run as low as 98.4 to as high as 98.7 degrees—all "normal" for them. Or we say that after childbirth the size of the uterus returns to normal. Does this mean that its size was abnormal during pregnancy? No. For that period it was of normal size for each of the stages of pregnancy.

On the other hand, science today can say that masturbation is normal, for not only do the facts show that no harm at all results from it, but research indicates that there are far more people who masturbate throughout or at some time in their lives than those who do not. Yet there are some people who choose to ignore these facts and who feel that masturbation is abnormal, perhaps especially in their own children.

There are, however, some aspects of sexuality that scientific researchers and sexologists might properly consider to be "abnormal" in the sense that it is not behavior usual to most people: rigid compulsiveness about cleanliness, for instance, with constant washing of hands or genitals; or compulsiveness about never appearing nude before a partner or about sexual intercourse always taking place in the dark. Here the "abnormality" is related not so much to sex as to the personality structure; it is not really an abnormality but a personality difficulty that can make spontaneous sex almost impossible and sexual life difficult for both partners, even though they may be happy together in most ways.

In the field of human sexuality, any behavior that cannot be related, however indirectly, to heterosexual intercourse is considered by some people to be a deviation from the "main" or "right" or "normal" way. However, to label any form of sexual behavior as deviant should not be taken to mean it is wrong, harmful, or despicable. The words *deviant* and *deviation* ought to be used scientifically with no moral or values connotation. Unfortunately, for many people these words have taken on negative meanings. That is why the terms abnormal or perversion or deviation are no longer used by sexologists. These words have the connotation of something "bad" or "sinful," and value judgments have no place in science except for acts that are damaging to others. That is why the preferred word is now *variation*.

There is no way to deal with sexuality as a vital force in the lives of all of us unless we understand the full range of sexuality and sexual behaviors in our society and put them in proper perspective. It is only in the past ten or fifteen years that the kind of information that is in this book has been uncovered by research, and most people are probably either unaware of it or, more likely, do not want to believe it. Once we know more about various kinds of human sexual behavior and how some of them develop, we should be able to deal better and more constructively with our own sexual behavior and with that of others, especially of those nearest to us.

Homosexuality

Homosexuality is a state of being in which a person seeks erotic satisfaction with a member of his or her own sex instead of with a member of the other sex. A female homosexual is referred to as a *lesbian.* Homosexuality is a difficult thing for many people today to deal with, yet we cannot pretend it does not exist, even though only about five to ten of every hundred men and three to five of every hundred women are *exclusively* homosexual. To insist on ignoring this six percent of the total population is unrealistic, especially when we accept—as we must if we are honest—that the state of being homosexual is in reality no more voluntary than is the state of being heterosexual.

Both homosexuality and heterosexuality are to the best of our present knowledge programmed in some way during the first five to seven years of life. Those who have done a great amount of research in this field honestly say that the actual origins of heterosexuality and homosexuality still cannot be explained.

It does not appear to be a matter of heredity; neither has it been shown to be a matter of hormones—unless it should turn out to be something that happens before birth. If it were merely a matter of imitation, then there would be little or no homosexuality, because for centuries almost all people who are homosexual have come from heterosexual families. And research is now showing that up to now the incidence of homosexuality among the children brought up by a homosexual parent is the same or less as among children coming from heterosexual backgrounds. (Such research is only beginning, for until recently, a parent who admitted her or his homosexuality was rarely permitted to continue to act as a parent. Today, however, the courts are not necessarily taking children away from a parent just because the parent is a homosexual.)

It is important to distinguish between a fixed state of homosexuality and the homosexual behaviors that many children and young people experiment with as they grow up. Youthful experimentation with a person of the same sex does not mean that either will ultimately be homosexual. Homosexual experimentation is more likely to occur when heterosexual social opportunities are not there—for instance, in schools, camps, reformatories, or prisons, in which young people and/or adults are segregated and meet socially only members of their own sex. This does not mean, however, that if both sexes were admitted to such one-sex institutions, all homosexual inclinations would be eliminated. The percentage of people who are exclusively homosexual throughout all their lives would remain about the same.

Such homosexual behavior as accompanies lack of opportunity for heterosexual relationships and experiences—unless it is the result

of fixed homosexuality resulting from early childhood programming —will almost always change back to heterosexual behavior as soon as the opportunity arises. This has been found to be the case in prisons or in the armed forces, where some men or women who have no opportunity to use their mental, emotional, aggressive, or spiritual energies, much less their sexual energies, in heterosexual relationships will become so desperate and lonely that homosexual behavior occurs.

A question many people are curious about is: "What do homosexuals do?" We are so conditioned to think of sexual activity only in terms of sexual intercourse in which a penis enters a vagina that it is hard for many of us to imagine anything different. Therefore a kind of folklore has grown up that intimates in hush-hush tones that homosexuals express their love for each other in all sorts of dark, mysterious, and ugly ways. Let's simply recognize that there are many ways by which human beings, whether heterosexual or homosexual, can make sexual love. Therefore, except for intercourse of penis with vagina, the ways in which homosexual men and women express their sexuality are exactly the same as the ways in which millions of heterosexual couples express theirs. The mouth, the vagina, and the anus in women, and the mouth and anus in men, are body openings that homosexuals find pleasurable to use—just as heterosexuals may and do.

There are some special problems that the homosexual faces, most of which are the result of the attitudes of society. We'll illustrate by taking an extreme case. Suppose heterosexuality were made illegal or deemed immoral and unnatural and all heterosexuals were told that they must immediately cease all lovemaking between the two sexes and begin to make love only with people of the same sex. What would happen? Consternation would reign. Why? Simply because once the heterosexual "set" has been programmed in a person, no weight of law or fear of persecution, or persuasion or seduction, can ever succeed in making a heterosexual person become homosexual. Heterosexuality would simply have to go underground—and this is exactly what has been happening with homosexuality throughout the ages in most cultures, until today.

We have seen homosexuality declared totally immoral and sinful, and that means labeling human beings, who cannot possibly help their homosexual programming in childhood, as immoral and sinful. We hear of police harassing and spying on young teenagers as well as adults who are homosexual, and trying to trap homosexual people into declaring themselves so they can be arrested, although such incidents are less common than they were a few years ago.

In the United States today the approximately six out of every hundred men and women (12 million or more, all told) who are homosexual suffer from the severe effects of hostility, cruelty, and denial of their civil rights. Up to the present, this has kept them underground, "in the closet," thus condemning them to lives of loneliness or furtive hiding, out of the mainstream of everyday life. These are indeed problems, not only for the homosexual but also for the rest of the society, which permits and even at times encourages such unwarranted persecution, to its own detriment.

Homosexuality will cease to be a "problem" to our society when we adjust to our present scientific understanding of homosexuality. In a sense, homosexuality might be compared to left-handedness. Not too long ago left-handed children were frequently branded and taunted and tormented to make them "change." As a result, severe problems, with reading or learning capacity, for example, developed with many of these children. Research eventually established that, just as in right-handed people the left side of the brain dominates, so in left-handed people the right side of the brain dominates. Therefore, if we tried to teach right-handed people to become left-handed, we would find them experiencing reading and learning problems too. Eventually we learned not to demand that left-handed people change but simply to adjust to the fact that they are different. Our acceptance of the difference is such that we even have left-handed scissors and can openers on the market. In other words, society has adjusted itself to that 10 percent of the population that is left-handed, rather than expecting left-handers to change in order to adjust to society.

Instead of trying to "cure" homosexuality, we need to educate society to the fact that homosexuals may need help in adjusting to homosexual life just as heterosexuals need help in adjusting to heterosexual life. Society can then provide such help for homosexuals who may need or want it.

Do we need to fear homosexuals? No. As a group, per capita they appear to be less likely than heterosexuals to be violent, to kill, or to rape. Neither do they "seduce," because it would only be possible to "seduce" someone who is already programmed to be homosexual, or possibly partly bisexual and curious to try a new experience. Hundreds of thousands of boys and girls must in the past have been exposed to people they did not recognize as homosexual—among clergy, teachers, pediatricians, scout leaders, youth leaders, and others. These people have served as "role models" without any noticeable increase in homosexuality among the youths they worked or lived with.

Fears based not on fact but on ignorance and bigotry tend to be hysterical, which can do a great deal of harm to young people. There is enough hatred and hysteria in the world without creating more.

It must be emphasized that homosexuality does not threaten the *norm* of heterosexual behavior and marriage. The overwhelming majority of people are heterosexual, and they get married. Some homosexuals are seeking marriage ceremonies as a way of making a commitment to each other, but there are no laws permitting such unions, even though some state laws do not specifically say that the marriage partners must be of different sexes.

An informed person will realize that heterosexuals and homosexuals are far more alike than they are different. Each of us comes in contact every day with homosexual people without ever being aware of it. Salespersons, bus drivers, lawyers, lawn-care people, physicians, nurses, government officials, clergy, football and tennis players, mail carriers, teachers, college professors, musicians, writers—there are homosexuals, male or female, in every walk of life. Homosexuals are not a segregated group. They are among us and, like heterosexuals, they want and need companionship, love, success, creative work, fun, a home, and friends, regardless of gender preferences.

Almost all heterosexuals and homosexuals enjoy the same kinds of sexual activities. And the person who is exclusively homosexual just accepts the fact that he or she cannot fall in love with and feel "turned on" by someone of the other sex, just as an exclusively heterosexual person cannot fall in love with and feel "turned on" by someone of the same sex. Parents of homosexual children need not ask themselves, "What did I do wrong?" That is not the right question. If they find that one of their children is homosexual, nothing has changed. The child is just as much in need of their love and caring and help— to become as good a human being as possible, able to find love, companionship, and fulfillment—as are their heterosexual children. Accepting all this in a rational way should bring a sigh of relief to countless people: one more thing we don't have to worry about.

In a report published for study by the Catholic Theological Society of America, five Roman Catholic theologians and teachers said:

Homosexuals have the same right to love, intimacy, and relationships as heterosexuals. Like heterosexuals, they are also bound to strive for the same ideals in their relationships, for creativity and integration. The norms governing the morality of homosexual activity are those that govern all sexual activity, and the norms governing sexual activity are those that govern all human ethical activity. . . . It bears repeating, however, without provision, that where there is sincere affection, responsibility, and the germ of authentic human relationship—in other words, where there is love—God is surely present.

This study has not yet been either accepted or rejected by the Catholic Theological Society of America and therefore speaks only for its five authors. But in speaking thus for themselves, they did provide us with guidelines with which many representatives of Protestant and Jewish faiths agree in principle.

Bisexuality

We have been talking about heterosexuality *or* homosexuality as states of being. Sex researcher Alfred Kinsey developed a scale of sexual experience, ranging from exclusively homosexual to exclusively heterosexual. We have been talking of the extremes at each end of this scale, with *0* the exclusive heterosexual, *6* the exclusive homosexual. In between are a series of scale marks in which *1* would be a person who has had some experience with homosexual behaviors but remained heterosexual in adult life, *5* would be a person who had had some experience with heterosexual behavior during growing up but remained homosexual in adult life. A *2* would be heterosexual by preference, but maintaining some form of homosexual experience in adult life on a small scale, with *4* the equivalent in the homosexual state. Point *3* on the scale would then be the people who are able to function comfortably either as homosexual or heterosexual, and today we are seeing more of this. We call it *bisexuality*.

Bisexual people can function in various ways: they can be married with children and carry on a full homosexual life in addition to the marriage, or they can live in a homosexual relationship and carry on an active heterosexual life as well. Or they can be bisexual in desire and attraction to other people, but choose to limit their sexual activity, say, to a single committed relationship. So far our society has not really recognized bisexuality, because it has not been studied as fully as homosexuality. We know that bisexuality exists and that bisexuals are no more freaks than are homosexuals; they are merely human beings, like everyone else. Just as we now know much more about homosexuality than we ever did before, so too the growing research into bisexuality will help us more fully to understand that orientation.

Sexuality and Aging

There are many myths about the effects of the aging process on sexual life that are harmful because believing them can actually make them happen. A recent letter one of us received from a 60-year-old man described his worry because his erections were not as strong as they used to be. He wrote, "I often wake up at night with an erection, but as soon as I start worrying that it will go away, it does." That's the problem in a nutshell. Periodic erections during sleep are entirely usual, and so is their loss because of interference in the sexual response process by his worrying. Had he upon waking simply enjoyed his erections, and capitalized on them by making love or by masturbating, this could have been a positive step toward retaining or restoring his capacity for sexual enjoyment.

What are the facts about the effects of aging on sexual capacity? As we age, our bodies and all their processes change and slow down somewhat. We tend to accept this, understanding that whereas formerly we could run the length of an airport to make a plane, as we move past age 50 we are less able to do this; so we allow ourselves the time for walking. Then too, females and males are different when it comes to aging and sexual performance. Women may not learn to experience orgasm until they are adults, sometimes not even until they are in their forties or fifties. However, whatever the level of intensity of sexual experience they do reach at any age, whether it be from pleasuring by the self or by another, they tend to maintain that same level until well into their seventies and eighties. By contrast, males are at their peak in their late teens and early twenties. Their capacity for erection is maintained, with a very gradual slowing mostly of frequency, until the fifties or early sixties, when strength of erection may also be somewhat diminished. By the seventies, perhaps a quarter of males have noticed that their capacity for erection has much diminished or even ceased. This proportion increases with age, but still some men remain sexually vigorous and capable into their eighties or even nineties. With both women and men, the most important single factor for retention of sexual capacity is desire and opportunity for sexual interchange with an interested and interesting partner.

In this connection, additional help comes from a zestful approach to life by both partners, so that if any inhibitions still remain in either, both can help maintain sexual interest and response by finding new ways or new and different occasions or places for renewing their mutual sexual experiences. Thus masturbation, mutual hand-genital or oral-genital sex, or variations in position can all be used to provide fresh feelings of interest and renewal, as can changes in locale: a different room or bed, in front of the glowing fireplace, in a hotel room, or even under the stars.

Of course in the older age-group, long or chronic illnesses or conditions are more common than earlier, and these can certainly interrupt sex life, sometimes for long periods of time. Here sex counseling may be important in preserving the sexual relationship for eventual return to it. Specifically, prostate surgery need not necessarily mean the end of sexual capacity and enjoyment, but specific questions about this should be asked of the doctor. After some prostatic surgery, the capacity for erection can be lost because the nervous pathways for erection may have been interrupted by the surgery. In such cases, sex counseling for the couple can assure them that this need not and should not interrupt other aspects of sexual life together, for there are many, many ways of making love through shared experiences, touching, caressing, and use of the lips and hands. In women, hysterectomy, unless accompanied by a very extensive removal that includes nerve connections in the pelvis, rarely affects postsurgery sexual enjoyment.

Hormone replacement is sometimes considered for women, and a gynecologist can advise on this. Many couples use artificial lubricants ("K-Y" or other greaseless creamy lotions) in the vagina, on the penis, and in the clitoral area, if natural lubrication has been reduced with aging, as frequently happens.

Family and social attitudes can play important roles. A critical attitude toward physical expression of sexuality among the elderly will be destructive of peace of mind and will inhibit continued sexual enjoyment by older people, for whom a valued sexual relationship can add greatly to life's later chapters. These men and women should find only dignity and pleasure in feeling that they are not "dirty old men" and "dirty old women" but simply sexually active older people—if they wish to be.

Separation, Divorce, Death

Every relationship must end, that is certain. And as more and more intimate relationships between two people come to an end—whether of marriage by divorce, or of a committed unmarried relationship by separation, or of either by death—the effects are very much the same: deep feelings of pain, loss, disorientation, and confusion. As efforts to learn how to live without the accustomed mutually dependent intimacy are made by a previously closely bound partner, despair and depression usually occur. In the case of death, the separation must be accepted as final, but acceptance is often difficult and the period of mourning and bereavement may be long. The same thing is equally true of separation or divorce from a still-living partner. Here the sense of loss, mourning, and bereavement may be felt not so much for the person as for the relationship that had existed—or that might have been.

Going through such an experience of bereavement for whatever reason is easier if one has a strong sense of the self, of who and what one is. Also essential are love and support from close family members and unquestioning friends—what is often today called a support system.

Until we need a support system in the case of loss by death or by life processes, we may not realize how vital it can be to our ability to continue and to rebuild a life shattered by a severe loss. There are many people today who do not have such a support system—people who are alone or who do not have families that have learned how to coalesce themselves, their caring, their concern for each other, into a system that can come to the aid of one member of the group who has been stricken in one way or another. Geographical distance is also a factor, but not the main preventive of such aid, for the long-distance telephone is there for lengthy, close conversations that can include such heartfelt remarks as "I love you," "I wish I were right there to hold you," or "I'm glad to hear your voice—it tells me that you're in a better place today than you were last week." These comments are particularly important because they mean that one is being kept track of as one moves along the path to recovery.

In such a stricken case, strangers, no matter how kind, just will not do. The greater the sense of loss for something that has been dear and familiar, the greater is the need for comfort and strength from sources that are also dear and familiar. Sometimes one can persuade oneself that a stranger is "the answer" to loneliness and despair, but this is rarely the case. Entering into new intimacy too rapidly can be most unwise and even dangerous, for one is really asking an unknown person to help handle suffering that must be worked out by ourselves.

The question of sex itself inevitably intrudes itself, especially if one has become accustomed to a full, regular, and satisfying sex experience. Women and men can both suffer cruelly from sexual deprivation, and if there is a haunting sense that this is unworthy or unbecoming, that one ought to be able to "sublimate," let it be remembered that the very ones who may be suggesting this are perhaps for the most part persons for whom the sex drive has not been a primary one.

This is when already established sound understanding and attitudes about the worth of self-pleasuring stand in good stead. Our bodies are our own, are always with us, were made to serve us in many different ways in case of need. Masturbation is far safer than rushing into relationships with comparative strangers, who should not be enmeshed in our own slow movement toward recovery of our sense of wholeness, of self.

All this has much to do with the many sexual aspects of life. Deep feelings of need, sexual and otherwise, that spring out of a deep relationship tend to match each other in intensity and power. These can help sustain in times of stress, whether there is the need *for* love and comfort felt by the stricken one, or the need to *give* love and comfort felt by a member of the support system. The more one has invested in relationships for mutual giving, the more one has to give to others in their crisis times.

6
Marriage

Marriage is something most people have; something most people want; something a great many people take for granted they will have; something a vast number of people consider to be the most wonderful thing they ever had; something some people would be better off never being involved in; something many people get out of after they're in; something others wish they could get out of but can't; something many people try a second time, usually more successfully than the first; something some people try even a third time or more; something many people don't *think* much about; and something most people do *feel* a lot about. In any case, marriage throughout the ages has been something very special in human life.

Marriage is not just the wedding, with the bride in white the center of attention. Nor is it an event which means romance will be the central force in two lives from that point on. For a great many men and women, romance can be a most important part of marriage and can help carry a couple through the difficult moments in living together. For others, a limited understanding of the part sex and romance play in marriage is likely to cause problems and disappointments. Too many people believe marriage is just a signal that they can at last have all the sex together they want and that the sexual part of their life together will always be perfect, without any effort on their part. They need to understand that romance is only a part of sex and that sex is only a part of romance.

The Role of Childhood Experiences

Marriage affects lives so deeply that it is far more than a ceremony in which two people say, "I do," the state says, "By this ceremony you are now legally bound to each other," and the church says, "By this ceremony you have now covenanted yourselves to each other in the eyes of God." In truth, the facts and conditions of a marriage begin not with the wedding itself but way back at those two moments when each partner was born, and they include all the moments in the lives of both since then.

Ever since two people who will eventually marry each other came into this world, all kinds of things have happened to each of them. These experiences will profoundly influence the kind of marriage relationship they will achieve.

In earlier times, when a girl was born, the mother and others in the family might begin weaving and embroidering sheets and other linens for what was then called a hope chest. A father might lay down some bottles of wine which, in the years before the newborn baby was expected to become a bride, would mellow and ripen and, he hoped, become a wine great enough for drinking as a toast at the wedding. The mother and father probably never realized that their own actions toward the baby in its first five years would influence the course of their child's future marriage more than their plans for the wedding.

Since early experiences are eventually reflected in what a person brings to a marriage years later, it is worthwhile for people to look back at such experiences to try to see how they will—or do—affect the marriage relationship. Good experiences can be used positively, but experiences that were not so good must be understood, so that a person can learn how to compensate for possible negative effects. It is important to learn how to change and adapt oneself, and how to grow in awareness and understanding—whether before marriage or within the marriage relationship—always bearing in mind that it takes two to make a marriage. In the words of Masters and Johnson, there is no such thing as an uninvolved partner, inside or outside marriage. That is why marriage and sex counseling can generally succeed only when both husband and wife are in counseling, or therapy, together.

What Makes a Good Marriage?

Let's look at two marriages that by now are familiar to millions of people in the United States. Are they "good" marriages? Why? Are they poor marriages? Why?

John and Olivia Walton and Archie and Edith Bunker are two couples just about as different from each other as any two real-life couples you could name. But there are some important similarities not only between the two couples but also to many real-life marriages.

Both the Bunkers and the Waltons have been married a good long time, and their marriages have lasted in spite of difficulties. For instance, neither couple has ever had much money—it's always been a struggle for them—but both take this fact in stride and expect to survive. The Waltons and the Bunkers are also alike in that the couples have a close relationship: they share with each other; they keep talking about both the easy things and the hard things; and in both marriages each member of the couple is *for* the other, believes in the other, cares about the other's welfare—and shows all this constantly.

"What!" you may be thinking. "Archie Bunker cares about Edith? Why, he's always telling her to 'stifle' herself, poking fun at her. John and Olivia Walton, now, they're different. You can *see* they love each other." John and Olivia do love each other—no question —and they show it. They look at and really see each other often. They communicate with each other, and in every program they touch each other. Their voices are warm and intimate and comfortable when they talk to each other. They do have differences, but these are resolved with no basic change in their relationship. They grow together. They are for each other, and both know it and are sure of it, as are their children and friends—and we who see them.

But Edith and Archie? Doesn't he speak roughly and put her down? Isn't he terribly self-centered? Isn't it always "I" and "me" and "my"—thinking of himself first? Indeed it is. Yet what is the very first thing he does when he comes into the house? As he hangs up his hat he calls out, "Edith, I'm home." Why does he do that? Because he needs her answer, hers and no one else's. And what happens? The few times she hasn't responded immediately he anxiously goes calling and hunting for her. This is because the thing he can count on is that Edith calls right back even as she's trotting from the kitchen to the dining room, "Archie, you're home! How are you? How was your day?" She runs to him and kisses him. Her voice says how glad she is to see him, her kiss is loving, and you know she means it and so does he. Even though he immediately launches into whatever is on his mind, she really listens.

These two also look and see and touch; they also are warm and intimate and comfortable with each other. They love each other, they are for each other. Their daughter and son-in-law know it. Everyone may wonder how it could be, with Archie the way he is, but everyone also knows that they love each other. And no matter how self-centered or angry or poisonous Archie may be, let Edith go into one of her rare episodes of depression or grieving or anger, and Archie is beside himself. He needs Edith, and at those moments he is never ashamed to show that he does. And he comes through for her in words and gestures that are tender and true. To know for sure that you are needed, that you are the most important person in the world to the person who is the most important to you—that is the rock on which a strong marriage is built.

Of course, a marriage relationship may not always be fifty-fifty. It seems to be more or less constantly so with the Waltons, but with the Bunkers, Edith is a more giving person than Archie. If their relationship is weighted perhaps sixty-forty, it's because Edith is a naturally open and giving person and because her sureness of his caring and need for her allow her to spill out on him all the giving and caring that she has joy in expressing and that he has therefore come to count on.

Where does the capacity for such an easy flow of giving and caring come from? From the very earliest experiences in life. The difference between the Waltons' fifty-fifty and the Bunkers' sixty-forty (or sometimes even seventy-thirty) could probably be traced back to their early childhoods. The baby who is eagerly awaited and received into the world, by two parents (or a single parent) who are mature enough to be parents, has a good start. As we have said, a baby requires not only feeding and bathing and a place to sleep but also recognition and meeting of its great need for touching, for talking— for communication, constantly in small but frequent doses. The parents have called the baby into physical being by the act of mating and the processes of conception and birth, but that is only the start. Parents play a continuing role. They must consistently call the baby's mind and spirit into being during the years after birth. This can happen only if at least one parent or permanent parent substitute is there to meet the deepest needs of the baby and the young child.

No matter how well a baby is bathed and clothed and fed, if it is left in the crib day after day for long periods of time, "so as not to spoil it," it will not develop into the best husband—or wife—material. A baby requires the continuing assurance that comes from being picked up, stroked, cuddled, and smoothed by a loving voice and welcoming arms; it needs to be looked at intently, close up, while being talked to, so that it can look back at the familiar face it can count on; it needs to hear voices that are not only loving and reassuring but laughing and gay, even when they are not addressing it. A baby and a young child need all these things over and over again, every day, from the same one or two persons who deeply feel them and mean them, and not just from casual strangers who are only performing a duty. Strangers can take over part of the twenty-four hours of care, and no harm will result. But parents, or permanent parental replacements, are needed for the rest of the time.

In the earliest months and years, babies and young children whose basic needs are consistently met are enabled to develop an increasing capacity to withstand what is called *separation anxiety*. Exploring as toddlers, at first they keep running back to the parent figure at short intervals, but if the trust is there, these intervals become longer and longer. Still, when they come home from school the first thing they do, as Archie does, is call out, "Mom, are you there?" or "Dad, where are you?" as the case may be. And although Mom or Dad may not be there, in those early years some Mom or Dad figure should be there to respond warmly, to be acceptable as a substitute for the real Mom or Dad who might be out working. None of this will hurt the child as long as it knows for sure that ultimately Dad or Mom will come home. In this way the child can move toward maturity with the sureness that comes from the conviction that the wanted, needed person is really there for him or her. In other words, the child is assured that he himself or she herself is a wanted and needed person.

Olivia and John Walton must surely have had this kind of childhood background, which made it possible for them to achieve a married relationship that not only fulfilled them both but enabled their children to receive from them the same kind of start in life. As a matter of fact, we can see John's background right there in the family: the strong, peppery, but real and loving relationship of Grandpa and Grandma Walton.

But what about Edith and Archie? Archie is certainly the one who causes us to wonder. All his actions tell us that he is unsure of himself. The louder he shouts and the more he puts people down, the easier it is to see that his babyhood and childhood may have been pretty rough, lonely, insecure, even painful. He has a need to want more than he gives, to be constantly reassured that he is an OK person, a wanted person, a needed person. He shies away from any efforts to change him, to open his eyes to himself and his relationships with others. He's afraid of being a giving person because he's afraid he'll never get anything back, except, of course, with Edith, who is secure in her love for him and her knowledge of his need for her. According to their expectations, it's a good marriage. And also, clearly, it's a marriage with enjoyable sexual moments that satisfy them both. From time to time Edith makes this known, and so does Archie, by his embarrassed refusal to admit it.

The Place of Sex in Marriage

Far more than a ceremony or a covenant, marriage is also far more than sex. Marriage means living together, growing together, building a relationship that is a source of strength for two people, not only a refuge *from* the world for them but also a springboard *into* the world. Intimacy—built on mutual need, mutual trust, between two people who are constantly saying, with or without words, "I need you, you are the most important person in the world to me"—is the ultimate refuge, the ultimate achievement of marriage. Love comes easily in this kind of intimacy, and so does sexual expression. Sex doesn't have to be constant fireworks with many orgasms. Although it can be, it can also be a loving, gentle experience that provides a kind of inner radiance for two lives, a warmth that others are aware of and that fully satisfies the partners.

Sex is only a part of marriage. For some couples, sex is perhaps the most vital part of their mutual need; for others it takes a lesser place; for still others it may be quite unimportant. But once mutual need and trust are firmly established for both, once lines of communication are opened up by talking and touching, the relationship is strong enough to stand the stresses that all living brings at one time or another.

Counteracting a Major Threat to Marriage

Among the many factors that threaten marriage today is the continuing pattern perpetuated by parents whose childhood experiences have not made them capable of achieving relationships that are giving, trusting, and intimate. These parents then have children, but they do not have the background to draw on to provide a good model for their children. Many efforts are being made to break into this self-perpetuating chain.

Besides psychotherapy for individual couples, there are groups of couples who help each other in the remembering and relearning process. These are known as marriage-encounter or marriage-enrichment groups, many of which are under church auspices. All these groups take up, among other topics, the topic of sex. They provide information and encourage discussion so that members of the group can come to see that the physical sexual relationship can be a highly pleasurable and comforting part of life that can even be strengthened by discussion. All such groups should be carefully checked to ensure that their leaders are well-trained people (see Sources of Help, pp. 315–320).

These groups also help people see that it is possible to change themselves and their lives for the better by being willing to remember and reexamine and evaluate all kinds of experiences, even those of earliest childhood and even—maybe especially—the most painful ones. When they are able to do this, with or without help, they can restructure their ways of relating to those who are most dear to them. Participation in such group experiences, by two people who can admit how important they are to each other even though they haven't been getting along well together, can serve to change the relationship so that a marriage that is hurting after ten, twenty, or more years can be salvaged.

More than being salvaged, such a marriage can be so strengthened and enriched that the two partners can find each other again— in a true sense fall in love again—and become for their children, their grandchildren, and all the members of their family, as well as for each other, sources of strength and joy and love.

But is marriage for everyone? Is marriage the only basis possible for the formation of a family? People used to think so, but today we are beginning to see a number of different kinds of "families." We talk about them in the next chapter, so right now is a good place to point out that everything in this chapter is as important for nonmarrieds who have entered into a committed relationship to understand as it is for marrieds.

A committee of physicians, working as a group convened by the World Health Organization, once defined sexual health as "the integration of the bodily, emotional, intellectual, and social aspects of sexual being, in ways that are positively enriching, and that enhance personality, communication, and love."

That's a fine definition of a good marriage, too.

7
The Family and Its Role in the Development of Sexuality

The family is probably the oldest human institution and society's most basic unit. It has always been the principal means for protecting and training children and rearing them to maturity. In most parts of the world, it is still the principal way by which property can be cared for, improved or increased, and passed on to the next generation. At its best, the family provides steady love and caring for each of its members. The family can make possible, also, division of labor and pooling abilities and talents of its members so that the educational, social, and economic welfare of each one is promoted. And, as we have already suggested, it is the principal environment in which the sexuality of husband and wife finds intimate expression and in which the sexuality of the young, as part of their minds and bodies, is first formed, to be guided and developed thereafter. Most of us, during our lifetimes, belong to at least two families, the one in which we were born and raised and the one which, usually with another person, we ourselves establish, by acts of love and intention.

The Family Today

In the United States, the most common as well as traditional definition of the family has been a married couple with children (the *nuclear family*). In another sense, family can also mean a group of people connected by ties of blood or marriage, such as one or more grandparents, cousins, aunts, uncles, nieces, nephews, in-laws, and so on (the *extended family*).

Over two thirds of the adults in the United States today live in arrangements that do not fit the traditional nuclear family pattern. According to the Bureau of Labor Statistics, in 1975 the living arrangements of U.S. adults were categorized in this way:

Nuclear families	*30%*
Married couples with children at home, two breadwinners	16%
Married couples with children at home, one breadwinner	13%
Married couples with or without children at home, no breadwinner (on relief, independent means, etc.)	1%

Non-nuclear families, and nonfamilies	*70%*
Married couples without children, or whose children have left home	23%
Single persons living alone (widows, widowers, persons never married, persons now separated or divorced)	21%
Single-parent families with children	16%
Extended families (one or more adults besides husband and wife, including those with and without children)	6%
Intentional experimental arrangements (groups, etc.), and cohabiting couples living together without marriage and with or without children	4%

From both groups you can see that at least 44 percent of U.S. adults live in homes where there are no children. So we have to be clear how many different sorts of "family" arrangements exist. As their variety has increased over the past fifty years, in response to new social and economic conditions and changing human needs, the proportion of traditional nuclear families has decreased. Today, the most comprehensive and helpful definition of a family, one that respects different kinds of people who have chosen different patterns to establish and support a family life-style, is: *Two or more people who, regardless of gender, age (although one must be legally an adult), or marital status, elect to live together in commitment and trust in order to care for and about each other.* Even so, we should repeat, the most widely accepted definition of a family remains the one into which most people in our culture have fitted at some point in their lives: *A mother and a father and their growing offspring.*

One thing is certain: regardless of the pattern of the family, what is always required of its members is to learn how to live together. And, especially where there are children, another thing is certain: given that the family's primary functions are to house, nourish, clothe, educate, and protect its members, one additional function stands out—to teach its members how to give and how to receive love and how to support each other in mutual development and fulfillment. You can put figures and measurements to how well families carry out their practical functions, but no one has ever learned how to measure love, devotion, development, and fulfillment.

During thousands of years of human history, there have been relatively few options for family members: men did what was considered men's work, women did women's work, and children were trained to fit this pattern. In 1847 the British poet Alfred Tennyson described it this way:

> Man for the field and woman for the hearth;
>   Man for the sword, and for the needle she;
> Man with the head, and woman with the heart;
>   Man to command, and woman to obey;
>   All else confusion.

Today in many parts of the world, including our own country, there remains considerable support for this kind of division of labor and functions, because of the fear of "all else confusion."

But over the past century, new developments have led to revolutionary changes in family life: the invention of machines providing both men and women with more leisure time and tending to make less important the greater body size and muscular strength of men; the change in the nature of productive work, with less need for physical strength (of which the average man has more than the average woman) and more need for special skills and training (in which men and women are relatively equal), so that today men and women can be equally productive; and the discovery of reliable means of contraception so that, as women need no longer face unlimited childbearing and rearing, they can, if they wish or must, join the labor force.

In short, it is now possible for women and men, and girls and boys, to choose with equal freedom what they wish to do with their lives, and they now have the same freedom in choosing how they will express their sexuality and arrange their groupings, their marriages, and their families. With these new freedoms it is now possible to make decisions for oneself rather than have one's life prescribed by tradition or necessity. Some people welcome these changes, some are troubled by them, but all have no choice but to adapt to them, for they appear to be here to stay.

In the United States, because of these changes, for our satisfaction and happiness in family life we have come to place more importance on the love and companionship we choose and less on the blood relationships and economic and physical necessities that once required us to stay together regardless of emotional needs and satisfactions.

Most people are now free to choose how, or even whether, to form a family, and, if they do form one, whether and when to add children to it, either natural or adopted. We have access to a vast range of ideas and information, and we see examples of all kinds of alternatives. We have fewer roots and we move around a lot. It is the exception to grow up in a single community surrounded by relatives and friends, younger and older, who grew up in the same community. More than half the women in our country are in the work force, rather than home-bound, and children are at home alone more often than before, in the care of people other than their parents, or at school or at a day-care center.

Despite the wide acceptance of diverse patterns of family living, there persists in the United States among many people a strong, deeply engrained sense of the "right" way for a family to be: the husband and father is "head" of the family and is the main breadwinner; the wife and mother takes care of everyone and is in charge of the home, except for major decisions; the two or three children, boys and girls, behave the way boy children and girl children are supposed to behave, which is not always "good" but is certainly not rebellious, except occasionally, when the boy children rebel more than the girl children.

That's the pattern still considered "typical" today by many middle-aged and older people, though not by younger people. Thus, as patterns have begun to vary and change has become more rapid, something of a gap has developed between generations, as has happened many times before. In the stable, unchanging, more isolated societies studied by many anthropologists, there exists little or no difference from generation to generation, but in our society—and in other "developed" countries today—such a gap is common. Furthermore, in countries now "developing" by rapid urbanization and efforts at industrialization, the communication gap between generations is becoming as marked as it is in the United States.

Parental Responsibilities

In spite of the influence parents can have on their children's development, there is no doubt that from the moment of birth, and even before, each child is his or her own being, a duplicate of no one else. Anyone who has had a number of children knows that from the very beginning some infants are placid and happy, some tense and irritable, some noisy, some quiet, some easy, some difficult. These qualities seem to be a part of the essential individuality of each child, not something conferred upon the child from outside. Thus, while parents do have a profound influence on their children, they do not form the basic stuff of the child.

Some parents make the mistake of feeling that they are responsible for everything their children are and everything their children do. They even try to live their lives for them. All that should be expected of parents is that they do their best with their children. While parents cannot live their children's lives for them, they can try to set good examples—without trying to masquerade as perfect. They can try to pass on to their children, as opportunities arise, the standards and values by which they live. The children think about these standards, try them out, reject them, return to them, discuss them with others; and all this helps young people mature.

Children will inevitably look outside the family for information, opinions, and experiences. Television, friends, books, magazines, visitors, and the like also reach them in their homes. Parents cannot and should not try to protect their children from outside influences, although they can rightly help to select the experiences their children will have. The main goal of parents should be to help their children equip themselves with information, with the capacity to reason about facts, with an awareness of where and when to make decisions, and with the ability to communicate, so that in the end the children learn to stand on their own. The age when a child must rely on himself or herself comes earlier than many of us think, in the middle and late teens. But even then the children must not be made to feel that their parents have abdicated their responsibilities, as did the teenage girl who told her friend, "My parents don't care what I do as long as it doesn't come to their attention."

Single-Parent Families

Because one out of every three marriages in the United States ends in divorce or separation, about 45 percent of children today spend some or all of their most formative years with only one parent, usually but not always the mother.

How does growing up in a single-parent family affect children? There is no simple answer. If the first six or eight years of a child's life have been spent with two parents who cared for and related closely to the child and to each other, much of the basic process of sexualization (gender identity, sex-role orientation, comfortable feelings about his or her body, sense of self-respect) has been accomplished. However, if the relationship between the parents has been hostile or distant, this is likely to leave a mark, but not necessarily an indelible one.

It is probably better for children to live with one loving parent than to live with two who are by daily example teaching poor human relationships. Children in a single-parent family have relationships with other families and other people who may be close to the parent. Thus there are many sources from which the children can learn about men and women, about what being "masculine" and being "feminine" can mean. With their own relatives, friends, and peers in the neighborhood and at school and, in turn, their families, the life of a child with only one parent need not be narrow or restricted.

About three quarters of divorced parents do remarry, and the process by which the parent develops a new relationship and then reenters marriage, while it may bring strains and fears and even jealousy, is observed and often participated in by the children involved, and they can learn from it.

When the single parent gives the children a sense of solid support and consistent love, and sees that they have opportunities to turn outward toward others for relationships and affection, a period of single parenting is not harmful. More depends on the quality of the children's relationship with the parents and others than on the number of parents. Healthy growth toward mature and responsible expression of sexuality can be fostered by many sources.

Sexual Feelings Between Parents and Children

Many a mother has experienced sexual arousal when she nursed her baby, and if this were understood by her as perfectly natural, it would not be so disturbing. Many parents also feel turned on sexually by their own children after they outgrow babyhood, especially when the children reach the age of puberty or later, and these feelings are usually disturbing to the mother or father. Children, too, can have sexual feelings toward their parents. It is helpful for both parents and children to know that such feelings are common and, if they are managed reasonably, are nothing to be ashamed of. They certainly should not be allowed to interfere with spontaneous gestures of affection between fathers and daughters and mothers and sons.

Anyone who thinks about it knows that feelings can cause actions, and families and society will work better if people, whether children or adults, develop a sense of responsibility for their actions. But what of the feelings that lead to the actions? Are we responsible for them? Not directly. They occur as a result of our thoughts and how what happens to us affects our thoughts. However, our thoughts can be subconscious or even unconscious—often we don't even know we have them. But if we can talk and think together about them, and then reflect alone upon them, or as we are helped by counselors with special training, or by caring friends and teachers, it is often possible to bring our subconscious or unconscious thoughts into consciousness so that we can understand how they affect our feelings and actions. The best way to change the way we feel, if we need to do that, is to do something about how and what we think. We are not responsible for our feelings because we cannot control them, so we need not feel guilty about them. What we must be responsible for is our actions, because it is possible to learn how to manage actions in such a way that no one will be hurt.

The Parents' Sex Life

Another area about which many parents feel some guilt is their own sexual life with each other; they somehow don't want their children to know that it exists. It is true that most children don't particularly

want to think about the lives of their own parents in sexual terms; most adolescents find it really hard to believe that their parents, much less their grandparents, actually have intercourse for enjoyment. In fact, quite a few children have the idea that their parents, if they have had three children, for example, have had intercourse only three times.

But there is no reason to conceal the fact that parents enjoy each other sexually. What a dismal impression of adult human sexuality some parents give by their asexual masquerade! This is not to say that parents should ever exhibit their sex lives to their children or discuss at the breakfast table how great (or otherwise) it was in bed last night. This would be harmful, artificial, and uncomfortable for everyone, for in our culture, intimate sexual activity is looked upon as a private matter, and children should learn this from the parents' example.

What if a child should happen upon his or her parents involved in what sometimes is alarmingly called "the primal scene"? The child is not likely to be adversely affected—unless the parents are upset and show it by such actions as slamming the door or shouting or scolding. The best way to handle the situation is to make clear that children should respect the parents' privacy, as parents respect the privacy of their children. Also, as soon as possible, it is important to tell the child that what he or she saw was an act of love, not an attack. (To a small child, intercourse can look like an attack of the father upon the mother.)

Adolescents and Growth Toward Independence

During puberty and on through adolescence, the need of children to establish independence from parents, even if well-managed, is likely to generate strains and stresses in family relationships. This is especially true when it comes to sexual matters. Parents feel they must protect the children from danger, while every child feels the need to be his or her own person, sometimes unaware of or unwilling to admit any need for protection.

It is important for parents to become aware that the period of adolescence, which covers six to ten years, requires young persons to accomplish at least four major tasks of growth:

1. They must separate from their parents and learn to stand on their own—without rejecting the parents. This task requires mutual respect on the part of both the adolescents and the parents, a respect

that is not always easy to come by, especially when the parents have a hard time letting go.

2. They must develop a strong and stable sense of who and what they are sexually: accepting their gender as male or female; understanding the appropriate gender role behavior and the actions, relationships, choices, and values that are consistently appropriate with this role and with the kind of person each one is; and coming to know for themselves where, how far, with whom, and under what circumstances they will go in testing and expressing their masculinity or femininity on the way to adult maturity.

3. They are expected to complete their formal education and be ready to present themselves as educated people capable of living in a world in which being educated is highly important.

4. They must prepare for earning a living.

Frequently, at least in our society, the accomplishment of these four very large and difficult tasks causes rough periods of separation, or seeming alienation, from the family. Awkwardness, open conflict, and feelings of suffering and loss will be common on both sides. But the period of abrasive criticism and conflicting immediate objectives usually passes, especially if all sides can manage to deal openly and rationally with expressions of anger and frustration and have learned how to center these feelings upon situations ("I can't stand the way you are acting!") and not upon persons ("I can't stand *you!*").

Young adolescents are not children and not adults; they are people on the way to becoming adults. They wobble in and out of behavior that may appear inappropriately childish. When they feel most childlike, they come to parents (if parents are open and flexible) in need purely and simply of comfort, bolstering, a listening ear, a warm hug, and even advice. They are probably as surprised and confused by their swings of behavior as their parents are, but the waverings provide rich opportunities for communication and teaching.

As children grow through adolescence, influences outside the family become stronger. This represents a healthy centrifugal force, an increased interaction with peers, with other families, with the world outside. Young people at this stage are fortunate if they are encouraged to get to know and be on intimate terms with other families, so that they can learn from inside how other families work and how different kinds of people relate to each other. Also, your own family may find itself invaded by young people from elsewhere who find you and your family a source of strength, variety, and satisfaction of curiosity. Members of your own extended family—cousins, uncles, aunts, grandparents, family friends, and so forth—can also help provide a wide variety of people with whom your children can interact and learn and from whom you as parent can also learn the various and changing ways of the world.

It is important that both parents and children accept adolescent sexual interests and urges as natural and good, while still agreeing on the need for limits to sexual behavior. As adolescents increase their capacity to take on responsibilities, the amount of freedom they are granted must increase. In this way they will gain the experience needed for maturity. The degree of maturity they can reach must serve to arm them for the time when the controlling forces in their lives will no longer be their parents but instead whatever knowledge, strength, values, standards, and capacity for giving and receiving joy they have developed with the aid of their parents. Inevitably, there must come the time when their only guardian is their own character.

Family Communication About Sex

How can parents and children learn to communicate with each other as the children work out standards for themselves regarding their sexuality? We have already said that much communication among members of the family takes place without words and even unconsciously, and that there is quite commonly little or no open, spoken communication on sexual matters. This is not a conspiracy of silence but an unspoken agreement to be silent, probably because some or all members of the family have gotten the message from each other that sex is a subject to be silent about. Members of a family need not feel guilty or inadequate or angry if silence is the pattern, but opportunities should not be missed to find ways to relieve the silence and let the words flow.

A good time to let down the silence barrier is any occasion of crisis—for example, when a parent is angry or worried about a sex-related occurrence in a child (genital play, too-early dating, use of the car for "parking," inviting a friend into a bedroom alone), or when a child is angry for being forbidden to participate in what seems like innocent activity. If the discussion can center on what actually happened, how each person feels about it, and what the motives and

consequences (both good and bad) were or are likely to be, it may be helpful talk. If the talk centers on the person or persons involved—their "goodness" or "badness" as people—rather than on the *actions* themselves, it is likely to be harmful. To express how you feel and how certain behaviors make you feel is fine, but it can be harmful if you get carried away in a spirit of accusation against the person.

If there is a heated exchange of words, it is best that parents not lay down the law while feelings are still hot. Instead, come back to the issues when things are calmer, and then work out some rules or standards or agreements together. A crisis can be the occasion for authentic, valuable communication, and exchange of true feelings, and we can be thankful when open crises, openly dealt with, result in keeping the doors open between people who love and care about each other and want to remain a family.

Answering Questions About Sexuality

When a child, especially an adolescent, asks a question, it is sometimes most fruitful to use the question as an opener for what may become a long and serious exchange of knowledge, ideas, and attitudes. At other times, it may be better to try to answer a factual question plainly, briefly, and factually, not going beyond the question but not hedging either. When you tell children what they want to know, you open the way to further questions and conversation. Be careful not to use a simple question as a springboard for a complete lecture on, say, human biology; if you do, you may turn off further questions. For example, four-year-old Sally points between the legs of her undressed little brother and says, "What's that?" A good answer would be, "That's his penis and testicles; they make him a boy, not a girl. You have a vagina and a clitoris; they make you a girl, not a boy." Later on, unless Sally asks more right then, you can find time to explain, "All boys and men have penises and girls and women have vaginas, and that's the way it's supposed to be. Little boys use their penises when they go to the bathroom"—you might say "urinate" if it doesn't seem too fancy a word)—"and when they grow up they also use them to help make babies. You don't have a penis, but you do have a uterus (or womb) inside you where a baby can grow. You see, it takes both a man and a woman to start a baby."

When questions and comments from the children do come, be

very careful not to overadvise or jump in too quickly. Parents should *listen* first to be sure they have correctly heard the question or comment before they answer. And of course, a sure way to shut off further questions is to respond, "Why do you want to know that?"—which may be heard by the child as "You shouldn't be interested in that" or "Have you been fooling around with something you shouldn't?" If you simply answer the question, the reason for the question may well come out sooner or later.

Giving Advice

If you feel you must give advice, and advice is often necessary (for example, if an early adolescent seems to be experimenting with sexual intercourse), let it come as information, not as negative or positive commandments. But when it comes to your own convictions and beliefs about sexual behavior, it is usually best to state these frankly. It is important, however, to label them as *your* beliefs and convictions, not as something you are trying to impose on your children.

By information, examples, and sharing of experiences, you may be able to convince a child to adopt your point of view, but you'll never succeed by insisting that the child think and behave your way only.

One advantage adults have over children and adolescents is that adults have lived longer and can probably see things more in perspective. A mature person doesn't tend to think the world is coming to an end quite as often as a young person does. Even if they haven't been explicitly told some things—about sex, for instance—children know a lot and have imagined or guessed even more. But much of what they think and believe is secret, incorrect, or out of proportion, and this is not their fault but ours for not providing factual information long before.

Parents can therefore be very helpful to their children by using conversation (at the dining table, in the living room, while preparing for bed, while driving in the car, while on a walk, during a TV commercial) to put things into context and to ask and answer questions or provide more information. Television shows, news items, school lessons, neighborhood gossip or events, remarks made by peers—all these are good opportunities for communication, sharing, and education. Such sharing is best done naturally and bit by bit, not in large doses of what seem to be prepared lectures.

We mustn't forget that some things that seem important or shocking to an adult are taken in a more matter-of-fact manner by most young persons (for example, news of a rape or an out-of-wedlock pregnancy). It is important to try to react so as to educate rather than frighten young people. Overreaction can easily distort and get things out of perspective.

Encouraging Young People to Talk

Sometimes it is obvious that a youngster doesn't have the courage to express an interest, to make a comment, or to ask a question. He or she may feel the subject is too personal or too embarrassing to talk about in front of the entire family. In this case it can work well to take the youngster aside later and begin a conversation or provide information or make it clear that you are ready to listen. If you let your child know you're ready whenever he or she wants to talk, eventually the child will get up the nerve to ask the question, sometimes of the father, sometimes of the mother. Make it clear you are always available—be "askable," as Dr. Sol Gordon of Syracuse University puts it.

Books can be helpful in encouraging youngsters to open up. There are a number of books that can be given or left lying around (but better given, with some explanation like, "This is a good book about sex, or at least I thought so. If you read it, then maybe we can talk about it.") The book you are now reading can be left around for any member of the family to pick up. (See page 299 for some other suggestions).

Other aids can be school or church programs. Learn whether they have a sex education program, what it is like, and how it is taught. Whatever you discover you will be able to use to advantage at home.

How Young People Can Improve Family Communication

Many adults would love to feel that young people are trying to keep open the flow of communication and would respond to this. Sometimes it is necessary for young people to take the initiative with parents who are shy. Here are some ways to do this:

1. Whenever possible, open up and share feelings.

2. Let the parents know how things are and what is going on in their lives.

3. Ask questions of fact or opinion.

4. When they think their parents (or other adults) are right, tell them so right out. This makes it unnecessary for parents to keep insisting they are right or to say "I told you so." It also puts the young people in a much stronger position when *they* are sure they are right; and they will be more likely to be listened to with respect.

Whether you are a parent or a child, if you are hesitant and embarrassed to talk about sexual matters, try to admit it. Don't pretend you know everything or have every issue about sexuality totally decided. If parents acknowledge their questions, children are likely to acknowledge theirs, and good discussion and sharing of information can result in mutual respect and growth.

Developing an Awareness of Differences

In some families all members feel reasonably free to talk together about sexual matters, and the children have learned to talk about body parts and sexual functions naturally and factually. This is a healthy state of affairs, but it can lead to problems when the youngsters go out into the neighborhood or visit other families where there is no such openness. Thus it is good for children to be taught, when they are old enough to understand, that not all families feel the same about what is proper to talk about and what is not, and that many people feel that matters having to do with the body and with sex are not good subjects to talk about. The children should realize that it doesn't mean their family is better than other families, just that it is a matter of differences in feelings and upbringing, and people's feelings should always be respected.

Privacy for Family Members

In most families, both parents and children value their privacy at certain times. If a parent is in the bathroom and really doesn't feel comfortable sharing it with a child, he or she can simply say so. There is no need to do this in a scolding tone. Simply explain, "I like my privacy, so please knock and I'll tell you if it's OK to come in. I'll do the same for you." Or, "I'll feel more comfortable if you knock first and wait for me to tell you to come in." Children can understand that; they often feel the same way.

If parents are in the bedroom together, even if they're simply reading or napping or talking, they may want privacy. Again, a "Please knock when the door's closed and wait to be invited in" is natural and clear and nonthreatening. It's just as important for parents to give the same consideration to their children—once they've reached an age where it matters, perhaps four or five—and to knock if the door is closed and wait to be invited in. A child will be grateful for the respect and understanding shown, and will learn to do the same.

Dealing with Sex Play and Experimentation

Infants quite naturally and quickly learn that it feels good when they touch and play with their genitals, and such play should not be discouraged or punished. Punishment will not stop the activity but will cause the baby to learn to be secretive and to feel guilty about it. Feelings of guilt about such activity may be quite heavy and long-lasting, affecting even the ability to enjoy sexual pleasure later in marriage.

Children in our culture must learn that sex and sexual touching are considered private matters. For example, if a very young child is engaging in genital play in the living room while other people are around, he or she can be picked up in an affectionate way, without the least hint of disapproval, and carried elsewhere. An older child can be told, "I'm glad you've found your body feels good, but when you want to touch your body that way, it's more private to be in your room by yourself." Some parents may ask, "But isn't this simply telling my child that it's OK to go to his (or her) room to masturbate?" The answer is yes, and we believe this is a good thing to reassure a child about. As we have said, masturbation is harmless, except when we make it otherwise by causing a child to feel guilty about it.

An even more difficult situation for parents to deal with is when young children engage in sex play with each other, either with another member of the family or with a friend. It is a fact that children are curious about each other's bodies and that they quite naturally want to satisfy their curiosity. Therefore, unless they are strongly inhibited from doing so, or explicitly forbidden, it is to be expected that they will want to see what another child's body looks like.

Some children will simply and harmlessly look at each other's genitals and perhaps touch them. Usually they will do these things in secret, which shows that they have already learned that any activity connected with the sexual parts of their bodies is taboo—wrong and unacceptable. Others will do their exploring through some sort of game, like playing doctor, to make it seem more acceptable. Such activity is rarely erotic (seeking physical genital pleasure); rather, it is research, learning, trying to find answers to questions, harmful only when adults happen upon it, become vastly upset, and express anger, fear, and the intent to punish. Then the children receive the impression that they are onto something really big and bad and fearful.

If they are observed by a parent, children will usually stop their sex play or genital exploration, and it is an appropriate response for them to do so. If parents feel comfortable enough about it all to say something like "It *is* interesting to find out how other people's bodies look, isn't it?" that's a suitable response. If they can go on to let the children talk about it with them and answer questions, or even to get a book with some diagrams and look at them together, so much the better.

Probably, though, most parents will not feel sure or comfortable enough to do more than put a gentle stop to the incident and then, we hope, find an occasion soon afterward to explain to the child or children what it is they want to know, by conversation or by looking at and reading a book together.

The main reason why parents are apt to make the mistake of becoming alarmed by childish sex exploration and sex play is that they read their own adult attitudes and feelings into the acts of the children. When adults, or late adolescents, engage in sex play, especially when it involves seeing and touching genitals, the activity is highly arousing and closely connected with the urge to have sexual intercourse. But with younger children this is not so. And it certainly does not signify the beginning of sexual promiscuity or "looseness." To them it's just a very interesting kind of looking and finding out. It is usually also part of "You be the Daddy and I'll be the Mommy" play. None of this kind of play upsets parents or other grown-ups except when it verges on the sexual. Then the children get frightened at the uproar, for they don't understand why something that was cute one minute is bad the next. And the fright and misery can stay hidden within them for years—until they marry, when it can rise up and cause problems.

When boys and girls who have reached puberty and can impregnate and become pregnant engage in sex play, it is much more than the relatively simple matter of small-child explorations. The urges are stronger, and the physical, emotional, and social consequences can be major.

By this age adolescents should have been provided with the straight facts about sexual activity and its consequences so that they will be aware of what they can be getting into. They should also have had previous opportunities to discuss the whole matter at home or at school, preferably both. Those who were unable or unwilling to discuss the subject of sex with their parents, and who had no opportunity to talk about it in a planned way at school or with anyone, will probably have talked about it in bits and pieces with their friends. They may have put together enough information to feel their needs are served, but their knowledge is probably only partial, and apt to be laced with errors or composed of elements quite out of perspective. If their information is not adequate, if they are "innocent" and yet exposed to the pressures leading to intercourse—or perhaps even unaware of what they are being led into—then they are at great risk and in need of help, and quickly, and parents ought to be the ones who can provide that help.

Parents should make clear where they stand on adolescent sexual activity. They should also make clear that they consider that they have the right to set the standards of behavior and limits for conduct within their home. If parents feel it's all right for a young couple to have the privacy of the living room or den for talking only, or for necking and petting, or even for engaging in genital sexual activity or intercourse, that's one thing, and some parents do feel that way. If they feel that it's entirely against their beliefs and standards to have direct sexual activity between their child and someone else's going on in their home, that's another thing, and they should set limits and explain their position as clearly as they can, allowing ample opportunity for questioning and discussion. It may be that their children will agree with them or can be convinced. Simply laying down the law is certainly not going to be as effective in modifying behavior as a conviction developed through information, discussion, and a firm position honestly and lovingly taken.

If parents are convinced that their adolescent children are going to be sexually active no matter what the parents think, then it is certainly better to have a nonpregnant or nonimpregnating sexually active adolescent than a pregnant or impregnating one. In other words, sexually active youngsters should be provided with contraceptive information, counseling, and methods (see Chapter 4).

If parents react to their children's experiments in sexual activity by anger, threats, or punishment, there are several possible consequences. Most likely, the sex behavior will simply shift to outside the home. Older children often react to strong disapproval that is unaccompanied by explanation and discussion not by conforming to the disapproval but by ignoring it, while at the same time continuing the behavior elsewhere. In fact, the most common response of young people to overrestrictive parents is to rebel, to do the opposite of what they are commanded to do. The "black sheep" of some families, young people who are heavy drinkers, users of drugs, or sexually promiscuous, may be examples of this kind of rebellion. Still another likely consequence of restrictions tinged with punishment is that the child will come to associate sex with disapproval, fear, and anger and will let sex be driven underground and buried in guilt. Later, this may make happy, pleasurable expression of sex more difficult, but not impossible. After some suffering and struggling to adjust, most people can overcome earlier disadvantages, especially if helped by a loving partner. But one other almost certain consequence of anger and punishment is that the whole area of sexuality will become a subject to be avoided with parents, a sad but quite common loss of opportunity to share caring and learning.

The alternative to anger and punishment is to try to reveal feelings and together to explore consequences. "I'm worried about the way you are experimenting, and I'd like to give you some information that you may not have. Can we talk about it?" is one opener that invites open responsiveness.

Language and Sex

We teach our children something about sex when they are first learning to name the parts of their bodies. Everyone is pleased when youngsters name their ears, nose, hands, "tummy button," toes, feet, legs, and knees. But the area between knees and navel is a different matter, and parents are not so sure that penis, testicles, vagina, and clitoris are acceptable words. It's a fortunate family in which all parts of the body can be named correctly without discomfort, thus facilitating communication. However, children need to know that the names of the sexual parts of the body are considered special and private by most people, just as are the actual parts themselves.

Children will learn that there are also "dirty" words for sexual parts and acts, words that have shock value. They may hear these words around the neighborhood and come home saying "fuck" or "prick" or "boob" or "pussy." They need to know that these words are not acceptable in most situations. It is important to convey that, although a word is merely a word—a set of sounds and letters that stand for a thing or idea, with nothing inherently bad or good about it—many words carry emotional overtones that arouse feelings as real as the words themselves. Just as people should be considerate in their use of any power—sexual, muscular, intellectual—so they should be considerate in their use of word power.

The same things are true of sex jokes. Human sexuality, like any serious, interesting human activity, is a rich source of humor, but of a kind that should be used with special care. A family may be one in which all kinds of jokes, including sexual ones, are enjoyed. There can be little objection to that as enriching and helpful in sharing laughter privately and keeping communication open. But everyone must understand that sex-related jokes are considered "dirty" by many people and that jokes appropriate in a locker room or in the family car are probably inappropriate with grandparents, another family, or in a classroom. Jokes should never be used to shock or hurt people or to put them down.

Many growing children, especially boys, collect magazines with nude pictures in them which are shared in secret with friends or simply pored over alone and then hidden away for future delectation. When parents come across this kind of thing, what should they do? Nothing. What harm can the pictures do if they are looked at in private?

Sometimes a boy, knowing that his father also has such magazines in the house, will offer to share his own trove with his father. A father should feel flattered at such evidence of openness, even though his enthusiasm for sharing the pictures may be mild at best. But the offer to share may accompany a willingness to talk and an opportunity to help the curious youngster not only satisfy his curiosity but also get things into better perspective.

If parents find a hoard of magazines and quietly remove them, saying nothing, the child may conclude that he has done something pretty terrible, so bad it can't even be talked about (which helps to tie sex and mysterious evil together), or he may resignedly understand that sex is just one more area where he can't talk with his parents. For parents to scold or punish the child for having such magazines is just as bad. A child might rightly protest that the magazines are his and ask what right his parents had to take them, but at least this could begin a dialogue and provide opportunity for each person to give his or her point of view. If curiosity seems to be the child's motive, why not satisfy it by some good factual talk and looking at some accurate drawings or pictures together? Or why not share the beauty of nude art by looking at reproductions of paintings and sculptures by great artists?

We want to reemphasize that it is good for parents to let their children know they do not need to feel guilty about any feelings they may have, because feelings or thoughts or fantasies cannot be completely controlled and guilt about such feelings can be destructive. Children should also know that they need not feel guilty about actions that do no harm to anyone—provided they also understand that harm can be emotional and intellectual, not just physical. Guilty feelings are, however, a good and appropriate response to an action that is harmful, especially if the feelings of guilt lead to an attempt to undo the harm and a resolve not to act in the same manner again.

8
The Different Ones,
the Lonely Ones

"Something there is that does not love a wall," wrote the poet Robert Frost. The people for whom this sentence will surely have meaning are those who are walled in by circumstances, or who have been walled in or out by others because they are different, or who have walled themselves in so they won't be hurt by the fact that they are different. These are the lonely ones.

We have talked about how from birth human beings have a great need and desire for continuing intimacy with at least one person. How is it, then, that some of us find ourselves alone, feeling empty, hungry, just plain lonely, aching for just one person really to need us and us alone because no one else will do?

Who are the lonely ones? They are those with disabilities of one kind or another: those who are mentally slow, who don't understand why they aren't like everyone else but who keep trying to be; those who are deaf, who have to put forth huge efforts day after day just to learn how to communicate; those who have physical disabilities, who have grown up feeling different and ugly, like the teenager with cerebral palsy who wept as he asked, "How can I even invite a girl to date when I'm always drooling?"; those who are disfigured, like the adolescent girl who was born with a harelip and wonders if any boy will ever want to kiss her; those born blind, who have no visual way to build good self-images as attractive girls or boys or to exchange the meaningful glances that are so often the beginnings of a human relationship.

The lonely ones, too, are those older people who may never have married or had a love experience, or who may have had and lost a beloved partner by incapacity, death, separation, or divorce, and now feel isolated by what our society looks upon as the ugliness of age.

And the lonely ones are those children who, through accident or death or abandonment, are deprived of the very people they most need to grow up to become adequate parents themselves. And they are those who, beaten, bruised, burned, and otherwise abused by one or both parents or caretakers, nevertheless are terrified at any hint of separation from the only people they know well enough to feel they belong to them. These children, even when seen again and again by hospitals and doctors because of their injuries, refuse to accuse or testify and so return "home," knowing that more of the same is in store for them. Their disabilities are not only the bodily scars but also the inner scars of emotions and spirit that can never be totally erased and can make it very difficult for them in adult life to achieve the very relationships they crave so much.

Among the many things the lonely ones have in common with the rest of the world is their sexuality, at the same ages and stages. This means that they have the same sex-related needs as all of us: they need a loving, caring person to be close to; they need the various forms of expression that relate to being sexual, such as tenderness, touching, kissing, stroking, caressing; and they need the soft words and the pleasure-giving expressions of sexuality, lovemaking, and sexual intercourse.

There is nothing in any book or medical teaching that says any of these lonely ones should be deprived of the possibility of a loving sexual life, including the kind of family experience that is the best preparation for it. For a fortunate few, there may be adoption in childhood, but for the groups we are talking about, adoption is rare. So here are these people of all ages, waiting for someone to care for them and love them, and waiting to give to someone else the caring and loving that waits inside them.

Many such fellow human beings have found some kind of love relationship, but the lonely ones add up to about 10 percent of our total population—one out of every ten people lost, lonely, sexually deprived, harassed, or abused. That's too many.

What can we do for these people? We need primarily to change our attitudes by increasing our awareness of the most up-to-date facts about sexuality. Professionals have already changed their views about the emotional and sexual needs of people with disabilities, both those who live in institutions and those capable of living independently.

Rehabilitative services for people with disabilities are now doing many things to enrich their lives. Nonprofessionals who are responsible for or close to someone in one of these groups can follow the lead of the professionals in dealing more wisely and caringly with that person.

At this point we would like to make it clear that many persons with disabilities resist the term *handicapped* and prefer the term *disabled.* A disability is some condition that makes life and its activities more difficult than otherwise. But people with disabilities are more and more expecting their disability *not* to handicap them, and as a result they may actually be more successful in life than some people who have no disability at all.

Sex and People with Disabilities

All too often we assume that people with a disability somehow do not have the same needs for physical affection, intimate relationships, and sexual expression that people without a disability do. In almost every case, however, they do have these needs, even though the way they have been treated may make them hesitant to express them for fear they may be rejected.

People with disabilities, given encouragement and training or sometimes even without these, quite commonly are able to accomplish things that nonhandicapped people would consider impossible under the circumstances. The capacity of the human mind and body to adjust to difficult situations is astonishing.

Of course, it is not helpful to lump all people with disabilities together, for each has his or her own special needs. As far as sex and sexuality are concerned, everyone who has a relationship with a disabled person or is in a position to be of help should remember that sexual feelings are there and that the need to give and receive love and affection, both physical and emotional, is also there. We should be sure that neither we nor others set aside someone with a disability as someone who is nonsexual.

Youngsters who have disabilities need sexual information and opportunities to talk about their sexual feelings and desires, just as adults do. They may need help and encouragement to reach out to others; they may need special instruction on ways to overcome or

compensate for the physical disabilities that might stand in the way of expressing their sexual natures in appropriate, responsible, and fulfilling ways. They need the same sort of sex education as everyone else, but it should be tailored to their special needs. Medical institutions concerned with rehabilitation are now moving toward considering and meeting the sexual needs of people with disabilities under their care.

People with Physical Disabilities

Awareness of the sexual needs of people who have various kinds of disabilities has been growing during the past ten years. Of the eighteen professional journals in the field of sexuality today, the most recent is titled *Sexuality and Disability.* To give you some idea of the scope of this professional awareness, here are some titles of articles in the first issue: "Sexuality and the Disabled Female," "Sexuality and the Spinal-Cord-Injured," "Sex Education for the Mentally Handicapped," "Mastectomy and Sexual Behavior," "Sexual Implications of Deafness."

Among the medical rehabilitation services of many medical schools and hospitals, education of health professionals in human sexuality and sexual rehabilitation is now included. In the Institute for Medical Rehabilitation, affiliated with New York University and made world famous by Dr. Howard Rusk, there is now such a unit. At the University of Minnesota Medical School under Dr. Theodore Cole, one of the first such services pioneered in producing teaching films to demonstrate clearly how those with spinal-cord injuries or other physical disabilities could be helped to achieve sexual relationships satisfying both to themselves and to their partners. These might not take the same sexual forms as before the injury, but when the films are shown to mixed groups of graduate physicians, medical and nursing students, religious counselors, and people with disabilities and their partners and/or parents, the message comes across clearly: Sexuality is a part of everyone, with no exceptions.

The same new attitudes that help those with partial or total hearing or visual loss have led to special programs in teaching institutions such as Gallaudet College in Washington, D.C., for the hearing impaired, and others where the visually impaired are being educated. The teachers in such programs have had training in the generalized techniques of teaching these two groups and are seeking specific training in human sexuality that can adapt contents, materials, and methods to the special needs of those groups.

People with Mental Disabilities

In our society, so much importance is attached to education that any impairment of the capacity to reach a certain minimum educational level constitutes a true disability. Those with intact mental faculties who are physically disabled can go to college or prepare themselves for a vocation or job, but the chances for people with learning disabilities are slimmer.

But people with mental disabilities should have the same rights to the happiness of an independent home and family life as the rest of us. Over the past ten years, sex education in institutions and schools for those who are mentally retarded has increased, with emphasis on competence and responsibility. Competence in dealing with oneself and others as sexual beings requires certain information and skills, and so does responsibility. Learning how to care for oneself during menstruation or how to use contraceptives during sexual activity combines knowledge and skills, just as does learning how to get, perform, and hold a job. All add greatly to the possibility of independent, happy living, and many who are mentally retarded can learn them, many more than we thought a few years ago.

Abused and Neglected Children

Children who are abused and neglected tend to become abusing and neglectful parents. Some observers say that it is almost impossible for such a deprived person to know how to form attachments later on or to move into caring relationships with others. One way to break this vicious cycle is to help young abusing or potentially abusing parents become aware of and deal with their feelings, in order to facilitate their capacity to nurture and rear their children. Good sex education can help to create good self-images; and people who have good self-images are better able to care for others.

The Single Person

Until the first twenty-five years of this century, a large family group could almost always find a niche for an extra single person. There is a tradition that these people turned into beloved "aunts" or "uncles," but the truth is that for every one who did, there was another who was barely tolerated or who was turned into a household drudge. The stories we like to believe about the "good old days" too often gloss over or hide the realities of situations that were cruel, heedless, or exploitive.

Social structures are different today. Families are smaller, and their members may be scattered all over the country or even the globe. And attitudes about what is or is not acceptable behavior are changing. We may be evolving into an age in which the individual will more and more replace the family as the basic unit of society.

One example of the change in the basic family unit is increasing acceptance of arrangements in which older, retired single persons form a household but do not marry each other because doing so might jeopardize their total Social Security benefits or their children's inheritances. But living together without marriage is not confined to older age-groups. Most of us know of one or more such arrangements, and people are not as shocked by them any more. Instead, the attitude is becoming more one of satisfaction and acceptance by many on behalf of two people who have eliminated loneliness from their lives by living together to care for and about each other, with the sexual part of it no one's business but their own.

One specific group must be specially identified: it consists of those unmarried persons who live together and who have made a decision not to have children. Generally they are persons who are concerned about overpopulation in the world or who find the world a difficult one in which to bring up children safely and with benefit to everyone concerned, or who have honestly admitted to themselves that they would make very inadequate parents. Both partners in such an arrangement are usually working, and neither perceives a necessity for formalizing the relationship by marriage. This kind of open relationship is called *cohabitation,* which simply means living together. Because cohabitation openly practiced is fairly new, studies of such relationships are far from complete. But the tolerant attitudes that society has today toward cohabitation, as compared to those of even fifteen years ago, is striking. We must remember that the United States is one of the foremost countries in the world to place the welfare of the individual ahead of the welfare of the state. This has been recognized by our Constitution and Bill of Rights, and we can expect that rugged American individualism will continue to assert that "my business is my own and not that of my neighbor"—provided no one else is harmed. We will have to wait for twenty-five or fifty years from now to learn from the research whether living together without marriage reduces the pain and suffering that come from loneliness in a crowded society.

The Elderly

Of the many lonely people in our society none are, as a group, more lonely than the older people who live alone—whether in their own homes or in their children's—or the 5 percent who live in institutions. We can understand that older people living alone would be lonely, and we can even understand that living in an institution might be lonely. But most people would find it hard to understand how living with one's own children could be lonely. Yet it can be. Why?

Because as you reach a time in life where you have more to look back on than to look ahead to; when you feel lost without your own possessions around you; when getting up in the morning means that everyone else bustles off to job or school and the day alone in a silent house looms frighteningly ahead; when you have no one to share your private concerns and anxieties with, no one really close and intimate; when day after day goes by without a touch, a kiss, or a hug from someone to whom you mean a great deal; and when the nights are long as you lie wakeful, remembering the comfort of a dear and loving person to reach for in bed—then you begin to wonder where you are going and if it's worth sticking around for. That's a pretty desperate state to be in at any time of life, but toward life's end it is worst of all.

We should do everything we can to make things better for such lonely people, and we can begin by recognizing that older men and women are exactly that: men and women. They have the same needs and wishes they always had, but they are no longer in a position to fulfill them alone. For instance, if they have lost a devoted life partner,

what social life can they develop? How can they meet new people? How can they learn all over again how to meet, date, and get to know someone well enough to develop a special relationship, when they may have no privacy for dating and no car (or driver's license either) to make dating easier? They need help for all these things.

In our society, too many of us think that an old man who is interested in sex is "a dirty old man," and that once a woman has passed menopause she is no longer sexy or interested in sex, or shouldn't be, since she's past the age when she can become pregnant. When older people become romantically or sexually interested in each other, their children and friends may treat it as a joke, or even with scorn, alarm, or distaste. What right have old people to be starting again, when they're supposed to be decently fading away?

Most homes for the aged, nursing homes, medical centers, and retirement communities have been organized on the assumption that the residents have no need for or interest in intimacy and privacy and sex. Even many doctors and other professions, when asked by older people about sexual problems or their declining ability to have sexual relations, respond with a friendly, amused comment, perhaps supposed to be reassuring and calming, like, "Well, at your age what can you expect?" instead of showing willingness to talk about the problem and to see what can be done—and often a lot can be done.

On the other side, there are those who so closely equate a high degree of sexual activity with the possibility of living a full, vigorous, rewarding life that they sometimes make older people who have less interest in sexual activity feel inadequate and old in every way. And there are many people, old and young, who may be relatively inactive sexually but are very active and creative in many other ways.

Researchers today almost all agree that the sexuality of the elderly is not very different from that of younger ages, that the need for sexual activity in some form and the capacity to enjoy it continues with many people well into old age. But perhaps even more important and universal than the continuation of genital sexual activity in older people is the need of the elderly for physical closeness, touching, stroking, intimacy, affection, and the actions and words of endearment. This is the same need that all of us have when we are born and most of us continue to have throughout life.

Some families may feel threatened if a new relationship for a parent or grandparent might result in a marriage that could mean loss of inheritance. While this is understandable, we believe that the children who feel responsible for an older person should be helped to understand that a new relationship could bring back laughter and sparkle and a sense of independence to two people who had thought these had been lost forever. If a marriage is planned, a premarital agreement can be formalized that will safeguard inheritance rights for both sides. And a surprising number of families are recognizing that what is most important is the happiness and well-being of two human beings and that in the interests of safeguarding Social Security payments and property rights, the marriage ceremony can take second place.

In any case, whether at home with family or in an institution, the early stages of a new courtship deserve the support of everyone and should never be subjected to the jokes that institution attendants or even families too often allow themselves in order to belittle the relationship. When a person is nearing the end of life, he or she seeks out experiences that can make the remaining years real and good. Love and work and playing a meaningful role in the lives of others or in a community—all or any one of these can give an older person a sense that life is still worth living. Institutions for the aged are recognizing this and are making strong efforts to educate their personnel to accept the reality of sexual interest in older people. It costs little or nothing to give the elderly every possible opportunity to enrich their lives.

9
Sex and Sexual Problems

Ways We Make Sex a Problem

Sex and human sexuality are not—or should not be—problems unless we human beings make them so. When and how do they become problems? In general terms, when they are used or expressed in ways that are harmful to any person or persons; when people are unable to express them in ways that they find satisfying and creative; and when they become associated with such negative feelings as anger, jealousy, fear, and guilt. Here is a summary, in no particular order, of some of the kinds of problems sex can cause and the ways sex can be made a problem:

• The basic lack of information among too many people, young and old, about what is known today about sex and sexuality, which can lead to various kinds of trouble. Often that ignorance is deliberately maintained.

• The obsession with the idea that the whole of sexuality is comprised of genital activity; that is, sexual intercourse and the steps leading to it.

• The strong social stimuli toward sexual activity but the few socially approved ways for responding to those stimuli.

• The conflicting messages we get from society to which our young are especially vulnerable: that sex is the best and most ecstatic, ennobling, status-giving, joy-creating activity, but that it's dirty and bad, so save it for the one you love or stay away from it entirely.

• The way this sexual stimulation acts upon boys and girls, especially during the many years between physical readiness for sex (puberty) and the capacity to form long-term, caring peer relationships that would warrant the full sexual act.

- Adolescent pregnancies—about 20,000 every week in the United States.
- The effects of unrealistic sex fantasies in films, TV, magazines, and advertising upon people whose real sexual lives are so different from those fantasies.
- The unrealistic expectations and requirements for "perfection" and "performance" that people impose on themselves and on others with respect to their sexual lives.
- The overreaction of families and society to sexual events, especially those in the lives of children.
- The tension and unhappiness within marriages in which people feel hopelessly bound yet unable or unwilling to seek help to change and possibly improve.
- The anguish of couples and their children involved in separation and divorce.
- The promotion of the idea, often through advertising or TV or films, that the measure of a man is the number of dollars and women he can make or, of a woman, the number of men she can seduce.
- Our mistaken idea that there can be sexual activity without consequences for human relationships—that sex can be lifted from its human context.
- Grouping sex with alcohol, drugs, tobacco, and violence as problems we should learn to avoid.
- The inability of many to respond sexually when they urgently wish they could.
- The inability of humankind to limit its numbers so that human beings can be decently supported on this planet without eventually destroying it.

Using Sex Selfishly

One of the main ways we make sex into a problem is by using our sexuality for our own purposes without thinking of or caring about the consequences for others. Here are some ways people do this:

One partner forces sex when the other doesn't really want it, either because of fatigue or illness or preoccupation with some stressful matter, or a need to talk or simply be stroked and held and comforted, without direct sex play or intercourse.

One partner is chronically unwilling to take the initiative in sex play that might lead to mutual pleasure. Instead, that person always waits to be wooed, not realizing that the other person may have a deep need to feel loved and lovable by being wooed occasionally instead of always having to do the wooing. This is an especially common complaint of husbands about wives; women often feel that it's the man's "job" to take the initiative, to woo, to make her feel "loved" in the physical sense. But men, too, often long to feel "loved" and wooed.

Some people hurry to get their own sexual satisfaction without thinking of the need for time and loving that the other person feels or needs. (This is an especially common complaint that women have about men: that the man gets his ejaculation and leaves the woman unsatisfied.)

Some people use their sexual attractiveness to lead another person to expect a genuine short- or long-term relationship, but actually seek only to exercise power or prove themselves attractive.

Some people use sex to put another person down, to make the other feel inferior or at fault, unattractive, insufficiently sexy, too sexy, or not loving or lovable.

Some people use "lines" (often really lies) to get sex: "Don't worry, I'm taking care of the contraception"; "Nobody will ever know that we're doing this"; "I love you"; "I don't have VD"; "You're the most attractive person I've ever been with"; "You're not a real man (or woman) if you won't have sex"; "I'm going to marry you"; "I'm not having sex with anyone but you"; "If you loved me you would."

Some people allow themselves to be overcome by their sexual urges and do not exercise control over themselves.

Some sexually experienced people use their sophistication and skill in lovemaking to overwhelm a less experienced person, without taking into account the other's feelings or the effects of the experience on the other.

Some young people use their attractiveness to get attention, money, gifts, and commitments from older people.

Some people are unaware of how the other person might feel or see things. They assume that their gestures and the words they say mean the same thing to the partner as to themselves.

Some people treat others as objects to be used and manipulated rather than as complex, feeling beings who are to be respected and considered at all times.

Some young people use sex to prove to themselves or to their parents that they are adults.

Some older people can be so preoccupied by their own ideas of what is right or wrong about sex that they selfishly block off attempts at communication by young people.

Some people tell tales about their sexual exploits in order to make their hearers feel inferior and inadequate. (Or, on the contrary, they may proclaim their own righteousness and invoke community standards to make others feel that their sexual patterns are bad.)

Negative Feelings About Sex

Some irreverent wag suggested that it would have been better for the sexual health of Americans if Plymouth Rock had landed on the Pilgrims instead of the other way around. By this he meant that we have inherited from the strongly and narrowly religious people who were important first settlers of our country (and who actually were known as Puritans before they left England and became Pilgrims to America) a rigorous and narrow set of values that set up piety and hard work as the supreme virtues and denied pleasure, especially bodily and sexual pleasure, as evil and animal-like. It is clear that in American society today there is still a strong current of thought that sex, except when used for procreation, is an evil and sinful thing, that it puts us on the level of the animals, and that we should feel guilty about enjoying sexual pleasure.

Dr. William H. Masters and Virginia E. Johnson wrote two books, *Human Sexual Response* and *Human Sexual Inadequacy,* which reported their pioneering scientific observation and studies of human sexual activity. Their goal was to discover why some married couples are unable to function well sexually, and to develop ways to help them. Masters and Johnson found that in the lives of couples who suffered from sexual dysfunction, a rigid religious upbringing often played an important part in the development of the guilt feelings that ultimately led to their difficulties. It did not seem to matter whether the couple in trouble was Jewish, Catholic, or Protestant. The trouble was caused by the way people interpreted the strongly orthodox "thou shalt nots" of their religion.

Some very religious people have no trouble at all with their sexuality; others, even those brought up in the same families, have great trouble and interpret sex as dirty, evil, sinful. If this interpretation becomes deeply ingrained when they are young, it is difficult later for them to overcome their negative feelings, even after marriage when their religion would then probably allow full sexual expression. Fortunate are the many who are able without too great difficulty to make the transition from premarital virginity to full enjoyment of sex after marriage in spite of such a rigid background. Fortunate too are those who find that having stuck by their conventional religious standards before getting married has only strengthened their marriage and increased their pleasure in it.

For people who find that the strictness of their religious background has tended to interfere with the healthy, responsible expression of their sexuality even in marriage, it may be helpful to know that some of the rules, the orthodoxy, of the Jewish and Christian religions were historically, and to a degree still are, based on a number of mistaken concepts about the biology of reproduction as well as on the need for human survival that no longer exists today. For example, at the time of the birth of Jesus, Jews and most other people believed that it was the man and his semen who provided the actual life, the "seed," and that the woman was merely the soil, so to speak, in which the seed grew to maturity to be born. It was considered almost like murder to allow the "seed" to be "wasted" through masturbation, homosexuality, or sexual intercourse without intent to procreate. It was also erroneously believed (and still is by many people) that semen, "the precious fluid," was limited in quantity so that if it was "wasted" the energy and strength of the man would thereby be reduced.

Furthermore, up until perhaps fifty years ago, human beings were convinced that anything likely to reduce the numbers of children born was evil because it would lead to a smaller tribe or nation and therefore a greater likelihood that the group might be defeated in war or killed off by disease. Many societies still feel this way. Of course today, from a world point of view, the real problem is not too few people in the human race but too many, in most places. It is our rapidly rising numbers that may destroy us.

Mindful of the facts now known to science that were not known several centuries ago, Rabbi Roland Gittelsohn writes in *Love, Sex and Marriage: A Jewish View* (published in 1976 by the Union of American Hebrew Congregations) that today Jews "must respect our tradition without necessarily following it. Most of the ethical concepts of Judaism are at least as valid today as when they were first conceived by our ancestors. In some areas, however, because we have knowledge that was unavailable to them, it becomes necessary to revise or even discard their judgment."

In other words, where religious laws or rules about sex were made on the basis of ignorance of facts now known, laws and rules need to be reexamined and recast to be consonant with these facts. Religious leaders in many denominations have been and are working carefully and intelligently on this reexamination. After all, when Moses and Jesus lived, they (and those among whom they lived) believed that the world was shaped something like our Frisbee, that the sun traveled over it, and that if you went too far you could fall off the edge. Religions have been able to adjust to the new facts here, and they are adjusting also to the new facts about reproduction, sex, and sexuality.

In the Christian religions, there has been an especially deep-rooted belief that the sexual urges of the body are somehow evil and should be put down and denied in favor of spiritual things. As Dr. Walter Harrelson, Dean of the Divinity School of Vanderbilt University at Nashville, commented in a letter to one of the authors:

> The Christian tradition, influenced by Hellenistic religious understandings of the Graeco-Roman world, lost sight of its Jewish roots and tended to spiritualize the Christian faith. One baneful result was the identification of the body as transient and belonging to a material world of less consequence than the spiritual. The solidly biblical understanding of all things as created by God and created good was compromised. The result has been a denigration of the sexual and a loss of that healthy regard for body and for bodily pleasure that ancient Israel understood as a gift of God.

Obviously religion cannot be blamed for all the deep and destructive antisex feelings and emotions that trouble so many people. But what should be blamed is the insistence on negative rules and regulations that can no longer stand in the face of present world conditions and known facts. As we said in the Preface, both of us are religious people. We agree with the thousands of religious leaders of all faiths who are convinced that religious values and insights, in the deepest sense, should not be looked upon as inconsistent with modern scientific knowledge about human sexuality. Instead, with recognition of those scientific facts, our religious values can help us not only to manage but also to express our sexuality in healthy, responsible, satisfying ways, and support our productive living together. We are thinking of such values as respect of the infinite worth of each individual, unselfishness, thoughtfulness of others, and use of our powers for the welfare and happiness of all people. Today many religious and church people are taking the lead in promoting and providing sound education and counseling in the field of human sexuality and working to enlighten a dark antisex dogma based on factual errors and conditions of life that no longer exist. They are also taking the lead in celebrating the fact that God did create us as men and women with the power of sexuality manifest in us from our earliest days of existence.

Talking About Sex

Sometimes sex becomes a problem because of our inability to talk openly and objectively about it. People who can't talk about a subject have more difficulty in sharing or getting the information and ideas they may need than do people who are more verbal. Yet the deep-rooted feeling of many people that sex is somehow dirty or evil, or that it should be kept totally mysterious and secret, makes calm discussion difficult. As the father in a cartoon said to his wife, "It's not that I'm opposed to sex education, but six is too young to start calling things by their right names."

Some people, perhaps especially the young, tend to use language about sex, both slang words and standard words, to shock, frighten, and anger other people. The generation gap in sex language helps make sex a problem, both for adults and for children.

It is interesting to note that in the vocabulary of some cultures there is a rich supply of entirely acceptable words to describe the varieties of sexual love and parts of the body especially involved in it. In our culture, however, the language is quite impoverished in this respect. Many of the words we do have are forbidden, so that with children we use terms like "your little thing," "your dicky," or "your bunny" instead of simply saying "penis"; or we go to the other extreme and use threatening words like "prick," "cock," "rod," or "pecker." There appears to be nothing between stilted medical terms or offensive slang terms. How much better if instead we had an ample, pleasant array of language with which to talk to each other about sex. Just as the Eskimos use over twenty words to talk about the varieties of that cold white stuff we know only as "snow," so we might be able to use as many words to describe the variety of activities which, now, we may politely call only "coitus," "sexual intercourse," "making love," or "sleeping together."

"Victimless" Crimes

Sex can also become a problem when the law treats as crimes sexual acts that are engaged in willingly and performed in privacy by the adults involved. In such situations there is no victim unless a complaint is made by one of the participants. Complaints usually come from observing outsiders whose moral sense may be offended. Crimes that do have victims—whether burglary, environmental pollution, reckless driving, or abuse or exploitation of children—certainly require the attention of law-enforcement authorities. "Crimes" that have no true victims—for example, selling pornographic materials to adults, adult homosexual activities mutually consented to, fetishism, prostitution, and sado-masochism—seem to many people examples of misuse of law-enforcement facilities. Such misuse is at best a waster of a scarce service and at worst an abuse of authority for the purpose of imposing the moral opinions of one specific person or group upon other adult persons or groups. What an outcry there would be if, for example, Quakers, who do not accept gambling of any kind, were to try to outlaw all gambling.

Personal Sexual Problems with Legal Implications

Child Molestation

Often confused with rape, but usually quite different from it, is child molestation, a sexual encounter between an adult (as a result termed a molester) and a child. Molestation is different from rape, because the happening is usually brief and it rarely involves violence or even sexual intercourse.

Most convicted molesters are men (though some women molest children), usually men who have little sexual experience and who are generally inept in their relationships with other people. Their average age is about thirty-five, though a few are old and senile and some are mentally retarded. Often the molester has been drinking before his offense. In general, molesters are not otherwise criminal types. For many, molestation is a compulsive, long-term tendency, though the event may happen only once or only a few times. About 85 percent of molesters are known to the children they molest as neighbors, friends of the family, or relatives. About 80 percent of the contacts occur either in the home of the child or in the home of the molester. (The stereotype of the stranger who uses candy to attract a child into his car and then molests the child sexually is largely false, but since such relatively rare events get wide publicity the public thinks of them as common.)

What is the nature of the offense? Sometimes the offense is exhibitionism (see next section), and does not involve any physical contact. Actual physical molestation, as we have said, usually is a brief contact, in which the offender may stroke the child and handle the child's genitals, and that is all. In only 2 percent of the reported cases of molestation is any physical harm done to the child.

What effect will molestation be likely to have on the child? According to the best evidence available (interviews with people who as children were molested), the molested children are hardly ever sexually excited by the experience. Their reaction is more likely to be quite slight and to involve puzzlement and a vague fear. The major effects of such incidents are caused not by the event itself but by the outraged, angry, fearful, and shocked reactions of the adults who learn of it, whether they be parents, relatives, or police. It is these immoderate reactions that may cause whatever psychological damage occurs. The problem seems to come from the fact that adults tend to react to such an invasion of the child's sexual innocence and privacy by projecting their own adult feelings onto the child. They may forget that children before puberty do not see or feel the event as a big, threatening sexual happening, for their experience and feelings are childlike, not adult. This is an example of how we often make sex a problem by assuming that others are feeling just the way we ourselves would feel in the same situation, instead of making a calm effort to put ourselves into the position, experience, and circumstances of the other person.

There is a widespread impression that, in the case of a homosexual molestation, a child's sexual orientation may be shifted from heterosexual to homosexual. As we explained in Chapter 5, a person's sexual orientation toward heterosexuality or homosexuality is established relatively early in life—although no one knows how—and certainly not by a single, brief, genital sexual experience.

It is difficult to make a single recommendation for the best way to deal with a child who reports having been sexually molested. Certainly, if the child is disturbed and fearful, he or she needs comforting. And children should always be assured that the event was not their "fault." It can and does happen that such children's needs as those for physical affection, for approval, for good grades, for having a feeling of control over adults, even for the good taste of candy or for an attractive gift, may cause them to act in ways that the children themselves see as merely attractive but that the adult may read as seductive and sexual. (That's why we enclosed the word *fault* in quotes.)

We should remember that children are even less likely than adults to report events accurately or completely. Therefore parents should probably, in a calm, objective, nonfrightening way, try to elicit information: What happened? Where did it happen? Who did it? Did you know him? What did he actually do? The parents should try not to appear greatly upset when suggesting to the child how to avoid such situations in the future: "It is always wise to steer away from men who approach you in an overfriendly manner or who go out of their way to touch you or try to persuade you in a secret way to be alone with them. This is true even if they are people you know quite well. Never accept gifts from strangers and certainly don't accept a lift in a stranger's car." But parents must be careful not to warn so strongly that the child grows fearful about meeting and being friendly with new people or about responding with physical affection to relatives and friends.

If the child is old enough, he or she will certainly benefit from being given some facts about the sexual side of life, but immediately after the stress of molestation is not the best moment to do this. Better wait until things have calmed down and an opportunity arises at another time.

If the event seems serious to you, the question of whether or not to report it to the police arises. Here parents must balance the advantages of having the molester apprehended and prevented from molesting other children (although the extreme punitive treatment that most molesters receive does little to remedy their condition and is more likely to make it worse), and the disadvantages arising from the likelihood that the child will have to give evidence to officials, perhaps even in court, which may increase his or her fears and reinforce the harmful emotional effects of the experience.

Let us repeat that the harm most likely to come from a case of molestation is not from the event itself so much as from the reaction of adults who may, by the example of their own emotions and even with the best of intentions, help to tinge all the child's subsequent feelings about sex with negative feelings and fear.

Exhibitionism

Exhibitionism involves the compulsion a man has to exhibit his penis, usually erect, to a woman or girl. There is no physical contact. In fact, the exhibition usually takes place from a distance, and as soon as he is seen by his "victim" (who is usually a stranger to him), the exhibitionist almost always flees.

Although the most common reactions to exhibitionists are surprise, puzzlement, scorn, disgust, fear, or panic, many females simply laugh off the whole thing as something done by "some sort of nut." Others are afraid that the exhibition may be a preliminary to attack and rape. Such fear is unnecessary, for exhibitionists are usually timid, harmless people who are very much afraid of actual sexual contact. They get their kicks in some unexplained way from the reactions evoked in females by the exhibition.

Exhibitionism is a truly compulsive act, for the man cannot help himself and often repeats it until he is arrested. When he is released, he is in many cases unable to resist the urge to repeat the offense. Many exhibitionists have been arrested and convicted a number of times.

Most girls are likely to encounter an exhibitionist at some time in their lives. Parents should not overreact but simply explain that the man is a disturbed person and that all the child need do is keep her cool and walk away toward other people. Women can leave the scene and should avoid showing the shock or surprise that is so important to the exhibitionist. They might decide to report the matter to the police in order to protect others from being so annoyed.

Incest

Incest is sexual activity, usually intercourse, between members of the same family. It is not as rare in our society as most people believe, and it is more frequent between brothers and sisters, and fathers and daughters, than between mothers and sons. The term *incest* covers sexual intercourse between a person and any close relative: brothers, sisters, uncles, aunts, grandparents, adopted children, stepparents and in-laws. In some societal groups, first cousins are included; in others they are not. In every culture that has been studied, there is a strong taboo against incest, and it is deemed a crime in every state in the United States.

The taboo is so deeply ingrained that we rarely stop to ask why it exists. A reason often given, but rarely true, is that children born as a result of an incestuous relationship are likely to suffer from hereditary diseases. Other reasons given are: If sexual intercourse were permitted between members of the same family, the inevitably resulting competition, jealousy, deception, hatred, and confusion might well destroy the family. Or, children would be subject to exploitation by older, stronger members and have no way to escape. Or, if a young person experienced sexual ties within the family, it could be more difficult for him or her to establish good sexual attachments outside the family in adult life. Whatever the reasons, the taboo exists and good research about incest is needed.

It is important not to confuse incest with the healthy, pleasant physical expressions of affection between members of a family. We have talked about the importance of body contact between young children and their parents, and especially between mothers and infants. The distinction between incest and healthy contact is found in the motivation for it. If the motivation is simply to express love and fondness and to give a feeling of comfort and support, it is healthful and good; if the specific motivation of the adult is sexual arousal and gratification, it is not. If young people find themselves in a situation where they are being pressured or seduced into sexual contacts within the family, they should seek counsel from someone in the family or outside.

According to psychoanalytic theory of psychosexual development as put forth by Sigmund Freud, as children develop they normally go through a stage of strong attraction, boys for their mothers, girls for their fathers. Most of us probably do not remember going through this stage, because we were very young and felt so guilty about it that we suppressed the memory. The attraction of son to mother is called the "Oedipus complex," after the Oedipus of Greek mythology who, as a result of many confusing events, married Jocasta, his own mother, neither knowing who the other was; when they discovered their relationship, Jocasta killed herself and Oedipus put out his own eyes. The attraction of daughter to father is called the "Electra complex," after another mythological figure, Electra, who avenged the death of her father, Agamemnon, by helping to kill her own mother, Clytemnestra. These historic myths serve to illustrate the concern of the ancient Greeks about people who broke the age-old incest taboo.

An interesting modern-day extension of the anti-incest feeling is reported among college students who live together in the proximity of coeducational dormitories, where the style of life and sharing somewhat resembles that of a very large family. In such situations, dating and sexual attachments are known most often to occur with people outside the dormitory. It may be that sexual attachments developing within the dorm are seen unconsciously as in some way violating the incest taboo, although dorm-mates would probably not think of it that way. Similar dating patterns have been seen among young people raised together from infancy in the same kibbutz in Israel.

One thing is certain: in any cases of sexual contact between a child and an adult, where there has been no force or violence, the greater the fuss and uproar, the greater the possible damage to the minor.

Pedophilia

Closely related to the problem of child molestation is a condition called pedophilia. The word comes from the Greek *paedo-* (child) and *-philos* (loving) and means sexual desire in an adult for children. A pedophile, then, is a child-lover, one who gets sexual gratification from contacts with children. Almost all known pedophiliacs are men. Only people whose strongest sexual feelings are aroused by children rather than by adults are pedophiles. Since sexual activity by adults with children is so strongly condemned by our society, it is quite possible that most people who have pedophilic feelings either suppress them or recognize them but never act them out. Pedophilic activity is a serious criminal offense.

There is both heterosexual and homosexual pedophilia. The common impression, doubtless conveyed by occasional cases highly publicized in the press, is that homosexuals are likely to try to seduce young boys. But the highest rate of seduction is of young girls by adolescent or adult males. Although the per capita rate of seduction is, according to the most reliable studies available, about the same for heterosexuals and homosexuals, the vast majority of homosexuals are active with adults only and scorn those who have, or attempt to have, sexual relations with young boys.

Pornography

What is "pornography"? No one is certain. The word is a combination of the Greek words *pornē* (prostitute) and *graphein* (to write) and meant, in ancient Greece, "the writing of prostitutes." Today it is often paired with the word *obscenity* to refer to writing and/or pictures designed solely to arouse the reader or viewer sexually. In a famous case in 1957, the U.S. Supreme Court defined as pornographic or obscene, material (1) whose dominant theme is designed to appeal to morbid or shameful interests, (2) which goes beyond contemporary community standards, and (3) which lacks any redeeming social value. This isn't a very helpful definition, because words like "morbid and shameful" and "social value" and "contemporary community standards" are so subject to individual interpretation. One Justice said, "I can't define pornography, but I know it when I see it," a common-sense statement with which most people might agree but which did nothing for understanding the decision and led someone to remark that pornography is "anything that turns the Supreme Court on." A more precise, descriptive term than pornography or obscenity is now used by researchers: *explicit sexual material*—material that portrays sexual behavior in words or pictures with specific intent to arouse. Whether or not it does so depends on individual reaction to it.

No one knows for certain whether pornography is a problem of sex or not. Many people make the confident statement that it is, and many say just as confidently that it isn't.

Let's summarize the arguments for and against explicit sexual material and the right to publish it:

For: With the possible exception of children, people have the right to read or look at any kind of material they wish—a right protected by the First Amendment to the Constitution. If we take away this right, what rights will we take away next? Forbidding is a dangerous business and not democratic. No one forces pornography on anyone; people can choose whether they wish to look at it or not. Pornography meets needs, it doesn't create them. For some, it provides entertainment and harmless and pleasurable sexual arousal and release; for others it can even be educational, showing or describing human sexual organs and activities that otherwise are kept unhealthily forbidden and mysterious. There is no reliable evidence that pornography causes people to commit sex crimes; on the contrary, research shows that people guilty of such crimes report having seen significantly less pornography than those guilty of other kinds of crimes. Pornography is a harmless human phenomenon, desirable and rewarding to some even though repulsive and shocking to others.

Against: It is only common sense that one who wallows in filth is going to get dirty, and pornography is filthy, a tasteless yet arousing depiction of promiscuous and disgusting genital sexual activity, produced for money and exemplifying sex glorified for its own sake, without love, caring, or commitment. Furthermore, pornography arouses sexual desires which are likely to overstimulate those exposed to it so that they go out and try the things they have seen; thus, it leads to rape, to sex outside of marriage, to the breakdown of families, to young people going astray, and to unnatural and repulsive sex acts. The authors of the First Amendment did not have in mind the legal protection of a kind of material they never could have imagined anyone publishing. People who commit sex crimes admit to having been stimulated by pornography, and many police officers, who are as close as anyone to crime, report that pornography leads to crime and that some criminals are found to possess pornographic material. Common sense and moral sense dictate that pornography, and the activities of those who profit from it, should be outlawed.

It is very difficult to define what is and what is not pornographic or obscene. One person's pornography may be another person's art. There are many Americans, both men and women, who desire and are willing to pay for explicit sexual materials of various kinds. About 85 percent of adult men and 70 percent of adult women have at some time in their lives been exposed to explicit sexual material, most of them voluntarily and with enjoyment, and many of them by the time they are eighteen years old. There are also many Americans who find any kind of explicit sexual material absolutely distasteful and immoral —even including the simple diagrams and explanatory text found in serious teaching manuals or books like this one.

Viewing explicit sexual materials does sexually arouse most people and, contrary to common belief, probably arouses females almost as much as males, although up to now most pornography has been produced to appeal to men. The arousal simply tends to cause people to be more active in their habitual patterns of sexual activity, whatever these are, whether within marriage, outside marriage, heterosexual, homosexual, variant (other than penile-vaginal intercourse), masturbatory, or other. But this response lasts for only a short time and does not change basic sexual attitudes or patterns of behavior.

Correlation does not mean causation. Indeed, one should be very surprised if those people of any age who had constitutionally stronger-than-average sex drives would not be more highly motivated than the average person, both to seek out pornography and to seek out sexual activity. The point is that there is no reliable evidence that the pornography *causes* the sexual activity. To reason that it does is like saying that because pouring rain and raised umbrellas are frequently observed together, raised umbrellas cause rain.

Explicit sexual material can be educational in that it plainly shows what human bodies, and especially genitals, look like, how they react, and how they are used in sexual activity. But pornography can seriously mislead the viewer if he or she takes it seriously, for it can give the impression that life is just a series of excuses or opportunities for genital acts. It can also give the erroneous impression that most people most of the time are panting for sex, and that they are endowed with very large sexual organs and extremely sexy-looking bodies. It also promotes the false idea that sexual activity is almost always orgiastically passionate and that it can be engaged in without human consequences and quite independently of human feeling and relationships.

We have heard practically no one argue in favor of exposing children to pornography, nor do we favor it. However, there is no solid evidence, except the urgings of common sense, that such exposure is harmful. There is no reason to go out of our way to introduce children to it, but neither is there any reason to get hysterically upset over it when they do seek it out—as many always have and still do today—or to deny even young children access to sound sex information when they want it, including simple pictures and diagrams to make it understandable.

It is difficult to determine whether the issue of pornography is a major one in the minds of the American people. In one survey, when asked to state what they thought were the two or three "most serious problems facing the country today," only 2 percent mentioned pornography; this was not surprising, given the many serious problems

our country faces. On the other hand, according to a Gallup poll, 85 percent of American adults favor strict legal control over sending pornography through the mails, and 76 percent want controls over materials exhibited on newsstands. In general, it would seem that people are ready to believe that pornography is harmful to *other* people but not to themselves. Studies have shown that young people and children tend to recommend that the group next younger than themselves be "protected" from pictures and diagrams of sex and reproductive organs, while insisting on their own right to have this information.

In 1967, the U.S. Congress created a Presidential Commission on Obscenity and Pornography which, after reviewing a vast amount of research, conducting some of its own, and engaging in extensive public hearings, released its report in 1970. The three most important findings were that (1) there is no evidence that exposure to explicit sexual materials plays a significant role in causing immediate or delayed delinquent or criminal behavior among youths or adults; (2) public opinion does not support imposing legal prohibitions upon the right of adults to have access to explicit sexual materials; and (3) sex education at home, in school, and in church would reduce the interest of the young in pornography and help individuals form a set of positive values and attitudes toward sexuality. (Three of the eighteen members of the commission, President Nixon, and sixty of sixty-five Senators voting all rejected the report vigorously; the rejecting three commission members issued a minority report in opposition to the majority.)

Prostitution

Prostitution is the exchange of sex for money. Although some prostitutes are men and some are boys or girls, the vast majority are women who use their bodies as a commodity. Prostitution is sometimes called "the oldest profession," for throughout recorded history there have always been prostitutes. (Two other words for a prostitute are *whore*, which today has become a put-down term, and *harlot*, now seldom used.)

In most parts of the world, prostitution is not considered a crime. In 1958 the United Nations passed a resolution calling for the universal decriminalization of prostitution, and in over one hundred member countries of the United Nations (including France, Britain, Italy, Japan, and Germany) it is not considered a crime, and the governments no longer attempt to regulate it. In all of the United States, however, except in certain places in Nevada, prostitution is outlawed in one way or another. Thirty-eight states outlaw acts of prostitution; forty-four outlaw soliciting business by prostitutes or their representatives. Despite this, prostitution is widespread in the United States, the best estimates being that there are between a third to half a million full-time prostitutes and many more part-time ones.

What kinds of people become prostitutes? We must be careful not to make sweeping generalizations, but scientific studies of prostitutes make possible some careful statements. Many prostitutes are poor and go into the work for economic reasons: to support their children, to get off welfare, to avoid the job discrimination that many women experience. Some prostitutes are drug users and need the earnings to pay for their addiction. Many prostitutes come from broken homes; a few are mentally deficient; many, when they are not on the job, show an active dislike of men. Prostitutes may stay in the business for only a few years, after which time they often marry and enter the mainstream of society.

Many people see prostitutes as emotionally ill people, unable to adjust to life in a normal way. The American Psychiatric Association, however, classifies prostitution not as a disease but as a "social maladjustment, without manifest psychiatric disorder." Although most prostitutes are not by ability and training very good at defending their profession in public (and, since almost everywhere in the United States it is illegal, it would be dangerous for them to do so), there are increasing numbers of prostitutes who refuse to accept for themselves the shameful role in which most of society has cast them. They reject the psychiatrists' classification of them as socially maladjusted, and they resent it when well-meaning people investigate their lives in the conviction that they are objects of pity leading a debased life and needing rehabilitation. What they need, they themselves say, is not rehabilitation but money and good jobs. Also, they maintain that they fill a genuine need (otherwise why would people be willing to pay them?) and help make rejected and lonely men feel satisfied and understood, and that they have a perfect right to do with their bodies what they choose. No one is forced to go to a prostitute, they say.

Prostitution is carried on in many different ways. There is the independently operating "streetwalker," who solicits her own customers. Other prostitutes work in houses of prostitution, also called brothels (or, in informal language, whorehouses), where facilities are provided for the customers. The woman who runs a brothel is called a madam, and people, usually men, who go out and solicit customers and control the earnings are called pimps. People who attract women to prostitution or help find a place to work for those who decide to become prostitutes are procurers or panderers. There is a common notion that prostitution is closely linked with the world of organized crime, but the business is not particularly attractive to organized crime, it being difficult to organize. Therefore, some women operate independently. Also, since prostitution is an underground activity almost everywhere in this country, prostitutes are seldom willing or able to defend themselves against assault or robbery by customers, because this would open them to arrest for the crime of practicing their profession. The prostitute is much more often a victim of criminal action than are her customers.

Some women, call girls, engage in a more sophisticated form of prostitution than that of streetwalkers and those who work in brothels. They have their own apartments, which are in many cases very attractive and comfortable, for providing entertainment and services, or they will go to the apartments of their customers. Call girls provide sexual services only by appointment, commonly arranged through a telephone "call" by a middleman, who shares the earnings. Another group consists of mistresses, sometimes simply called "girl friends," women who are supported on a long-term basis by one man, for whom they provide sexual services and perhaps meet other needs that society would expect usually to be met in marriage. Between men and their mistresses there may indeed be genuine affection, considerate sharing, and even love. (It is interesting that many prostitutes have somewhat similar relationships with their pimps; they love the man who obtains their customers for them, provides them with protection, manages their finances, and provides bail for them when they are arrested.)

Not all prostitution is by females. There are male prostitutes, more of them homosexual than heterosexual. Many male prostitutes are capable of erection and often ejaculation between three to six times in twenty-four hours. There are also men who are paid by women to provide companionship and sexual services. A term for such a man is gigolo.

Prostitution involving children is today being identified as especially objectionable. Runaway teenage boys and girls are all too often enticed into prostitution. Since they usually are desperate for money and some sort of love and security, and are unaware of the possible long-term consequences of the activity they are entering, they are easy to victimize. In large cities there are numbers of boy prostitutes, nicknamed "chickens," who are patronized by older adolescents and men, nicknamed "chicken hawks."

Dr. Alfred Kinsey reported in his study of male sexual behavior (published in 1948 and based on data collected in the early and mid-1940s) that intercourse with prostitutes comprised less than 4 percent of the total number of sexual outlets of those interviewed, but that 69 percent of those interviewed had actually had contact with prostitutes, typically only a few times during their lifetimes. Some 15 to 20 percent visited prostitutes frequently over a period of years. Most customers were thirty-five to forty years old or more and came from social groups not highly educated; far fewer college graduates patronized prostitutes. Kinsey calculated that in an average community of 500,000 people, 16,000 acts of prostitution would occur each week, which gives some idea of what a job the police would have if they attempted to enforce the laws against prostitution.

During the years since Kinsey collected his data, it appears that the prostitution business has declined. A number of trends explain this. Many more women now feel free to engage in sexual relations with men to whom they are not married, for their own satisfaction as well as for that of the men, and without pay. Also, there is probably a wider acceptance of masturbation as a normal, harmless activity to achieve sexual release. Perhaps an even more important factor is that married women—indeed, women in general—have become more ready to see sex as something to be enjoyed by both sexes and are therefore better prepared to be satisfying sexual partners for their husbands, who thus have no need to seek sexual gratification outside their marriage.

Why do men go to prostitutes? Many men know of no other way to satisfy their sexual urges. Some have a deep feeling that masturbation is sinful, harmful, or somehow unmasculine, or they do not find it satisfying. Other men find a fascination in trying something new, something forbidden. Still others prefer, at least from time to time, a sexual encounter where there is no complicating human relationship and where they can get whatever kind of sexual service they want, without hang-ups. Some are just plain curious and turn to a prostitute for sexual experiences different from those they have with their wives.

Prostitutes are most commonly arrested and prosecuted for *solicitation* of customers. But in many states a woman need not be caught in the act of soliciting or engaging in sexual relations to be arrested. If because of previous acts she can be proved guilty of *being* a prostitute, she can be convicted and punished. The usual punishment is a fine and then release—usually to go right back to prostitution. About 30 percent of the females in American jails are prostitutes. In jail they seldom decide to give up their profession; instead, they may become more closely tied to the criminal world and return to the streets or brothels after their release.

It is interesting that the law considers the activity of the prostitute to be criminal, and in some states that of her customer as well. One could ask why it is that *both* the partners in the act are not always considered equally guilty, or equally innocent. The American Civil Liberties Union states that "laws against prostitution represent one of the most direct forms of discrimination against women in this country today. The woman who sells her body is punished criminally and stigmatized socially while her male customer . . . is left unscathed." It is also interesting to note that when a man whistles at or propositions a woman it is not considered a crime, even though it is solicitation, but when the woman solicits it is considered criminal.

A common notion is that prostitutes are a principal cause for the spread of venereal disease (VD) in our country. In fact, the VD rate among prostitutes is somewhat higher than in the general population, but not nearly as high as that in the group of the general population aged fifteen to thirty, which group accounts for 84 percent of the reported VD cases in the United States, according to the U.S. Public Health Service. It is not possible completely to eradicate VD among prostitutes, because even if they are examined and treated frequently, one customer who has gonorrhea, the most common major venereal disease, can reinfect the prostitute immediately, and she can then infect the next customer, even though she has no symptoms. Most prostitutes, however, are quite aware of the danger of venereal disease and take every precaution to avoid it, to be examined, and, if necessary, to be treated. Robert M. Nellis of the San Francisco City Clinic says, "Prostitution is not where it's at with VD today; it's Johnny next door and Susie up the street." (See pp. 199–205, on Venereal Diseases.)

An important question to consider is whether or not prostitution should be decriminalized in this country, as it has been in most other Western countries. Here are the main arguments:

In favor of decriminalizing prostitution: Prostitution should not be considered a crime. A prostitute has the right to do with her body what she wishes, and the state should not interfere with her privacy or the privacy of her customers. The purpose of the law is to protect people and property, not to legislate individual moral conduct. Outlawing prostitution does not prevent it; it only drives prostitution underground. The history of the prohibition of alcoholic beverages demonstrates the impossibility and vast expense of trying to enforce laws against any activity for which many people feel a need and to which they are convinced they have a right. Furthermore, prostitution cannot be a crime since there are no victims (except in the case of associated violence or robbery); all parties enter into it voluntarily to meet what they consider to be their own needs.

Against decriminalizing prostitution: Prostitution is an immoral and debasing human activity, both for the prostitute and for her clients. It separates sex from love and tends to break up marriages by providing sexual satisfaction outside the marriage bond. It commercializes and trivializes in the most crass way what should be a meaningful, deep, unifying experience within the context of love. If the state says yes to prostitution, it is saying yes to sexual license and permissiveness, yes to the breakup of the family, yes to those who go against all accepted moral standards. If prostitution is decriminalized it will increase, because it will be available to people who now, restrained by the law, stay away from it. It is a responsibility of the state to use its laws to strengthen and uphold the commonly accepted standards of morality and to protect the structure of the family. To decriminalize prostitution would do just the opposite.

Rape

Any human activity can become a problem when it is mixed with violence, and sex is no exception. Rape is primarily an act of violence, with sex organs used as the weapons to express that violence. It is sexual intercourse or oral-genital sex forced upon another person against that person's will. Usually the victim is a woman, although boys and men are raped, most frequently in prison and by heterosexuals. On rare occasions even babies and very old women are raped, and it is not unknown for grown women to force sex upon adolescent boys, which could be considered a kind of rape.

The facts we present here about rape are based on *reported* rape cases. However, government authorities estimate that only one tenth to one twentieth of all rapes are reported, probably because of fear, shame, ignorance, and feelings of hopelessness on the part of those who are raped. Much more study on this subject is needed.

Generally, rapists are young men (average age about 25), and their victims are young women (average age about 24). In more than half the reported rapes, the rapist was drinking alcohol before committing the crime. In 48 percent of the rape cases, the victims and their rapists are known to each other, and some rapes take place even on social dates. In many cases, the rapist and his victim meet on the street, and he entices or forces her to go to his place of residence, where the rape takes place. Also, quite frequently, the rapist enters the residence of the victim and rapes her there. Well over half the rapes are planned in advance and occur in a residence.

There is no simple, single explanation of why some men (and even a few women) become rapists. Many are people whose behavior is generally oriented toward crime and violence. They often lack a moral sense and are prone to aggression. Not a few are true psychotics, deeply troubled people who need psychiatric help and from whom society needs to be protected. Many male rapists feel an overwhelming need to find a victim to dominate and terrorize; otherwise they cannot perform sexually. Many have histories of relationships with women, often starting right within their own families, which have left them fearful and resentful of females generally. Still others believe, in a distorted way probably accentuated when they see a woman whom they find sexually provocative, that the woman they select as victim really desires to have sexual intercourse with them, that she is "asking for it," even when she struggles and protests. Also, there is a good deal of evidence that acts of sexual violence like rape originate in emotional deprivations suffered by the rapist in early childhood.

Obviously, a woman should try not to allow herself to get into situations where she might be raped. That means avoiding dark, lonely streets or city parks, whenever possible; it means not acting or dressing in a sexually provocative manner in situations where a rapist might see her; it means staying aware of her surroundings and noticing whether she is being followed; it means not showing herself to be alone in a house or apartment, and keeping doors and windows locked; it means having her keys ready when she gets to her door or, if she's inside, always finding out for certain who's at the door before opening it; and it means, in the longer run, working with community organizations to try to make a safer environment.

Rape crisis workers generally agree that it is most important for a woman to look confident, strong, and purposeful and, even in the most tense, threatening, and emotional situation, to stay cool if she can. It will also be well for her to try to think out in advance what she would do if she were threatened with rape.

An experienced counselor who has worked for several years in a rape crisis center wrote us some wise words about the question of what a woman should do when faced with a rapist. She said:

> Please be very careful about giving specific advice on what to do. There is great disagreement on the subject. Some rapists say that if a woman had screamed or resisted loudly, they'd have run; others report they'd have killed her. Self-defense training is valuable in that it helps a woman feel and act more assertively, but it is risky in that none of us really knows how we would use it when scared to death—and badly or ineffectively used active self-defense could get us killed. Some say it is best to seem to give in quietly so as to avoid being injured or killed, and to try to calm the rapist, to win time, so that escape is more likely should the opportunity arise. The trouble with telling a woman she *should* resist and yell is that she adds to her already large burden of guilt if she does not do so, and it plays into the hands of prosecutors and those who insist (against the law) that a woman isn't really raped unless she is beaten up or shows signs of struggle. I think it is best to give various options and then say that each woman and each rapist and each situation are unique, and the woman should respond in whatever way she thinks best.

Cruel and psychologically devastating as rape is, it does not mean the end of the world for the woman, who knows it is not her fault. Although she feels the shock and will never forget the experience, she is alive and probably not seriously injured physically. It is important that she be helped to get over the experience by talking with someone, preferably a skilled counselor, so that she may receive the support she needs. There are a number of organizations across the country that deal with rape. Most are locally organized, and they have various names, such as Women Against Rape or Women Organized Against

Rape (WOAR). To find the one nearest you, look in the telephone directory under "Rape" or "Rape Crisis Center." Usually there will be a hot-line number to call and women on duty twenty-four hours a day to give confidential advice and help (see Sources of Help, p. 315).

If a woman has been raped, what should she do? The Philadelphia WOAR gives the following advice:

> If you are raped:
> 1. Tell what happened to the first friendly person you meet.
> 2. Call the police. Use the emergency number. Give your location and tell them you were raped.
> 3. Try to remember as many facts as you can about your attacker: clothes, height, weight, age, skin color, etc. Try to remember his car, license number, the direction in which he went, etc. Write all this down right away.
> 4. *Don't* wash or douche before the medical exam, or you destroy important evidence. *Don't* change your clothes, but bring a new set with you if you can.
> 5. At the hospital you will have a complete exam, including a pelvic exam. Show the doctor any bruises, scratches, etc.
> 6. Tell the police simply but exactly what happened. Try not to get flustered. Have a friend or relative accompany you if possible. Be honest and stick to your story.
> 7. If you do not want to report the rape to the police, see a doctor as soon as possible. Make sure you are checked for pregnancy and venereal disease.
> 8. If you need help or have questions, call WOAR. We're here 24 hours a day.

An important thing to remember is that reporting the rape to the police is not the same thing as pressing charges against an accused rapist who has been caught and identified. A woman has to decide whether she wishes to press charges; that is, to attempt to have the rapist convicted of a crime. If she does, there must be an investigation and hearings, for it is not unknown for women to engage willingly in sexual relations with a man and then claim to have been raped, and every person, under our system of justice, is presumed to be innocent until he or she has been proven guilty. The accused rapist has civil rights, too.

STATUTORY RAPE

"Statutory rape" is the term for sexual intercourse with a girl who is below the legal age of consent, which varies from state to state between the ages of 14 and 21, most commonly between 16 and 18. The girl may have been an entirely willing partner in the intercourse, but because of her age the law does not consider her responsible and considers the man as having raped her; that is, if she, her family, or someone else brings a complaint. Obviously, millions of girls under the age of 18 are willingly having sexual intercourse. Their male partners, if it is clear that they are physically mature enough to achieve penile penetration, could be found guilty of statutory rape. Complaints are rarely brought, however.

Sado-masochism

Sadism, in the sexual sense, is the condition in which sexual gratification depends largely upon inflicting physical pain on others. (The term derives from the name of the Marquis de Sade, a Frenchman who practiced and wrote about such activities.) *Masochism,* the condition complementary to sadism, is the condition in which sexual pleasure depends upon undergoing physical pain or humiliation.

Sadists and masochists, whether heterosexual or homosexual, thus match each other as partners, and as long as each satisfies the needs of the other, there seems to be no great problem. Usually the masochist more or less controls the relationship, not allowing the infliction of pain to go further than he or she wishes, since if it did, the sadist would lose a desired partner. Sadists use, and masochists consent to, whipping, gagging, chaining, and other restraints such as leather wrist and leg straps, sometimes called "bondage."

Obviously, if a person with sadistic tendencies gets involved with or marries a person who is not a masochist, serious problems can develop, for in the eyes of the law, sadistic activity is criminal, whereas masochism is not. There are more sadist and masochist heterosexual males than there are females to match.

Transvestism

A transvestite is a person who dresses in clothes of the opposite sex in order to be able to perform sexually and achieve orgasm. Like voyeurism and exhibitionism, transvestism can be considered merely a "public nuisance offense" in that it may be annoying or repulsive but is otherwise harmless. Transvestites are almost always males.

Many transvestites confine their cross-dressing to their homes. Often they are married men; others are homosexuals. But whether heterosexual or homosexual, the transvestite can get into trouble with the law if he publicly flaunts his behavior in female clothing. Transvestites are quite clear that they are not transsexual (see pp. 195–196).

Voyeurism

A voyeur (a French word meaning "one who sees") is a person, almost always a man, who gets sexual satisfaction from looking at a sexual act or at a person undressed or undressing. Being sexually aroused by seeing people doing sexual things or dressed (perhaps undressed) in a sexual manner is certainly nearly universal among men and increasingly common among women. Often the voyeur masturbates while he is looking, or soon afterward.

Voyeurism is considered a deviation only when the seeing is preferred to sexual intercourse, when it is done at considerable legal risk to the voyeur (and thus contains an element of the forbidden), and when the person or people being seen are unaware they are being observed. Usually voyeurs watch strangers, and they are for the most part entirely passive and harmless, except as they are considered nuisances or offensive. Voyeurs are in most cases reported to the police by neighbors rather than by the person being observed.

A common term for voyeur is "Peeping Tom," the name coming from Tom the tailor, who according to an eleventh-century legend was the only villager who failed to close his shutters but "peeped" out when Lady Godiva rode nude down the main street of Coventry, England, as a gesture to persuade her husband to stop oppressively taxing the poor.

Personal Sexual Problems Without Legal Implications

Fetishism

Fetishism means experiencing sexual stimulation and gratification from touching, fondling, or just looking at an inanimate object that is not in itself sexual, as for example pieces of clothing, leather garments, chains, or shoes. In some ways it can truly be considered that, in our society, women's breasts, although not inanimate, obsess men to such an extent that they are treated almost as fetishes. Fetishism is a condition of men, very rarely of women. How a fetishist becomes fixed upon a certain object is not always clear, but it does have to do with some kind of conditioning, association, or deeply affecting experience during the very early years—sometimes before memory.

It is usual for the fetishist to masturbate into or onto the inanimate object that is the fetish. However, a fetish should not be confused with what might be called a "masturbation aid"; say, a picture or recording that stimulates the fantasies that often accompany masturbation.

Transsexualism

Transsexuals are people who wish they were, or are convinced that they are, of the sex that is opposite from that shown by their anatomy and chromosomes. They are genetically of one sex but psychologically of the other. No one knows the origins of transsexualism.

There are three to four male transsexuals to every female transsexual. A male transsexual is convinced that he is "a woman imprisoned in a male body" and has a compelling and never-ending desire to have his body reconstructed to what he considers to be his true sex. His condition is to him serious and is not to be confused with the wish of some men and women that they had been born as members of the other sex. The medical profession is learning how to study, appraise, and test the transsexual's compelling drive for a sex-change operation.

Many transsexuals, usually after long periods of suffering followed by much counseling, achieve the surgery. In sex-change surgery the penis and testes are removed entirely, and an artificial vagina is constructed which usually functions very well sexually. The patient has already had female hormone treatment to modify as far as possible his secondary sex characteristics toward femaleness, and this results in growth of the breasts and change in body-fat distribution. Hormone treatment must continue for the rest of male-to-female life. He is also required to live for a full year as a female before surgery is granted. Finally, as a woman, a male-to-female transsexual can legally marry, can enjoy penile-vaginal intercourse, usually with orgasm, but naturally cannot become pregnant.

People often confuse transsexualism with homosexuality, but the two are entirely different. Homosexuals like their own maleness and enjoy sexual love with people who have the same sex organs as themselves. Transsexuals are also interested in members of the sex they were born into, but this interest is actually heterosexual. They wish to be transformed into the other sex they truly believe they are. They want their bodies to be reassigned as far as possible to the other sex to conform with what they are convinced is their true gender identity so that thereafter their sexual relationships can, in fact, be heterosexual.

Female-to-male transsexuals also exist, request surgery, and where appropriate receive it. This includes removal of uterus, tubes, ovaries, and vagina, inclusion of plastic testicles in a scrotal sac constructed out of the labia, and a penis constructed from skin. Even though the surgically constructed penis cannot function as successfully as the surgically constructed vagina, many female-to-male transsexuals legally marry women, and many such couples are able to lead contented lives.

Drugs, Alcohol, and Sex

When sexual activity becomes associated over a period of time with the use of drugs or alcohol, problems arise. Drugs used for nonmedicinal purposes, and alcohol (which medically is considered a drug, even though it has wide social acceptance), tend to lower people's capacity to reason straight, to make responsible decisions, or to have the willpower to carry out those decisions. When this effect is injected into a sexual situation, tragedy may well be the result, especially if the sexual activity that may be affected is carried on outside the context of a stable relationship like marriage.

Insofar as sex is concerned (and many other human activities too), it is not possible to separate the actual physical effects of drugs and alcohol from the psychological effects. If a person thinks that a drink or a drug will make sex better for him or her, then quite possibly it will seem to do so, in spite of the fact that for others the capacity to perform sexually may actually be lowered.

One of the main effects of drugs and alcohol is to reduce people's inhibitions, to make them feel more relaxed. Since inhibition, worry, and tension about sex, conscious or unconscious, make it difficult for some people to enjoy their sexuality, anything that reduces these may temporarily increase pleasure. But if inhibition is so reduced that a person loses his or her sense of judgment and responsibility, trouble can result. Also, if there is dependency on drugs or alcohol for the enjoyment of sex, that can be a serious problem requiring professional help.

Here are some facts about specific substances that affect, or are believed to affect, sexual behavior. Keep in mind that different people are affected in different ways by different substances and that for some people there is a greater factor of risk than for others.

ALCOHOL

Alcohol lowers the capacity to reason and to make sound decisions, increases vulnerability to sexual or other impulses, reduces inhibitions, and may temporarily increase a person's sense of pleasure. However, even small amounts lower the capacity—from a purely physical point of view—to perform sexually, especially in males. Large amounts of alcohol produce temporary impotence in males and have a negative effect on sexual desire.

MARIJUANA

Marijuana is believed by many of its users to enhance their sexual pleasure and reduce inhibitions. Long-term use, if excessive, impairs mental faculties and sexual judgment.

HEROIN

Heroin temporarily decreases desire and potency. As a person becomes addicted, his or her capacity to enjoy sex is greatly impaired. This impairment may continue even after the habit is kicked.

AMPHETAMINES AND COCAINE

At first, amphetamines and cocaine tend to increase sexual desire and activity. With their continued use, however, the ability to perform and to enjoy is reduced, as exhaustion, nervousness, and even serious irrationality set in. In the female they can cause vaginal dryness and irritability.

LSD AND OTHER HALLUCINOGENS

The effects of LSD and other hallucinogens are highly unpredictable; the nature of the hallucinations depends on who is taking the drug. No generalizations about the effects on sexual feelings and behavior can be made.

SPANISH FLY (CANTHARIDES)

Spanish fly is a powder made from dried beetles, commonly believed to stimulate sexual desire. It does not have this effect. Instead, it is actually an irritant to the urinary system which may initially seem like an exciting stimulation but which actually can produce inflammation acute and damaging to the entire system. This is a very dangerous substance, and its use can be fatal.

SALTPETER

Saltpeter is a tasteless substance sometimes allegedly put in food in the belief that it will reduce sexual desire among soldiers or even, it is rumored, at boys' boarding schools. In fact, it has no effect except to increase the amount of urine.

Venereal Diseases (VD)

Venereal diseases (VD) are diseases spread primarily by close sexual contact and sexual intercourse. (The word *venereal* means "having to do with sexual intercourse" and comes from the name of Venus, the Roman goddess of love.) Today many prefer the term *sexually transmitted diseases* (STDs). Most people, when they think of VD, think only of two diseases, syphilis and gonorrhea; actually there are a number of others.

One problem in dealing with the venereal diseases, both in writing and medically, is that they are so closely related to sexual behavior. Most people, doctors included, find it hard to be objective about sex and sexual behavior, so it is difficult for the average person to get accurate information about the diseases; for example, how they are spread and how widespread they are. Thus, although doctors and public health people are legally required to report all cases of gonorrhea and syphilis to the public health authorities, the U.S. Public Health Service estimates that only one case in four that is medically treated actually is reported and entered into the statistics.

If it were possible for people's attitudes about sex and sexual information to be more understanding and realistic, health workers and others interested in public and individual health might be more successful in their efforts to control the STDs. There must be sober acceptance that sexuality and sexual behavior are facts of life and that many people of all ages, for better or worse, are and will continue to be sexually active—as they have always been. The job of the VD health worker is not to deal with the morals of the situations he or she is concerned with—important as these are in other kinds of work and teaching—but to deal directly with the problems of prevention, control, and cure of the diseases.

We speak of venereal diseases or sexually transmitted diseases, and yet it is often not accurate to say that certain diseases are sexually transmitted and certain ones are not. An unborn baby will contract syphilis from its syphilitic mother; or, if not protected immediately after birth by drops or ointment applied to its eyes (as almost all babies now are in the United States), a newborn can be infected with gonorrhea in its eyes as it passes through its infected mother's birth canal, with the risk of permanent blindness. Yet neither of these transmissions of disease is sexual. On the other hand, a person may very likely catch a common cold if the person he or she has sexual relations with has one, yet no one thinks of a cold as a venereal disease.

In general, the organisms causing most venereal diseases can live only in the warm, moist conditions found inside the human body. They die almost at once if exposed to air or allowed to become dry or cool. The organisms of VD are transmitted mainly by contact between the warm, moist *mucous tissues* of an infectious person and those of another person, as in sexual intercourse or heavy petting. The mucous tissues are the soft, moist linings inside almost all the passages of the body that open to the outside, in the penis, the vagina, the rectum, the mouth, or the throat. The germs can also enter through the eyes or through those parts of the skin that are quite delicate, like the skin on the penis or in and around the genital area or on the face or the nipples. Syphilis germs can enter the body through a cut, a scratch, or an opening in the skin; gonorrhea bacteria can be transmitted through using towels or sheets immediately after an infectious person has used them, and while they are still damp *and* warm. The germs of VD cannot be transmitted by means of toilet seats, doorknobs, swimming pools, or drinking glasses. (An exception would be the rare circumstance of a person using a glass immediately after its use by another person with a syphilitic sore on the mouth.)

Everyone who is sexually active should have some knowledge about the symptoms of the main venereal diseases. In the Concise A–to–Z Encyclopedia at the back of this book, we give a summary of the information about the most common of the STDs, each in its alphabetical position. The diseases explained are the following, arranged here in order of their *annual incidence* (the number of people who become infected each year), as estimated by the U.S. Public Health Service, starting with the disease of highest incidence:

> Trichomonas vaginalis (3,000,000 new cases per year)
> Gonorrhea (2,700,000 new cases per year)
> Nonspecific (or nongonococcal) urethritis (2,500,000 per year)
> Venereal warts (700,000 new cases per year)
> Syphilis (80,000 new cases and 350,000 untreated continuing
>   cases per year)
> Herpes progenitalis (300,000 new cases per year)
> Crab lice (300,000 new cases per year)

There are other STDs for which the Public Health Service has not published figures of annual incidence. These are:

Lymphogranuloma venereum
Granuloma inguinale
Chancroid
Monilial vaginitis (yeast infection, probably the most common
   of all vaginal disorders)

Self-treatment of any venereal disease should never be under-taken. If you suspect you have the symptoms of or may have been exposed to a venereal disease, go promptly to a physician, either your own or one at a public VD clinic. To find a clinic, look for the telephone number and address under "Health" or under the name of your city or town and then "Health Department." If you or any people you know have questions about symptoms, diagnosis, or treatment and where to go to get help, you may call, toll-free, the VD National Hotline (see p. 320), seven days a week. The calls are confidential. No names are asked, no records are kept. But the VD National Hotline has available in its office the names, addresses, and hours of service of VD clinics throughout the United States.

Most of the venereal diseases can be cured by one or more injections of penicillin or another antibiotic. The cure is usually quick and inexpensive, and free of charge at a public clinic. Examination, testing, and treatment are done confidentially. Even if they are minors, young people may be diagnosed and treated entirely legally without their parents' knowledge.

During and after World War II, the venereal disease rate in the United States went way down as the result of the discovery of penicillin and other antibiotics, and most people began to believe that the VDs were on their way out. But in the late 1950s, as people became complacent and as sexual intercourse outside of and before marriage and with more than one partner became much more common, especially in the age-group of 15 to 24, the rate of syphilis infection began to rise. The rate of infection by gonorrhea soared from about 130 cases per 100,000 population in 1957 to almost 500 in the late 1970s (and remember, only about one fourth of VD cases are reported). Gonorrhea is now considered epidemic throughout the United States, especially among young people, and it is estimated that 50 percent of Americans have contracted it at least once by age 25.

The Prevention of Venereal Disease

While VD is not the worldwide disaster it was before the discovery and application of antibiotics, it is still a terribly serious health problem. For instance, although antibiotics can cure syphilis, it cannot repair the serious damage it may already have done. Also, there is every possibility of reinfection after a cure. As far as prevention of venereal disease goes, there are two parts: individual protection and public protection.

INDIVIDUAL PROTECTION

There are a number of ways by which you as an individual can help to protect yourself and your partner from venereal diseases:

1. *Don't have sexual intercourse or engage in heavy petting with just anybody.*

2. *Be sure you and your sexual partner are free of VD.* The only way to be certain is to be tested at a clinic or by a doctor and then have intimate sexual contact only with your partner, and your partner only with you.

3. *Use a condom if you have sexual intercourse with a person you are not certain is free of VD.* (See p. 83 for instructions on this.)

4. *Know the symptoms of the sexually transmitted diseases.* These symptoms are described in the Concise A–to–Z Encyclopedia in the back of this book. In general, if you have in your genital area soreness or pain, severe itching, inflammation, unusual discharges, ulcers, warts, or any other unusual conditions, especially if you are sexually active, assume that you may have one of the STDs.

5. *Get diagnosed and, if needed, treated.* If you have symptoms, go at once to a clinic or doctor and follow the instructions you receive. If you don't know where to go, call the VD National Hotline (see p. 320). Do not try to treat yourself. It can be dangerous.

PUBLIC PROTECTION

The U.S. Public Health Service's Center for Disease Control, in Atlanta, Georgia, and various state and city public health services attempt to keep track of the spread of venereal diseases in the United

States. They publish the latest information about the extent and location of the diseases and the ways of diagnosing and treating them. One of the most important aspects of this work is locating all people who have VD and confidentially treating and curing them. You can assist in this work by being sure that if you become infected this is reported by you or your doctor to the public health authorities. You should also report, again confidentially, the names of all your sexual contacts, so that if infected they can be diagnosed and treated. The chain of infection cannot be broken without this contact tracing.

A chain of infection describes the way a single person with VD can be responsible for starting its spread to many other people. Chart 2 diagrams an actual VD outbreak at one U.S. high school.* It shows how in one school the disease of syphilis (and the same sort of chain might be diagrammed for a gonorrhea outbreak) spread from person to person until it had affected forty-one people, all from Boy 1. Of these, fourteen became infected and infectious, and twenty-seven were treated preventively before they developed symptoms. Twenty-five of the people on the diagram were not infected.

Information like that on which Chart 2 is based is gathered confidentially by public health contact tracers. Contact tracing involves interviewing each person who comes to a public health clinic and getting the names and locations of that person's sex contacts. The names are kept entirely confidential, and when the contact tracer finds the people, he urges them to come to the clinic for testing and treatment. When they come, each one is also interviewed for his or her contacts. The people whose names are given are not told who gave them—only that they have been exposed to VD and that they should come to the clinic. Thus, through the persistent efforts of the interviewer and contact tracer, exposed persons are found, treated if necessary, and the outbreak can be brought to a halt.

The contact tracing cannot be completely effective unless each person interviewed gives the names of every single one of his or her contacts. It is in a person's own interest to do this, otherwise he or she might be the victim of what is sometimes referred to as "ping-pong" infection. For example, although it does not show in the diagram, Boy 1 might have been treated and cured but then might later have had sexual contact with one of the people in, say, Row D and have become reinfected. This reinfection would not have happened if all involved

*Adapted from a diagram published by the American Social Health Association.

Chart 2.
Syphilis outbreak at an American High School
(adapted from a diagram published by
the American Social Health Association).

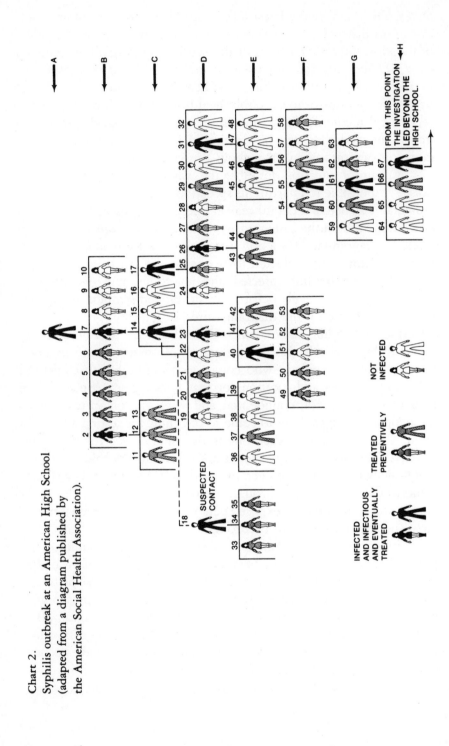

had come as soon as possible for testing and treatment and had given the names of their sexual contacts.

Contact tracing is a very effective method of stopping epidemics, but it is also enormously costly. Lack of trained contact tracers and money to pay them is a major problem in controlling the present nationwide VD epidemic. There is no question that our country needs better public health services, more adequately staffed and financed, to come as close as we can to eradicating the most serious sexually transmitted diseases. But our country also needs people who, if they are sexually active, will be as informed and responsible as possible about this activity.

The Biggest Sex Problem of All

We have said a good deal about ways that sex can get turned into a problem by human beings. The length of this chapter is an indication of how often this happens. But undoubtedly the most important of all are the fear and guilt that our society attaches to the expression of human sexuality, as the result of the ignorance—today—about the simple and complex physical and emotional facts about sexuality. All too often this ignorance is willfully and stubbornly maintained by individuals who refuse to read, listen, and learn and who thus deprive themselves—and usually their children—of the calm, informed attitudes and understanding about sex that might give them sexual peace and happiness in their lives.

And that brings us to the subject of our next chapter.

10
Planned Sex Education Programs

The following exchange of letters recently appeared in the "Dear Abby" column:

Dear Abby: I may be old-fashioned, but I can't see teaching sixth and seventh graders sex in the schoolroom. They are a long way from needing that kind of information. Why rush them? If you start putting ideas about sex into their heads, first thing you know, they'll start experimenting.

No wonder we have so many unmarried mothers among teenagers. I read in your column that venereal disease is now an epidemic in this country.

What can be done to stop all this sex education, Abby?

Concerned in Illinois

Dear Concerned: If there really were all the sex education you claim there is, we'd have less teenage pregnancy and VD—not more.

No one has to put "ideas" about sex into the heads of children. It's there already. Sexual feelings and curiosity about sex are natural and normal in all children. And so is experimenting.

Ideally, parents should provide their children with a proper sex education, but surveys show that most of them do not, so some schools provide it. Unfortunately, the only states that have laws requiring sex education in the schools are Hawaii, Kentucky, Michigan, Maryland, Missouri and North Dakota.* (Louisiana expressly forbids it.)

The old saying, "What you don't know can't hurt you" is not true. On the contrary—it can hurt you. And it's hurting all of us.

---

*But even in these states many local communities refuse to abide by the mandate because of the very attitudes and misunderstandings reflected in the letter to Abby.

Although Abby makes her point strongly and clearly, we doubt that "Concerned in Illinois" was, or could ever be, convinced. The fear that Concerned expresses—that information leads to ideas which in turn lead to experimentation which in turn leads to illegitimate babies and VD—is widespread, deep-rooted, and based on error.

Why Sex Education Outside the Family?

We have already explained how parents are their children's primary sex-educators, whether or not they know it or want to be. Most of the education is done unconsciously, by example and attitudes, rather than directly in words. There are, however, a number of reasons why today it is widely considered beneficial to children to have available a sex information program outside the home, not to replace but in addition to home teachings:

• Some parents—or their children—are so embarrassed when a sexual subject or action comes up in family or community life that they are simply unable to discuss the matter. ("My mother says, 'Go talk to your father,' and my father says, 'I'm busy.' ")

• Some parents keep waiting for their children to ask the questions, but the children never do, or else the parents fail to recognize implied questions.

• Some parents simply do not have the information—beyond the simple facts of where babies come from—to answer their children's questions. (This book is one resource for all family members to use when information is needed, for not all parents will wish to be directly involved in providing the necessary information found here.)

• Information and opinions can often be shared more easily in a clear, friendly, and objective way by people trained as educators than by parents, who are quite naturally and properly very emotionally involved with their children.

• Once children reach puberty and begin to struggle with the four tasks of adolescence (see Chapter 7), sex and sexuality become an area in which they feel they must try especially hard to achieve independence. They resist the idea that their parents might be worried about their sex lives. They very much want and need physical and psychological privacy with respect to sex, yet they need to be able to talk about it with each other and with respected authority figures.

• In most families there is little chance for the children to talk about sex and sexuality with people their own age, but this is an important skill for people of any age to learn. Such talk helps to prepare boys and girls for communicating with their future mates and for the responsible, intelligent choices they must learn how to make.

• A classroom can provide a "safe," somewhat structured situation in which young people can speak out more easily than in the more intimate environment of the home. It also provides the opportunity to be silent and learn from listening to the exchange of ideas by others.

Many parents worry that a sex and family-life education program will promote or suggest ideas they would not approve of. But we must remember that, as the Dear Abby column pointed out, ideas and feelings about sex and sexuality are already in the heads of normal children. However, it would certainly be wrong for a public school to promote any given point of view or set of morals, other than the basic one of responsibility for one's own actions *and* their consequences. Generally, the fear in this connection is that teachers, in their enthusiasm, will promote a pro-sex, go-out-and-try-it point of view. In actual practice, this has not proved to be the case; in the rare instances where it has happened, the community outcry was so immediate and vigorous that it soon stopped. A far greater danger is that the subject of sex and sexuality will be grouped with "problems"—like drugs, alcohol, and smoking—or that it will be taught by teachers who are not trained to deal with the subject. Parents are quite right to be concerned about this.

Essential Elements for Planned Sex Education

It would be a mistake for anyone to prescribe a sex education program, since the content should be developed by a school's educational staff in cooperation with a broadly based committee from the community, as far as the basic approaches and areas are concerned. Community needs and degrees of readiness do differ from place to place. However, here are the elements we consider to be essential to any sex education program:

1. The complete biological facts of sex and reproduction.

2. The basic facts of birth control and family planning. Even people who are for religious reasons opposed to the medical birth control methods need to know these facts, for if they don't they will accept rumor and half-truths.

3. The differences in sexual behavior between other animals and

human beings. The sexual behavior of animals is largely programmed by instinct and innate physiology, so they have no choices to make, whereas the sexual behavior of human beings is mostly learned, humans can make choices about how they will behave sexually, and they are therefore directly responsible for the results of their choices. Too many youngsters, aware of the copulation of animals, conclude that the sexuality of men and women is the same as the reproductivity of animals.

4. The differences between men and women, not just the biological differences but the differences in sexual roles, in sexual response, in personality, and in what society expects. In other words, sex education should primarily be about sexuality, not just about sex (see p. 1).

5. The facts about masturbation. This subject is unlikely to come up spontaneously in class and therefore needs to be introduced, if only to make sure that misconceptions about its role throughout the life cycle are cleared up.

6. Such facts as we now know about homosexuality, and a discussion of the rights and special social problems of people with homosexual preferences.

7. The facts about venereal diseases—not to scare young people but to help them protect themselves against a real and widespread health danger.

8. The possible results, both good and bad, of sexual intercourse, and the steps that lead up to it.

9. The place of sex in family life.

10. The place of sex in the social life of teenagers.

11. Through discussion and through literature, the recognition that the feelings experienced by one individual are often not the same as those experienced by another individual. Students need help in putting themselves in the places of other people.

Sometimes it is helpful to give students a form sheet on which they can indicate what they would like to talk about. We have reproduced one here, for use with modifications appropriate to the specific situation.

Sex Education in the Public Schools

We have suggested that teachers should stick to facts and preside over the discussion, making sure that the major issues get discussed. But mere facts and discussion are not enough. They need to be undergirded by a set of values. (We use the word *values*, not beliefs or dogmas. A church or church school has the right to teach a specific set of religious beliefs, dogmas, or rules about human sexual behavior, but a public school does not have that right.) The following six values should be acceptable to any community in our American democracy.

The value of information. Correct information is better than ignorance or the wrong information; it makes responsible action possible, while ignorance can lead only to irresponsibility. There is no evidence that sound knowledge leads to experimentation and trouble, for those who get into what we call "trouble" are usually those who are not truly and fully informed. There are people in every community who will argue for ignorance in matters that concern human sexuality, but we believe that the great majority favor information. Imparting information, and teaching people how to get it and use it, is a main function of the schools.

The value of responsibility. An action, sexual or otherwise, taken in the light of all its possible consequences, good and bad, present and future, can be called responsible. An action taken without regard for the consequences is irresponsible.

The value of control. Sex is a power, and, like any other power, it can be used for good or for bad. Therefore it must be controlled by the individual for good purposes. (Automobiles and fire are two other examples of power where responsible and knowledgeable control can mean the difference between benefit and tragedy.)

The value of consideration. The welfare and needs, both short-term and long-term, of oneself, of others involved, and of society, must be considered in whatever a person does.

The value of each individual person. The infinite value of others is worthy of our most caring and loving consideration.

The value of communication. It is good to have opportunities to talk over our questions and ideas, to test them out against the ideas of others, to make our feelings known and to learn the feelings of others through discussion and conversation.

Teaching According to Age Level

In general, we have found that in kindergarten through about fourth grade it is best to proceed in sex education somewhat as an enlightened family would proceed at home; that is, (1) deal with questions as they come up, (2) answer them briefly and factually (either before the entire group or simply to the individual who asks them, whichever seems most natural), and (3) ask if there are any other questions. This is the method of using opportunities as they arise, taking advantage of the moments of teachability. If classrooms have animals (hamsters, mice, guinea pigs, rabbits, and the like) that from time to time mate and have young, this is a good extra resource for teaching, as much for teaching how animals and human beings differ as for teaching reproduction. (But the birth of baby rabbits, for example, should never be explained by saying that the mommy and daddy rabbits got married.) It may also be useful to read aloud, look at together, and discuss a carefully chosen book written especially for children in kindergarten or first grade. (See list beginning on p. 299.)

By fifth grade, children are ready for a planned unit on the facts of human reproduction. Children of this age are in that wonderful period of life when they are enthusiastic about all sorts of facts, can learn them without discomfort or silliness, and are likely to have lots of serious questions. Very few will have reached puberty, so their interest will still tend toward the facts rather than toward their own emotional involvement. A number of books are available for this age-group.

Beginning with the upper elementary grades, the planned portion of the sex education program really has two parts: (1) use of the entire school curriculum to deal with questions and information about human sexuality as they come up, and (2) definitely scheduled units of instruction and discussion. The curriculum-centered part can make valuable use of such subjects as social studies (history, current events, anthropology, sociology, and the like), English (especially literature, which is rich in the materials of human behavior), and science (especially biology), as well as opportunities that arise in counseling situations. To make intelligent but not excessive use of the curriculum, it is important for faculty members from time to time to discuss together what information and understandings they wish to be ready to convey or develop, so that they can have in their minds an informal agenda of items relating to sexuality. In such faculty discussions it is useful, too, for the staff to share and talk about classroom experiences that have been especially successful or unsuccessful.

In the ideal school, the curriculum-centered approach would perhaps be sufficient, and it does have the advantage of not setting sexuality off as something apart from the rest of life. In most schools, however, what is everyone's responsibility turns out to be no one's, and so for the teenage years it is well to plan definite units, perhaps once every two years—say grades 7 or 8, 10, and 12. Grades 7 and 8 are crucial years, in which more children reach puberty than in any other, when interest in the social as well as the physical aspects of sexuality becomes high, and yet before many students are deeply involved personally (most are still only thinking about getting involved). A month- or six-weeks-long unit, planned on the basis of the content suggested, with reading, discussion, and writing and with the students being tested on facts, is a valuable focal point.

By Grade 10, students have grown in maturity and experience and are ready to discuss again, at new levels, the factual and behavioral aspects of sexuality. A shorter planned unit is probably sufficient here —say, ten days. Then in Grade 12, as students are about to experience the greater freedom of the world outside of school, on the job or in college, they should be helped by another planned unit to prepare for being independent and for meeting with value systems other than their own.

Learning by the Discussion Method

As we have said, schools and other public institutions serve best if they do not promote a certain point of view or set of morals, other than total personal responsibility for one's own actions. Teachers should stick to established facts; where the facts are not known, or where they do not know them, the teachers should be frank and say so. For example, no one can or should say that it is a fact that premarital intercourse does or does not improve a person's chances of having a happy, satisfying, and long-lasting marriage. Research on this question has come up with no consistent evidence one way or the other.

If a student asks, "Is it OK for a boy and a girl to have sex if they're in love and know what they are doing? Will it hurt them later when they get married?" some teachers, afraid of parental reaction, might be inclined to answer, "Well, if you have sex with somebody you're not married to *before* you are married, you are likely to go on having sex with people you're not married to *after* marriage, and that's bad for marriage, isn't it? Also, it's immoral." Other teachers, not wanting to cause hang-ups in the children, might say, "Well, I don't know, but you certainly don't want to get so turned off about sex that when you get married you will have difficulty enjoying the sexual part of your marriage." The best way to handle a question like this is to say only that it's a very good question and then turn it back to the class for discussion, making sure that all aspects of the question get talked about. Such an approach emphasizes that questions like these have to be answered by each individual for himself or herself, and also that there are some things the teacher—or science itself—just doesn't have answers for.

This student's question, when discussed fully, freely, and openly by the class, provides almost enough material for an entire unit of sex education. Look at the questions in it:

What do you mean, "having sex"?
What does "OK" mean? OK with whom?
What does "in love" mean?
What do you mean, "know what they're doing"? Know physically? Know emotionally? Know intellectually?
What do they need to know? How do they know that they know it? What were their sources for finding out?
What do you mean by "hurt" them? In what ways could it hurt them?
In what ways could it be good for them? How could it hurt, or be good for, their eventual marriage?
What makes a good marriage?

In our experience, a discussion of subjects like these, if there is free expression of all points of view, is likely to result in a balance of opinions and the gradual emergence of a clear wisdom of the group. The main benefits are two: the chance to hear the views of others, especially of others of the opposite sex, and the chance to think through, with others, various issues of behavior and feeling—what to do and what not to do, and what the consequences are likely to be. This process requires teachers skillful in facilitating group discussions. The main role of the teacher is to be the moderator for the discussion (only one person talking at a time), to correct any misstatements of fact or to inject any factual knowledge that may enlighten the discussion, and to make sure that questions raised keep being turned back to the class for further exchange. Thus, without preaching and without forcing, a maturity of thought, opinion, and choice-making develops in the group and in each individual, even among those who prefer listening to talking (see also Chapter 11).

Teachers of Sex Education

Who should teach about human sexuality? Not necessarily the persons with the most factual knowledge. Facts can be mastered rather quickly by persons chosen and trained to teach. Nor should teaching about human sexuality be the monopoly of any traditional field. It can become integral to courses in English, history, social studies, biology, general science, physical education, health, or family life. Thus it need not be specifically the province of the pastor, the doctor, the psychiatrist, or the nurse.

People who teach sex education should

• be able to communicate simply, openly, and truthfully with boys and girls.

• feel unembarrassed by any aspect of the topic and comfortable in a dialogue-centered classroom.

• be secure in their own sexual feelings and have developed for themselves a set of values that they feel confident about.

• be willing to communicate these values, when appropriate, but without trying to impose them.

• be skilled in facilitating discussion and especially be able to resist talking too much, giving all the answers, or providing advice.

• be ready to acknowledge that there are things they don't know (which make it easier for the students to admit that there are things *they* don't know).

• be able to maintain a nonjudgmental attitude especially about things they feel strongly about, for criticism of student ideas of behavior will destroy rapport and communication. Rather let the students criticize themselves.

• be nonshockable, which is not the same thing as being insensitive.

• absolutely respect each student's right to silence and to privacy. Certainly, any faculty member who does not feel comfortable in discussing matters of sexuality and sexual behavior with a class should not be asked to do so.

Training in Teaching Human Sexuality

As to courses in human sexuality in schools, churches, or other institutions, parents are right to inquire who will be teaching these courses and what their training and qualifications are. In recent years, more and more courses in human sexuality are being offered in institutions that train teachers, doctors, nurses, social workers, and clergy in ministering to people's needs.

Many summer training courses are available for periods of one week and longer in universities across the country, and each year the March issue of the *SIECUS Report,* the publication of the Sex Information and Education Council of the United States, lists these training opportunities. Certain university centers offer courses that can lead to master's or doctoral degrees in human sexuality. Among these is New York University's School of Education, Health, Nursing and Arts Professions in New York City. The SIECUS library of two thousand volumes, now housed at this school, is available to accredited professionals. There is also the Institute for Advanced Study of Human Sexuality in San Francisco, which was established in 1977 in response to the 1976 California law that requires all health professionals to have training in human sexuality. The Institute, accredited by the State of California, gives advanced degrees in three aspects of human sexuality: research, therapy, and education. The Institute for Sex Research of Indiana University at Bloomington provides postgraduate summer training courses every year for psychiatrists and other professionals. This institute was founded as a result of the work of Dr. Alfred C. Kinsey, and its library is probably the most complete in the world.

Professional organizations such as the American Medical Association; the American College of Obstetricians and Gynecologists and its adjunct, the Nursing Association of the American College of Obstetricians and Gynecologists; the American Psychological Association; the American Psychiatric Association; and numerous others often provide for one- or two-day workshops on training and the reporting of research in conjunction with their annual meetings. Other important organizations are the Society for the Scientific Study of Sex (SSSS); the Sex Information and Education Council of the U.S. (SIECUS); and the American Association of Sex Educators, Counselors and Therapists

(AASECT). Each has had a leadership role. The Society for the Scientific Study of Sex was founded in 1957. Its primary interest is reporting research in the field of human sexuality; it publishes the *Journal of Sex Research.*

SIECUS, the Sex Information and Educational Council of the U.S., was founded in 1964. Its board of directors has always included leaders in psychiatry and other medical fields, sociology, anthropology, psychology, education, clergy of the three major faith groups, and the business community. It publishes the *SIECUS Report,* which contains lead articles by authorities on various aspects of human sexuality and reviews of current professional books and audiovisual aids. SIECUS has had no programs for use in schools but has dealt specifically with the education of professionals in human sexuality.

The American Association of Sex Educators, Counselors and Therapists was formed in 1967 as a membership organization. It is not possible to belong to AASECT unless one has been trained and accredited by the association. AASECT has set up standards of qualification and accreditation for three groups: sex educators, sex counselors, and sex therapists. The organization itself conducts national, regional, and local training workshops and provides certificates for those attending them. It maintains a geographical directory of sex educators and counselors and a separate list of therapists certified as qualified by AASECT.

The general public is probably not aware of the great and growing numbers of professionals in all the health and caring professions who have received training. In Connecticut alone, six hundred teachers have attended sexuality training courses at the University of Connecticut at Bridgeport. Many seminaries of all faiths and denominations now provide such training to help qualify the clergy to minister more effectively to those who come to them with sexual problems. Social service workers in various national and local welfare and youth organizations have also been receiving this important training.

The result is that in almost all large and medium-sized cities and in many smaller towns there are now well-trained people to respond to the needs of those who seek their services, whether for education, counseling, or therapy.

The Relationship of Sex Education Programs and the Home

Some parents fear that teaching outside the home about human sexuality will somehow take from them their right and duty to bring up their children to believe and behave as they, the parents, want them to. Parents who feel this way can be assured that a school's provision for sex education does not mean it is attempting to take over the parents' role as the primary sex educators of their children. As far as sex education is concerned, educators see it as their job to supplement and complement the education that has been going on at home since the birth of each child. When schools follow guidelines like those suggested earlier in this chapter, there is no danger. The real dangers lie in the unplanned, distorted, sensationalized messages of society, whose onslaught on children is continuous, and in the gossip, rumors, and assorted revelations of fact and fancy that circulate among young people of school age. Many children need help from the school as well as from their families in the task of separating fact from distortion and in making judgments in the light of full scientific information and in the perspective of open discussion.

The School's Obligations Toward the Parents

To deserve and win the confidence of parents, educators should provide full information in advance about any sex education program, so that parents may know what its objectives are and what to expect. Parents should have an opportunity to see and comment on all materials to be used, to hear an explanation of the teaching methods, to know how and where the teachers have been trained, and to be told exactly when their children will be studying a given unit on sex education. (The *when* is important because it enables parents to take advantage of the school's program to open up discussion at home. Otherwise children often will say nothing about it, and good chances for communication will be lost.)

If some parents do not want their children to participate in the program, the school should respect this wish and furnish an alternative, even if it is only a supervised study period. Sex education is a sensitive area for some parents, and thus it should remain optional. Experience across the nation has shown that, given this option, 2 to 3 percent of parents ask that their children not participate.

The school should be open to suggestions and objections from parents, and to acting upon those that give promise of improvement. And it has the obligation to provide a well-thought-out program taught by trained and qualified teachers who are sufficiently secure, mature, and sensible enough to deal well with the many important questions that may come up in discussion. The program must stick to facts and a discussion of facts, issues, and values. It must not present a certain point of view as the right one. Facts and discussion are the essentials of a program; propagandizing should have no place in it.

How Parents Can Encourage Sound Programs

Many teachers and especially school administrators hesitate to start a sex education program for fear that parents will object. So if parents want to have a sex education program in their school, we suggest that they first discuss the matter with other parents who are likely to feel the same way. Then, very early in the process, they should talk with the principal or superintendent to find out what his or her thoughts are, to explain their views, and to ask for advice on how to proceed. The administrator will appreciate being brought in at the earliest stages. Next, the parents may want to assemble an informal committee of lay and professional people—some teachers, perhaps a doctor or two, some clergy, maybe a couple of lawyers and other professional people, some school administrators, a cross section of parents, and perhaps a thoughtful eleventh- or twelfth-grader or two.

It would be unwise to prescribe a course of action from this point on. What parents do will depend on the community and on people's attitudes and convictions. They may find that once the administrators know that a responsible group of parents is ready to back them, they will go ahead and take the necessary steps themselves, keeping parents informed. Or they may want to continue to have parents involved up until the program is established. Of course, no such program is ever finally established, for it will need modification over the years, as those involved gain experience, as conditions in the community change, and as new research knowledge becomes available.

Furthermore, we must remember that no sex education program can succeed if it goes beyond what the community is ready or can be educated to accept. This does not mean giving in to the objections of a small group of determined objectors (whose children, as we suggested, need not participate); it means letting the program grow, with guidance and organization, out of the values of the community itself and its sense of what it needs. Many a program has been wrecked because it was launched without the necessary preliminary discussions or because those teaching it allowed themselves to get out of touch with the community.

If some parents have been influential in getting a program started, it is important for them to remember that it is the school people who will be carrying out the program. Once the climate of acceptance is created and communicated to the school, the detailed development of the program and its teaching are the responsibility of the school, not of the parents. It is, however, the responsibility of the school and the parents to keep their communication going, so that parents never feel things are happening behind their backs.

What to Do If You as a Parent Have Objections

If you have objections to the school program, what is the best way to get heard and to get constructive results? First, be sure you have the facts straight. The first place to go for information is your own child. Find out as calmly as possible exactly what took place. (But remember what one teacher reportedly said to parents at a first PTA meeting: "If you will promise not to believe everything your children tell you happens at school, I'll promise not to believe everything they tell me happens at home.")

If your objection is to something said by another student in class, think twice before doing anything. The school is not responsible for what children say in class, only for how this is dealt with by the teacher. In a healthy school discussion of human sexuality, many points of view will be expressed by different children. This is good, because young people must develop discrimination and skills in dealing with opinions and assertions they come in contact with and, putting them into proper perspective, in deciding whether they agree or disagree and why.

If you wish, you might check with another parent to see if you are the only one who is disturbed, but be sure that the other parent is responsible and unexcitable. It is never a good idea to call ten parents and ask, for example, "Did you hear that Mrs. X is having those sixth-graders look at illustrated, dirty sex books and discuss them, and what are we going to do about it?"

If you are sure of your facts and still firm in your objection, the best policy is first to make an appointment with the teacher concerned. After talking together, both you and the teacher may be better educated about the feelings and purposes of the other, and the matter may be settled right there. If the teacher does not want to talk with you, or if you do not feel satisfied after your talk, then it would be well to ask to see the principal, not as a threat but as a way of getting the objection dealt with sensibly. There's no doubt that teachers do from time to time make errors in judgment—they're as human as anyone else.

Only rarely are there situations that cannot be resolved by frank, calm discussion. If you feel you must organize support for your view, do it with the full knowledge of the school authorities and the officers of the PTA, so that the discussions can be well-informed and constructive action will be likely to result.

If you are a parent who feels that a small group of people is making a large fuss over a minor event, and if you basically agree with the school and disagree with the objectors, let the school know and offer your help if it is needed. Too often the strident protests of a small group of parents, or even of outside people, have weakened or wrecked a good sex education program because those who were in favor of it did not make themselves known.

Sex Education Programs Outside the School

According to the best estimates, only about 15 percent of American students are offered any planned sex education in school, and that 15 percent includes those whose courses deal only with the facts of human reproduction, plus some information on the dangers and treatment of VD, with very little opportunity for the kinds of discussion of human sexuality that we have been talking about. Since so many teachers, administrators, and school boards are afraid or unwilling to provide adequate sex education in the schools—often because they feel they have enough troubles without facing the objections of the minority of parents who oppose it—we can be thankful that there are other ways to provide opportunities for boys and girls to learn about and discuss human sexuality under expert leadership and outside the home. Many churches offer excellent, carefully planned programs, as do the YWCA and the YMCA, the Big Brother Association, the educational outreach departments of some hospitals, and many Planned Parenthood affiliates.

If you find that no schools in your community provide sex education acceptable to you, we suggest that you investigate other community organizations to see what they can offer. You may find it possible to join forces with other parents and families to encourage organizations with which you have connections to provide what is needed.

Planned programs of sex education to complement the education at home are not panaceas. They can inform, enhance communication, and put matters in perspective, but they are not likely, by themselves, to shift a selfish, exploitative person to responsibility and altruism or to free a fearful person from crippling inhibition and guilt, although they might provide nudges in these directions. We think, though, that the results can be more than merely modest. Stated briefly, good sex education can develop in boys and girls knowledge and attitudes that will enable them to make sound choices about the use of their sexual powers—choices that are intelligent, because they are based on solid information; responsible, because they are made in light of all possible consequences; and moral, because they are not harmful to the decision-makers themselves or to any others involved, now or in the future. In this way, young people will begin to learn not to fear the sexual part of their natures but to understand and accept it and to be prepared to manage it and use it as a part of life and for the good of life.

11
Making Sexual Decisions

This chapter is addressed to young people especially. What kind of sexual person would you like to be, and how can you become that kind of person?

In his play *Hamlet,* Shakespeare wrote:

> This above all: to thine own self be true,
> And it must follow, as the night the day,
> Thou canst not then be false to any man.

What does it mean to be true to one's self in all that concerns sexuality? Does it mean telling the truth to oneself? That certainly is part of it—actually the very first step in decision-making. Lying or fabricating to oneself about sexuality makes it impossible to get a clear and true picture of it, especially if one needs to make clear-cut and well-grounded decisions about one's sexual life. Insisting on remaining ignorant of the known facts about human sexuality also leads to difficulties in decision-making. That is why in this book our aim has been to present only the facts about sex and sexuality now known through responsible research. So the first question is: How best are you going to use the facts that you read in this book and elsewhere or that you experience? The answer lies largely with you, for no one else can answer your questions as well for you as yourself.

Next comes a second question: How well do you know yourself? Well enough to predict how you will make decisions about sexual situations in the light of all the facts? And are you strong enough to carry out what you decide? What kind of sexual person would you like to turn out to be—or turn into from what you already are?

Of course, it is possible to get away with making very few decisions at all in life about anything, to slide along and live from day to day, taking what comes and doing things on impulse. Most people can get away with this when it comes to unimportant things, but should such an important thing as your sexual life be left to chance and luck? Certainly no more than trusting to chance and impulse about how you would make your living if you left school, say, at the age of 10.

Or maybe you could choose to drift along about sexual decisions as long as you are the only person involved. But sooner or later, sex almost always involves at least one other person, and as soon as that happens everything changes; involving someone else in your life, especially sexually, means that you are affecting the life of that person as well as your own. Are you ready and able to accept responsibility for that?

Feeling comfortable about oneself as a sexual person is important. But how does one decide what's right and what's wrong about sex? How do any of us decide what we'll think or imagine or wish or feel or do about our sexuality? As with most of our actions—past, present, and future—there are only two ways of answering these questions: One is, when a moment for sexual decision descends on us, to rely on inspiration, intuition, or impulse and hope for a good answer, one we can feel comfortable with for the rest of our lives. The second is to develop a set of moral values that we would choose for governing all our life's actions and relationships, including the sexual ones. Once we are aware of what these values are, and have accepted them for ourselves, nothing should be able to catch us off base; that extraordinary computer, our brain, can sort out the elements in any decision we face, including a sexual one, test these elements against the values we have set for ourselves, and give us an answer. That answer may not be the one we would like it to be, and so we may try to put it through the computer again. But we must face the results of our reasoning process honestly, and this is where knowing one's self is so important. How good are you at accepting responsibility for your actions, at being aware of how what you do or think can affect others? If you drop your clothes on the floor and walk over them, who is affected if you live alone? If you have a roommate? If you buy your clothes out of money you earn? If your parents buy them?

To be involved with others every day in our activities is inevitable, and the involvement is tinged with sexuality, for we relate to each other never as a non-woman or a non-girl or a non-man or a non-boy but always, in part, as the sexual person we are, female or male. How we relate, though, depends on the kind of person each of us is—dependable or not dependable, honest or cheating, willing or unwilling to take advantage of others, caring or not caring, open to learning or closed to it. And the kinds of people we are is always reflected in the way we go about making our decisions, especially those that affect other people's lives.

There are certain ethical principles that are basic to all the great religions: respect for human life and dignity; putting yourself in the other's place; modifying your actions and demands to fit the rights and needs of others even though this may interfere with or postpone your own immediate wants. The Old Testament puts it this way: "Thou shalt love thy neighbor as thyself" (Leviticus 19:18). In the New Testament, Jesus of Nazareth put it this way: "All things whatsoever ye would that men should do to you, do ye even so to them" (Matthew 7:12).

Treating others as we would like them to treat us is easier said than done, whether we're talking about little things or big things. Sex is a big thing for almost everyone, and when another person is involved, it becomes much bigger. When one knowingly risks involving not one but two persons in one's sexual life, the need to make moral decisions rather than purely selfish ones is imperative. For example, sexual activity before marriage risks pregnancy. Each year an estimated 1 million young women under the age of 19, or 1 out of 10, became pregnant, and 600,000 of these young women deliver babies. This is still happening, at the rate of almost 20,000 pregnancies every week in girls under 19—20,000 babies conceived, usually unwanted, most of whom will have to be cared for by someone other than the teenage boy and girl who begot them.

Mature thinking would have meant avoiding intercourse, or protecting against pregnancy by taking the trouble to use contraceptives because "A baby really needs two people to bring it up—a mother and a father who can take care of it until the age of 18 at least." Reasoning in this way would have shown awareness that their own actions did not involve just themselves but might also do harm to a third person —a baby brought into the world when they were not ready to be a real mother and father to it.

Learning how to reason in arriving at decisions can help us develop a system of moral values to rely on in making sexual decisions, not only to analyze our own reasoning processes but also to see how other people reason. Research has found that most people seem to prefer to accept a set of rules someone else has made, although they may not always be able to live up to them. Rule-minding spares such people from having to think out carefully *why* they are or are not going to do a certain thing. If the rules are good and the circumstances favorable, reasoning by rules may work.

But in a very real sense, moral decision-making, whether about one's sexual actions or about anything else, must eventually involve growing beyond unthinking obedience to rules. It requires accepting responsibility for thinking through your own wishes, needs, decisions, and actions in the light of the needs of all the other persons involved, and you must have made and tested your own rules to live by. That is your responsibility to yourself.

We can come back to the questions we posed at the beginning of this chapter: What kind of sexual person would each of us like to be—and how can each of us become that kind of person? Bound up in the answers each one of us would make to those questions are our dreams. We all have our own dreams, and so must find our own answers. Some of us will have someone in our lives to live our dreams with and to help us find answers; others of us once had that someone but no longer do; and still others have not yet found that someone, and may or may not. But to turn Shakespeare's thought around: when you play straight and caringly with all other people, you are then really being true to your own best self. And your self is the one person in the world you can count on to be there for you, no matter what.

So think of all the things you would like to have be part of your sexuality. The suggestions that follow are like pieces of a puzzle thrown on a table. Pick up your own pieces and make your own pattern, one that fits *you,* in whatever relationships you may choose to have with others, now or in the future.

Concise A-to-Z Encyclopedia

In the main chapters of this book we tell in as readable and connected a way as possible everything that members of a family might be interested in finding out about human sexuality. But people often want to know about a specific matter, and quickly. Arranged alphabetically, the items in this Encyclopedia will help you find out immediately what you need to know.

Many of the subjects in this Encyclopedia are discussed in the main part of this book more completely or in a different context. Refer to the General Index to find where else in the book a subject is discussed.

Words set in SMALL CAPITAL LETTERS the first time they appear in an entry are also separate entries in the Encyclopedia. Look them up for more information as you need to.

A

ABDOMEN. The area of the human body, both the external part and the internal cavity, that lies between the diaphragm and the PELVIS; the belly.

ABNORMAL. Not average, typical, or usual. The word is carelessly and often harmfully used to label unfavorably certain sexual behaviors or conditions of which the person doing the labeling may not approve. Two other words carelessly used as put-downs are *deviant* and *perverted.* The best word to use scientifically is *variant,* which is a neutral descriptive term meaning "different." *See also* NATURAL/UNNATURAL; NORMAL.

ABORTIFACIENT. Anything that causes an ABORTION, *-facient* coming from the Latin word *facere* (to do). The term is usually reserved for drugs or procedures specifically used to terminate a PREGNANCY after IMPLANTATION has taken place.

ABORTION. The premature expulsion or removal from the UTERUS of the products of CONCEPTION, that is, of a FERTILIZED EGG, an EMBRYO, or a FETUS. A *spontaneous abortion,* often called a MISCARRIAGE, is an abortion that occurs without intention on the part of the PREGNANT woman and without the use of any artificial method. An *induced abortion* is one intentionally brought about by medical or surgical means. A *self-induced abortion* is one deliberately brought about by the pregnant woman herself, usually by methods that are dangerous and can result in her illness or death. *Therapeutic abortion* is a medical term used for an abortion induced to protect the life or health of the prospective mother or to prevent the birth of a baby likely to be deformed or incurably diseased. *See also* DILATATION AND CURETTAGE; SALINE ABORTION; VACUUM ASPIRATION.

ABSTINENCE. To abstain from any action. With respect to sex, it generally refers to not having SEXUAL INTERCOURSE. Abstinence is one of the principal methods of CONTRACEPTION, especially by people before they are married. *Periodic abstinence* during that part of a woman's MENSTRUAL CYCLE when she is FERTILE—that is, may become PREGNANT—is the basis for the method of BIRTH CONTROL called NATURAL FAMILY PLANNING. Note that abstaining from sexual activity does not necessarily mean abstaining from sexual urges. *Permanent abstinence* (CHASTITY in the case of women or CELIBACY in the case of men) is held by some religious groups to be the only holy way to deal with one's SEXUALITY, as with nuns and priests, for example.

AC-DC. A slang term referring to BISEXUALS. It comes from the initials for the two types of electric current, alternating current and direct current.

ACNE. A condition of the skin, especially of the face, that causes pimples, often rather deep ones. It seems to be the result of the chemical changes in the body during PUBERTY, when the oil glands in the skin begin secreting increased amounts of an oily substance that clogs the pores. The condition is more common in boys than in girls and, fortunately, is usually temporary. Although it is generally more noticeable to the sufferer than to his or her friends, it can be very embarrassing while it lasts. The severity of acne can be lessened by frequent washing of the skin with soap and water, which helps to unclog the pores. If acne becomes severe (with many painful, deep swellings), infections and scars may result. Therefore, if acne persists, the young person should seek a doctor's advice about treatment. A simple well-balanced diet with ample fruits and vegetables and a minimum of sweets and fats can help reduce or avoid acne. There is no connection between acne and sexual activity, except that acne and the beginnings of desire for sexual satisfaction both happen to come at about the same time in the lives of most persons.

ADOLESCENCE. From the Latin *adolescere* (to grow up). The period of time between PUBERTY and adulthood, when a person is neither a child nor an adult but at various times behaves in ways characteristic of either or both.

ADOPTION. The process by which a person, usually a child, is legally made a part of a family into which he or she was not born. The person can be of any age from newborn up and can be a blood relative, relative by marriage, relative by out-of-wedlock birth, or unrelated. Adoption meets the needs of an unwed mother who does not want to or is unable to raise her own child and does not wish to have an ABORTION. When children are adopted, they have full legal rights as members of their adoptive family. Most adoptions in the United States are arranged through licensed social agencies, although quite a few are arranged by physicians or lawyers. Before a social agency approves an adoption, it makes a thorough investigation to be sure that the family will be a good one for a child to grow up in; in most states the child spends a trial period of from six to twelve months in the adoptive family before the adoption is made final. Adoption agencies generally agree that parents should tell their child that he or she has been adopted, although there is no agreement as to what age is best for this. Children should be told as soon as they are old enough to understand, certainly before they go to school, and they should be told as simply and naturally as possible. *See also* FOSTER PARENTS.

ADULTERY. The historic and legal term for SEXUAL INTERCOURSE between a married person and someone who is not his or her wife or husband. The term preferred today is EXTRAMARITAL sexual intercourse. Adultery was formerly one of the few grounds for DIVORCE; today, however, irreversible breakdown of the MARRIAGE is generally accepted as more realistic and humane. *See also* EXTRAMARITAL SEX.

AFFAIR. A romantic relationship, usually but not always of brief duration, between two people who are not married to each other.

AFTERBIRTH. The product of the third stage of labor, when the UTERUS expels the PLACENTA and with it the sacs or coverings that contained the AMNIOTIC FLUID in which the baby floated during GESTATION. In animals, the afterbirth is usually eaten, for it provides the mother with HORMONES that stimulate the milk flow to nourish the baby animal. In humans, the afterbirth is disposed of. The hormone needed to establish LACTATION is produced by the PITUITARY GLAND at the base of the brain.

AGING AND SEX. Though people are sexual beings all of their lives, with advancing years their sexual interest and capacity for performance tend to decline. In addition, menopause, when women lose their capacity to become PREGNANT, may bring with it the message that it is somehow no longer acceptable to enjoy sex. Actually, aging and menopause do not mean the end of sexual desire and the capacity to enjoy sexual pleasure; in fact, with no further need to bother with CONTRACEPTION, many women enjoy sexual activity even more than before. With men the peak of capacity for sexual performance is usually reached in the late teens or early twenties, with a very gradual reduction in capacity as the years pass, depending on health, circumstances, and interest. Research has proved that many women and men can and do continue to lead active sexual lives well into their seventies and beyond, especially with the availability of an interested and interesting partner, and of circumstances of privacy. Families can help by understanding and respecting the sexual interests and desires of their older members. So can friends, doctors and nurses, and directors and staffs of institutions for the elderly. Older people can be helped to realize that there are many kinds of pleasurable physical contacts besides those that lead to intercourse, and that these can be deeply satisfying expressions of love and sources of comfort: hugging, stroking, KISSING, MASTURBATING, for instance. On the other hand, some older people suffer needlessly by being made to feel that they are somehow inadequate if they are *not* sexually active. Clearly all of this should be a matter of freedom to exercise personal preference. *See also* CHANGE OF LIFE; CLIMACTERIC; MENOPAUSE.

ALCOHOL AND SEX. Many people believe that alcohol increases the SEX DRIVE and the ability to perform sexually. Actually, alcohol is a depressant, and its initial effect is to depress feelings of shyness, inhibition, and control. Thus people whose tensions, worries, and emotional conflicts about sex prevent them from relaxing and enjoying it may be helped by a modest intake of alcoholic beverage. But taking more than a moderate amount of alcohol in a sexual situation may also seriously impair judgment and good sense and cause a person to do things that he or she will later regret. For young and inexperienced persons, it is certainly foolish to mix alcohol and sex. Far from improving sexual performance, too much alcohol has actually been found to be a major cause of decreasing a man's capacity to have an ERECTION and a woman's ability to have an ORGASM. *See also* MARIJUANA.

AMNIOCENTESIS. A procedure by which a doctor inserts a hollow needle into the ABDOMEN directly through the wall of the PREGNANT UTERUS and into the AMNIOTIC FLUID surrounding the FETUS to draw out a small sample. Analysis of this fluid can in certain cases provide information important to the coming child's welfare—for instance, whether the child will be a male or female, but unless there is a very high probability of a GENDER-linked genetic disorder, the procedure is never done for this purpose, because any such procedure has certain risks: possible infection, possible damage to the fetus, and possible induced ABORTION. *See also* GENETIC COUNSELING.

AMNIOTIC FLUID. *See* AMNIOTIC SAC.

AMNIOTIC SAC. Also called the *amnion.* The thin membrane within the cavity of the UTERUS forming a closed "bag of waters" that surrounds the developing baby during PREGNANCY and cushions it from bumps and shocks. The "waters" are called *amniotic fluid* and, during LABOR, rupture of the sac allows the fluid escaping through the VAGINA to act as a LUBRICANT for the passage of the baby.

ANAL INTERCOURSE. A form of SEXUAL INTERCOURSE in which the PENIS is inserted into the partner's ANUS. It is practiced by HETEROSEXUAL as well as HOMOSEXUAL couples as one of the ways of having sexual pleasure. It is one of three forms of sexual activity to which various states apply the legal term SODOMY. Unless considerable care is taken about soap-and-water cleanliness, anal intercourse preceding VAGINAL intercourse can result in vaginal or URINARY infections.

ANAPHRODISIAC. Anything that decreases sexual desire; the opposite of an APHRODISIAC. It is usually sought by people who wish to reduce sexual activity, especially that of others. SALTPETER is the best-known supposed anaphrodisiac, but it doesn't work at all. Some tranquilizers and other drugs, and alcohol taken to excess, have anaphrodisiac effects, as does poor health. Bodily uncleanliness, mouth odors, unkindness, and anger can all be anaphrodisiacs.

ANDROGEN. The HORMONE that produces the male sex characteristics and influences the growth and development of the male body. It is also responsible for the level of the SEX DRIVE (LIBIDO) in both male and female. Derives from the Greek word *andros* (man). *See also* ESTROGEN; TESTOSTERONE.

ANDROGYNOUS. Containing or exhibiting the characteristics of both sexes; BISEXUAL, not specific to male or female. The word can refer to physical characteristics, to behavior, to clothing, etc. It is a combination of the Greek words *andros* (man) and *gynē* (woman).

ANUS. The opening in the human body leading from the lower end of the intestines to the outside. Through this opening passes the solid refuse of digestion (bowel movements, or feces) in the process called defecation. See Figure 8, p. 44.

APHRODISIAC. Any substance that is believed to stimulate SEXUAL DESIRE, such as odors (*see* PHEROMONES) or certain foods or drugs. For centuries, people have searched for substances that would increase sexual excitement, but not one has been found that works consistently or safely. It has been said that the most important sex organ is "between the ears" and that, therefore, if a person really believes a certain substance will increase sexual desire then it probably will, at least temporarily. Some substances that have enjoyed popularity over the years are potatoes, oysters, ground rhinoceros horns, pigs' testes, finely ground beetles ("SPANISH FLY," a very dangerous substance), and peanuts. Some drugs are considered by uninformed persons to be aphrodisiac when in fact they are not. The best advice is not to search for a magic aphrodisiac substance, because disappointment and possibly danger will almost certainly result. The best aphrodisiacs are good health, good diet, positive attitudes toward SEXUALITY, freedom from emotional tension, and a partner who turns you on and is turned on by you. *See also* ALCOHOL; ANAPHRODISIAC; MARIJUANA.

ARTIFICIAL INSEMINATION. The injection of SEMEN into the VAGINA or UTERUS by means of a syringe. The procedure is used to inseminate a woman who desires a child but who may be unable to have one by means of SEXUAL INTERCOURSE, perhaps because her husband's SPERM COUNT is too low or of poor quality. The semen may be collected from several EJACULATIONS by MASTURBATION, quick-frozen, and stored in a glycerine solution until sufficient sperm have been collected. Then the collection is used to inseminate the wife. If the husband produces practically no sperm at all, donor sperm from another man—who is usually anonymous—may be used, with the consent of both husband and wife. It can be taken from a SPERM BANK or directly from a donor who is known only to the physician performing the insemination, never to the woman being inseminated or to her husband.

AXILLARY HAIR. Hair under the arms. Its first appearance is one of the signs of approaching PUBERTY. Axillary hair usually appears somewhat later than the first PUBIC HAIR.

B

"BAD BLOOD." *See* SYPHILIS.

BARTHOLIN'S GLANDS. Two small GLANDS, one located at each side of the entrance to the VAGINA. During sexual excitement they may provide, in some but not all cases, a drop or two of LUBRICATION.

BASAL BODY TEMPERATURE (BBT). The usual body temperature. In many but not all cases, the BBT rises very slightly at and just after OVULATION. If a woman takes her temperature at the same time each day, preferably immediately upon waking up in the morning and before getting out of bed, and keeps a chart of her readings, she may be able to tell when she has ovulated. The BBT method of NATURAL FAMILY PLANNING is more useful for telling when ovulation *has* occurred than for predicting when it *will* occur. Minor illnesses like colds or even emotional stress can throw off the normal BBT pattern. *See also* NATURAL FAMILY PLANNING.

BESTIALITY. Engaging in SEXUAL RELATIONS with animals; also known as ZOOPHILIA. According to the KINSEY studies, 17 percent of farm men have reached ORGASM through sexual activity with animals. Whether the sexual satisfaction some men and women obtain by sexually caressing house pets or being licked by them should be labeled true bestiality is hard to say, but probably not.

BIRTH CANAL. The passage in the female body through which the baby is pushed during the process of being born, in other words, the VAGINA. It begins at the exit from the UTERUS, that is, the upper end of the cervical canal (*see* CERVIX), and ends at the outer opening of the vagina. In all, it is not more than 3 or 4 inches in length. See Figures 6 and 18a, pp. 42 and 68. The walls of the birth canal are capable of expanding greatly to accommodate the baby's head.

BIRTH CONTROL. *See* CONTRACEPTION.

BIRTH RATE. The number of births each year per 1,000 population. In the United States in 1980 it was 14.7; in West Germany, 9.8; and in Nigeria, 49.3. Comparing the birth rate with the death rate, one can figure the rate of population increase (or decrease). In the United States, for the same year the death rate was 8.9; in West Germany, 11.9; and in Nigeria, 22.7. Thus the net population increase rate for the three countries was 5.8, -2.2, and 26.3, respectively. Any good yearly almanac gives up-to-date figures for the major nations of the world.

BISEXUAL. Sexual attraction to people both of one's own sex and the other sex, or a person so attracted. It is likely that most people in their FANTASIES, even though not in their actual sexual behavior, have bisexual potentiality. People who are bisexual may vary in the kind of bisexuality, at times preponderantly active with their own sex, at other times preponderantly active with the other sex. Only rarely does an absolute fifty-fifty situation exist at all times. *See also* HETEROSEXUAL-HOMOSEXUAL BEHAVIOR RATING SCALE.

BLADDER (URINARY). An expandable, muscular sac into which the two kidneys secrete urine through tubes called *ureters*. The urine is accumulated in the bladder until the sensation of pressure leads to emptying by urination through the URETHRA. The opening and closing of the urethra is controlled by two muscles, the internal and the external urinary sphincters. The urinary bladder is not related to the gallbladder. *See also* CYSTITIS.

BREAST-FEEDING. *See* NURSING.

BREASTS. Two milk-producing organs on a woman's chest, known also as *mammary glands*. The breasts contain many lobules (sacs) which, after a woman gives birth and is NURSING her baby, manufacture milk. The milk is led by many small ducts to a small reservoir just under the NIPPLE, so the baby has a constant supply to suck. As the time for giving birth approaches, the breasts' glandular tissue increases to supply more milk. Women with small breasts are just as successful at nursing their babies as those with large breasts. The pink or brown area surrounding the nipple is called the *areola*. The breasts of both men and woman are EROGENOUS ZONES. In our society there is preoccupation with breast size as a symbol of the supposed sexiness of a woman. There is, however, absolutely no relation between the size of a woman's breasts and the degree of her SEX DRIVE. Preoccupation with breast size on the part of both women and men is unfortunate, since it is unconnected with the meaningful aspects of relationships between them, sexual and otherwise. *See also* NURSING.

BROTHEL. A house of PROSTITUTION.

BUTCH. A slang term for a female HOMOSEXUAL who tends to dress and behave in a MASCULINE manner.

C

CALENDAR METHOD. A method of NATURAL FAMILY PLANNING based on a woman's carefully keeping a record of the dates each MENSTRUAL PERIOD begins. Theoretically, this enables her to estimate when OVULATION will occur, so that she knows when to abstain from SEXUAL INTERCOURSE if she does not wish to become PREGNANT. The method works fairly satisfactorily only for those women with a regular MENSTRUAL CYCLE. However, absolute menstrual regularity can rarely be counted on, since stress, fatigue, or even a cold can unexpectedly lengthen or shorten the cycle. *See also* NATURAL FAMILY PLANNING.

CALL GIRL. A PROSTITUTE with whom an appointment may be arranged by a telephone call.

CARNAL. A word deriving from the Latin word *carnalis* (fleshly). Generally used in the sense of "having to do with the pleasures of the flesh," principally sexual activity. "Carnal knowledge" means SEXUAL INTERCOURSE, especially in legal or biblical language.

CASTRATE. To remove the SEX GLANDS—the TESTICLES in a male, the OVARIES in a female. Castration of males used to be a method of STERILIZATION, but VASECTOMY has taken its place. Castration has also been used as punishment for sex criminals, and it still is in some of the less developed parts of the world. Castration can be necessary to save the life of a man who develops cancer of the testicles, and this usually results in the loss of SEXUAL DESIRE. Also, because the body of a castrated man no longer receives the

HORMONES produced by the testicles, his voice may become higher, his beard sparser, and he may gain weight. Hormone replacement therapy that might correct these conditions cannot be used if the original reason for the castration was cancer of the testicle or of the PROSTATE.

CELIBACY. Voluntary ABSTINENCE from SEXUAL INTERCOURSE. Historically there has been a strong current in Christianity and in some other religions to attribute the nobility and holiness to the celibate way of life. Catholic priests and nuns take vows of celibacy. *See also* ABSTINENCE.

CERVIX. The lower end or neck of the UTERUS that constitutes the passage between the uterus and the VAGINA. SPERM pass upward through the cervix and into the uterus during and after SEXUAL INTERCOURSE, unless certain methods of CONTRACEPTION block the passage. In the other direction, from uterus to vagina, pass the MENSTRUAL FLOW and, during birth, the baby. The cervix's powerful muscle holds the FETUS in the uterus until birth, when it relaxes to become an extraordinarily flexible passageway.

CESAREAN BIRTH. *See* CESAREAN SECTION.

CESAREAN SECTION. Also, *Cesarean birth.* Delivery of a child by means of a surgical incision through the ABDOMINAL wall and the UTERUS. A cesarean is performed when the doctor determines that childbirth via the BIRTH CANAL may be dangerous to the mother or the baby. This might be because the mother's bony PELVIC opening is too small or the baby's head too large to permit a normal birth, or because the baby is positioned in the uterus in such a way that the birth would be very difficult. In the United States, from 10 to 15 percent of all births are cesarean, and cesarean babies develop just as well as those born the usual way. A mother may have several children by this means, or occasionally a cesarean birth may be followed at another time by a normal birth. (The name cesarean comes from that of Roman Emperor Julius Caesar, who according to tradition was born by this method.)

CHANCROID. One of the sexually transmitted diseases (*see* VENEREAL DISEASES). Occurs most often in men. Also called *soft chancre,* as distinguished from the firm, "hard" chancre of SYPHILIS. *Cause:* bacteria *(Hemophilus ducreyi). Symptoms:* one or more shallow, painful sores on the GENITALS which bleed easily. Usually causes painful enlargement of lymph nodes in the GROIN, which may break open and drain pus. *Time from contact to first symptoms:* one week or less. *Method of diagnosis:* microscopic examination. *Complications:* can destroy tissues of the genitals.

CHANGE OF LIFE. A now rather old-fashioned term for MENOPAUSE and CLIMACTERIC. Change of life refers mainly to that time when a woman ceases to OVULATE and MENSTRUATE, commonly between forty-five and fifty-five years of age. Many people used to assume that along with a woman's loss of capacity to become PREGNANT went a loss of SEXUAL DESIRE and attractiveness. Now we know that this is not necessarily so. *See also* AGING AND SEX; CLIMACTERIC; MENOPAUSE.

CHANGE OF VOICE. The lowering of the voice in boys during PUBERTY. Increased male HORMONE from the TESTICLES makes the voice box grow larger, resulting in a lower voice. At the same time, the ADOLESCENT boy's whole body usually undergoes a rapid spurt of growth. Most commonly, the change of voice becomes noticeable some time after a boy's first EJACULATION of SEMEN. While a boy is adjusting to his new voice, he has a tendency toward sudden, brief breaks into falsetto. This experience should not be, but too often is, cause for embarrassing jokes and laughter by those who hear it. Females have a similar deepening and maturing of the voice at puberty, but not in such an obvious way.

CHASTITY. The state of being chaste; abstention from SEXUAL INTERCOURSE. The word comes from the Latin *caste* (pure, clean), and it implies a connection between sex and impurity or uncleanness, as if not having had sex means being pure and clean. The word is most commonly used in reference to women—nuns take vows of chastity, monks and priests vows of CELIBACY. In the Middle Ages some women wore iron chastity belts, locked on by the husband to prevent his wife from having sexual intercourse during his absence.

CHILD MOLESTER. A person, usually a man, HETEROSEXUAL or HOMOSEXUAL, who seeks sexual satisfaction from physical contact with young girls or boys. Often the children are not aware of what is really happening, for the molestation may be only simple touching of the GENITALS. Molesters behave compulsively in this respect and need help, but they are rarely dangerous. Most often they are older relatives or friends rather than strangers. Young people will do well to steer clear of contact or being alone with such people, and to go immediately to someone they can trust, to tell them about the experience. It will probably make them feel better, and it may make it possible for the molester to get help. A young person can be helped to know that the molesting was not his or her fault and that there is no reason to feel guilty about it. Child molestation is a crime against a minor (defined by the American Law Institute as a person under age sixteen), provided the molester is at least four years older than the child. *See also* PEDOPHILIA.

CHILD PROSTITUTION. Selling the sexual services of children, male or female. *See also* PROSTITUTION.

CHROMOSOMES. Minute rod-shaped bodies in the nucleus of every living cell. The number and shapes of the chromosomes are characteristic for each plant or animal species of life. Each chromosome carries the thousands of

GENES that determine the characteristics a person inherits from his or her parents. One pair of the chromosomes always determines the sex of the child: the female's OVUM chromosome is always X, but SPERM are of two kinds, X or Y. An X-bearing sperm uniting with the ovum (always X) will produce an XX, or female, baby. A Y-bearing sperm uniting with the X ovum will produce an XY, or male, baby. Thus it is the sperm from the male which determines the sex of the baby. *See also* HEREDITY.

CIRCUMCISION. A minor operation that removes the FORESKIN of a boy's or man's PENIS. In the United States it is usually done on the second day after birth. The operation is performed for reasons of cleanliness and, among Jews and Muslims, for religious reasons. Research has not shown that circumcision in any way affects later sexual response.

CLAP. *See* GONORRHEA.

CLIMACTERIC. The group of physical and psychological changes that occur around the time of MENOPAUSE in women, which is the time of reduced production of ESTROGEN, or female sex HORMONE. Climacteric, a very difficult phenomenon to define, both as to time and effects, can show itself in a combination of ills and miseries, both physical and emotional. In women, emotional effects are mostly related to loss of feelings of sexual adequacy. In some men, similar effects can be traced to a feared loss of sexual attractiveness and power, especially in those segments of our society that are highly competitive. *See also* AGING AND SEX; CHANGE OF LIFE; MENOPAUSE.

CLIMAX. The high point of sexual excitement and pleasure—whether during SEXUAL INTERCOURSE, SEX PLAY, MASTURBATION, FANTASY or dreaming —when ORGASM is reached.

CLITORIS. The small, very sensitive, erectile organ in the female, located just in front of the opening of the URETHRA and under a hood at the top of the small lips of the VULVA. It becomes ERECT when the female is sexually stimulated. The nerve endings in the clitoris are quite similar to those in the head (GLANS) of the PENIS. Pleasurable stimulation of the clitoris is an important part of the process by which a woman reaches ORGASM. See Figure 8, p. 44.

CLONING. A technique in which the nucleus of an OVUM is replaced with the nucleus of a body cell, the "donor" cell, and the resulting EMBRYO develops into an exact copy, or clone, of the donor. A "donor" cell can come from either a male or a female, and no SPERM is involved. The ovum with its new nucleus is placed within the WOMB of the "host" mother to develop in the usual way. Cloning can be done with simple forms of life such as frogs but not at present with mammals (including human beings), despite rumors and stories to the contrary.

COHABITATION. Literally, living together. In terms of human sexuality, the term usually refers to a couple (sometimes more people than a couple) who live together, having SEXUAL INTERCOURSE, as a way of discovering whether or not they wish to marry. But many couples these days cohabit simply as a matter of pleasure and convenience, with no commitment to serious consideration of MARRIAGE.

COITUS. *See* SEXUAL INTERCOURSE.

COITUS INTERRUPTUS. *See* WITHDRAWAL METHOD.

COLOSTRUM. The substance ready in the BREAST of a mother immediately after birth, even before the infant has suckled. It is slight in amount, yellowish and watery but rich in protein, and helps the digestive system to begin normal functioning. It also provides the infant with immunity to infectious diseases during its first few months. Within two or three days after birth, the baby's sucking stimulates the breast GLANDS to make true milk that is more nutritious.

COMMON-LAW MARRIAGE. A MARRIAGE without a religious or civil ceremony, or a license, in which, after a certain number of years (differing from state to state), a couple which has been living together as wife and husband is considered, by law and by the community, to be legally married.

CONCEIVE. *See* CONCEPTION.

CONCEPTION. FERTILIZATION, the moment at which the SPERM and OVUM join, at which the woman is said to have *conceived.*

CONDOM. (Also called *rubber, prophylactic, safety.*) A sheath, usually made of rubber, which is placed over the ERECT PENIS before SEXUAL INTERCOURSE to prevent the EJACULATED SPERM from entering the VAGINA. If properly used, it is a very effective method of CONTRACEPTION and also provides good protection against VENEREAL DISEASES.

CONTRACEPTION. The use of any device (CONDOMS, IUD'S, DIAPHRAGMS), the PILL, VAGINAL SPERMICIDES, or action (WITHDRAWAL or NATURAL FAMILY PLANNING) designed to prevent CONCEPTION. Another term for contraception is *birth control.*

CONTRACEPTIVE. A device or medication used to prevent CONCEPTION. *See also* CONTRACEPTION.

COPULATION. SEXUAL INTERCOURSE. The term copulation is usually used to refer to the sexual activity of animals, sexual intercourse being used to refer to that of people.

CORPUS LUTEUM. Yellow cells in the OVARY which develop in the GRAAFIAN FOLLICLE after it has expelled the OVUM by OVULATION. The corpus luteum (Latin for "yellow body") secretes the HORMONE PROGESTERONE that helps prepare the UTERUS for receiving the FERTILIZED ovum and maintaining the PREGNANCY.

COUNSELING. The formal or informal process by which a professional who has been trained in counseling talks with a person, couple, or family to help them become aware of and solve or manage their problems. Besides sex counseling, there are a number of kinds of counseling that might be related to human sexuality: MARRIAGE counseling, singles counseling, ABORTION counseling, CONTRACEPTIVE counseling, RAPE counseling, and various combinations of these. A distinction is usually made between the skills of counseling and those of THERAPY and the training necessary for each.

COURTSHIP. The period before MARRIAGE when, in traditional terms, a man woos a woman in the attempt to persuade her to marry him. In different cultures the forms of courtship vary greatly and in many are quite strictly defined and prescribed. In the United States, the practice of formal courtship has largely disappeared, although a period of developing acquaintance between the prospective mates is still common and undoubtedly important.

COWPER'S GLANDS. Two GLANDS in the male, one on each side of the URETHRA near the PROSTATE GLAND. Cowper's glands secrete a slippery substance which becomes a part of the SEMEN and which sometimes oozes down the urethra after ERECTION of the PENIS and LUBRICATES its tip.

CRAB LICE. A sexually transmitted insect that lives in the warm, wet folds of the body and lays eggs on the PUBIC HAIR. Also called *pediculosis pubis, crabs, cooties, lice. Cause:* tiny lice and eggs (or "nits"); lice barely visible, nits invisible. *Symptoms:* intense itching, especially in pubic hair; pinhead blood spots on underwear. *Time from contact to first symptoms:* four to five weeks. *Method of diagnosis:* examination. *Complications:* none. *See also* VENEREAL DISEASES.

CRABS. *See* CRAB LICE.

CREAM. *See* SPERMICIDE.

CROSS-DRESSING. *See* TRANSVESTITE.

CRUSH. A brief, romantic fixation or infatuation, often by a younger person toward an older person. Quite commonly the older person is entirely unaware that the younger "has a crush on" him or her. Crushes can be same-sex or other-sex. The concept of and behavior involved in the crush seems to some people old-fashioned, but it still happens.

CUCKOLD. An almost obsolete term of mockery for a husband whose wife is committing ADULTERY, when he is said to be cuckolded.

CULDOSCOPY. *See* LAPAROSCOPY.

CUNNILINGUS. The act of using the tongue or mouth to stimulate the VULVA of a female, one sort of ORAL SEX, a common practice for both HETEROSEXUAL and female HOMOSEXUAL couples. The word derives from two Latin words, *cunnus* (vulva) and *lingere* (to lick). *See also* FELLATIO; ORAL-GENITAL SEX.

CURETTAGE. Emptying the UTERUS by means of a curette, a spoonlike instrument used for scraping. *See also* DILATATION AND CURETTAGE.

CYSTITIS. Infection and inflammation of the BLADDER caused by invasion of the bladder by bacteria, usually through the URETHRA. The symptoms are painful (burning) and frequent urination. It should always be treated by a doctor. Cystitis is more common in women than in men, because a woman's urethra is very short and therefore bacteria can easily and quickly enter the bladder.

D

D & C. *See* DILATATION AND CURETTAGE.

DEATH RATE. *See* BIRTH RATE.

DEFLORATION. The tearing of the HYMEN during first SEXUAL INTERCOURSE. An equivalent term is *deflowering*. Both terms, now somewhat old-fashioned, used to signify that a woman had been deprived of the "flower" of her VIRGINITY.

DELIVERY. The act of giving birth to a child, including the assistance given to the woman while she is delivering.

DEPRESSION. A state of feeling downcast, gloomy, lacking initiative or energy. Almost everyone feels depressed from time to time, often without any easily recognized reason for it. Some women feel depressed at certain times during their MENSTRUAL CYCLES, most often during the days just before MENSTRUATION or while MENSTRUATING. Also, many women suffer from POSTPARTUM DEPRESSION, or "postpartum blues," a brief period of feeling low and discouraged during the week or ten days after childbirth. Depression during the period of MENOPAUSE is common too, as it is also after a terrifying and traumatic experience such as RAPE. In relation to human sexuality, almost any frustrating or difficult problem, and many of the chemical changes in the human body, can cause depression. If depression is severe, frequent, or of long duration, the depressed person would be wise to seek COUNSELING. Most periods of depression, however, are brief and easily dealt with.

DES. Diethylstilbestrol, a strong ESTROGEN which used to be prescribed as a "MORNING-AFTER" CONTRACEPTIVE. Because of the danger of harm to the female offspring of women who took it while PREGNANT, it is no longer used.

DESIRE. *See* SEXUAL DESIRE.

DEVIATION. A sexual behavior that is considered by the user of the word to be not "NORMAL." Deviation and sexual deviancy tend to be put-down terms. Terms that are more scientific and less judgmental ones are *variance* or *variant see also* ABNORMAL; VARIANT SEXUAL BEHAVIOR.

DIAPHRAGM. A CONTRACEPTIVE device—a round rubber cap—about 2 to 3 inches in diameter, which a woman places in her VAGINA to cover the CERVIX before having SEXUAL INTERCOURSE. Used with a SPERMICIDE (cream, jelly, or foam), it prevents SPERM from entering the cervix.

DIKE. Also *dyke.* A slang term for a female HOMOSEXUAL, or LESBIAN, generally referring to a homosexual woman who assumes a MASCULINE role. The concept of male and female roles among homosexual couples is far less common today than a few years ago. *See also* BUTCH.

DILATATION AND CURETTAGE. Often called *D & C.* Stretching open the CERVIX to permit surgical curettage, which means scraping out the lining of the UTERUS and any contents of the uterus. There are three primary reasons for a D & C: to diagnose possible disease, to correct habitual heavy bleeding during MENSTRUATION, and to perform an ABORTION. For abortion, the method has now been largely replaced by VACUUM ASPIRATION.

DILDO. An artificial ERECT PENIS. Dildoes are used by a man who is unable to achieve an ERECTION so as to give pleasure to his partner, or by a woman for self-stimulation during MASTURBATION, or by two women for mutual stimulation.

DISABILITIES AND SEX. Many people with disabilities tend to be regarded as not being sexual, having neither legitimate sexual needs nor the capacity for sexual enjoyment. This view is contrary to fact, and today it is recognized that regardless of the nature of the disability, such people need special help. With such guidance they may enjoy the sexuality that is legitimately theirs in the way most appropriate to their life situation and without harm to themselves or others. Medical schools have special services for rehabilitation of people with disabilities, including sexual rehabilitation.

DIVORCE. In the legal dissolution of a MARRIAGE, divorce releases both the husband and wife from all marital obligations to each other and returns them to the single state.

DNA. Deoxyribonucleic acid, a chemical substance making up the GENES that are carried on the CHROMOSOMES and that determine the inherited characteristics specific for each living organism.

DOPE. *See* MARIJUANA.

DOSE. *See* GONORRHEA.

DOUBLE STANDARD. The concept that there is one standard of sexual behavior for men and another for women. In the traditional double standard, society has tended to view PREMARITAL or EXTRAMARITAL SEX as acceptable for men but not for women, and to expect that men will actively seek many sexual contacts, whereas "nice" women will limit sex to marriage. The double standard is much less widely accepted in the United States now than it was a generation ago, but it still persists, often in subtle forms, despite the efforts of believers in equality of sexual rights, pleasures, and obligations to eradicate it. *See also* SEXISM.

DOUCHING. Cleansing or rinsing the VAGINA with a jet of liquid, usually squirted from a douche bag or syringe. A totally ineffective means of CONTRACEPTION, and unnecessary in the healthy vagina.

DREAMS. Images, thoughts, emotions, and imagined happenings that pass through the mind during sleep. Many dreams are sexual, either directly or symbolically, and the psychoanalyst Sigmund FREUD was a pioneer in the effort to interpret dreams. Everyone dreams—everyone must dream—even though many dreams are not remembered after people wake up. Periodic ERECTIONS in men and VAGINAL LUBRICATION in women do occur in sleep, and ORGASM in both may occur during dreams. Many young boys at PUBERTY and during ADOLESCENCE also experience "WET DREAMS," during which they have a sexual dream and awaken to find that they have EJACULATED. *See also* NOCTURNAL EMISSION.

DRIP. *See* GONORRHEA.

DRIVE. *See* SEXUAL DESIRE; LIBIDO.

DYSFUNCTION. When used in connection with sexuality, the term means a problem that interferes with or prevents a satisfying sexual life. (The prefix *dys-* comes from a Greek word or affix meaning "bad" or "ill.") The most common sexual dysfunctions are in the male IMPOTENCE and PREMATURE EJACULATION, and in the female DYSPAREUNIA (painful SEXUAL INTERCOURSE), VAGINISMUS, and inability to reach ORGASM.

DYSMENORRHEA. Literally, painful MENSTRUATION, which may involve cramps, headache, backache, and nausea. The cramps are probably caused by spasms of the muscles of the UTERUS or CERVIX. In most cases, dysmenorrhea disappears after the age of twenty or after the birth of a woman's first child.

DYSPAREUNIA. Painful SEXUAL INTERCOURSE. The most common cause is fear, tension, and anxiety accompanying intercourse which can make the VAGINAL muscles tighten. There are several medical causes possible that should be diagnosed only by a GYNECOLOGIST.

E

ECTOPIC PREGNANCY. A PREGNANCY that implants somewhere outside the UTERUS in the ABDOMINAL cavity. A pregnancy in a FALLOPIAN TUBE is known as a *tubal pregnancy.* The *ectopic* means "out of place," from the Greek words *ec* (out) and *topos* (place). The most common cause of ectopic pregnancies is scar tissue in the fallopian tubes that is the result of an infection by GONORRHEA or other bacteria, so blocking the passage that, even if the SPERM can proceed up the tube, the much larger FERTILIZED OVUM is unable to pass down it and into the uterus to IMPLANT. An ectopic pregnancy is very painful and may cause death of the mother from bleeding, especially if the fallopian tube ruptures. It must be recognized early and terminated by surgery to avoid this.

EFFEMINACY. A term used to describe male behavior that appears as a caricature of FEMININITY.

EGG. *See* OVUM.

EJACULATE. To eject SEMEN from the PENIS at the male CLIMAX resulting from SEXUAL INTERCOURSE, MASTURBATION, NOCTURNAL EMISSION, or other sexual activity. Ejaculation comes in a series of quick spurts caused mainly by contractions of the PROSTATE GLAND and the muscles around it, as well as the muscles at the base of the penis. In a healthy man, one ejaculation contains about a teaspoonful of semen containing from 150 to 600 million SPERM.

ELECTRA COMPLEX. The feelings of EROTIC attachment that, according to FREUD's theory of psychosexual development, a young girl, usually age three to five, experiences for her father. (In Greek mythology, Electra was the daughter of Agamemnon, King of Mycenae.) *See also* OEDIPUS COMPLEX.

EMBRYO. The unborn young from the time of IMPLANTATION in the UTER-INE wall until, in human beings, about the end of the second month of PREGNANCY, after which it is known as a FETUS.

ENCOUNTER GROUPS. A group of people who meet under the leadership of a COUNSELOR or THERAPIST who, through a series of close interactions with each other involving the relatively free expression of thoughts and feelings, are helped to understand and so resolve problems of personal relationships, many of which may be closely connected with the sexual aspects of living.

ENDOCRINE GLANDS. In contrast to GLANDS such as the salivary glands that deliver their product through ducts, the endocrine glands secrete their products, called HORMONES, directly into the bloodstream. The PITUITARY, adrenal, and thyroid glands are among these, as are the TESTICLES and OVARIES, which secrete the sex hormones TESTOSTERONE and ESTROGEN, respectively.

ENDOMETRIUM. The soft, velvety lining of the UTERUS, richly supplied with small blood vessels. Into this the FERTILIZED EGG implants itself and begins its development. If no egg is implanted, the lining, along with the blood and blood vessels that are a part of it, are discarded monthly through the process called MENSTRUATION.

ENGAGEMENT. A period during which a man and a woman have a formal understanding that they will be married at some time in the future. Engagement is usually marked by the gift of a ring from the man to the woman. It is looked upon as a period during which the betrothed (engaged) couple become better acquainted with each other as preparation for their eventual MARRIAGE.

EPIDIDYMIS. (plural, epididymides). A collection of about a half mile of extraordinarily tiny tubes coiled behind and against each TESTICLE. In these tubes the SPERM that have been manufactured by the testicles are stored, to mature before they pass into the VAS DEFERENS, ready for EJACULATION. See Fig. 2, p. 36. *See also* SEMEN.

EPISIOTOMY. A small surgical incision made in the PERINEUM, usually toward the end of the second stage of LABOR. This is done to enlarge the VAGINAL opening and thus prevent the tissues from being overstretched and possibly tearing as the child's head emerges. After DELIVERY, while awaiting the AFTERBIRTH, the OBSTETRICIAN stitches the episiotomy. Such clean incisions heal faster than would an accidental tear in the tissues.

ERECTION. Erection occurs when, during sexual stimulation, a supply of blood becomes temporarily trapped in the spongy tissues of a usually limp

SEX ORGAN. Such stiffening and enlargement of the PENIS usually occurs as a result of sexual excitement. The CLITORIS also becomes erect during sexual stimulation, as do the NIPPLES. When the erection is over, the blood supply returns to the body. One interesting fact about male erection is that penises that are varying sizes when they are not erect all tend to approach approximately the same size in erection. Many boys and men, whose unerect penises vary in size, often worry unnecessarily about this, especially if their penises appear small in comparison to those of others. In any case, a large erect penis is a no more effective giver of pleasure, or of SEMEN and PREGNANCY, than a somewhat smaller erect penis. The area of the VAGINA in which the pleasure-giving nerve endings are located is the lower part, and whatever the size of the erect penis, it will stimulate that area.

EROGENOUS ZONES. These are the areas of the body which are especially sensitive to sexual excitement, such as the GENITALS, the BREASTS, the mouth, and the inside of the thighs. People vary in their responses, however, and almost any part of the body if touched or stroked in a sensual manner can prove to be an erogenous zone.

EROS. The ancient Greek god of love. When not capitalized, eros refers to SENSUAL love or SEXUAL DESIRE. The ancient Romans called this god Cupid.

EROTIC. Having to do with arousing SEXUAL DESIRE. Erotic material is anything—prose, poetry, pictures, music, perfume, etc.—that causes, or is designed to cause, sexual arousal. *See* EXPLICIT SEXUAL MATERIALS; PORNOGRAPHY.

ESTROGEN. One of two HORMONES produced by the OVARIES. It is the hormone that produces the female sex characteristics and affects the way a woman's MENSTRUAL CYCLE functions. Synthetic estrogen is one of the chemicals in the contraceptive PILL which mimics the state of PREGNANCY and therefore suppresses her OVULATION. Synthetic estrogen can be prescribed for older women during MENOPAUSE, when their ovaries cease to produce natural estrogen, to reduce the physical and psychological effects of menopause. Its use after menopause is still open to question by physicians, who are not sure yet what the long-term effects may be.

EUGENICS. A science that attempts to improve the quality of future generations by controlling HEREDITARY factors, by identifying people who ought or ought not to be encouraged to have children. It is not a well-developed science and remains highly controversial, since it involves making judgments about the relative worth of various kinds of people.

EUNUCH. A CASTRATED male, that is, one whose TESTICLES have been removed. The word derives from the Greek words *eun* (bed) and *-ouchos* (keeping) and literally meant "guardian of the bed," when eunuchs were often used as guards of the women in harems.

EXHIBITIONIST. In the SEXUAL sense, a male who feels a compulsion to expose his PENIS publicly and who derives sexual satisfaction from so doing. Exhibitionists are almost always harmless and tend to keep a safe distance from their "victims." However, their activity often is disturbing and frightening to people who do not understand it, and to most people it is upsetting. Exhibitionism is a minor crime and more of a nuisance than a menace.

EXPLICIT SEXUAL MATERIALS. This is the term preferred today to describe printed and audiovisual materials that are designed to be EROTIC in nature and to which the term PORNOGRAPHY is applied by some. The word *explicit* means clear, detailed, and unreserved. *See also* PORNOGRAPHY.

EXTRAMARITAL SEX. SEXUAL INTERCOURSE by a married person with someone other than his or her SPOUSE. The legal and religious term for it is ADULTERY. It should not be confused with PREMARITAL SEX (strictly speaking, sex before MARRIAGE between two people who expect to marry each other) and NONMARITAL SEX (sex between two unmarried people who do not expect to marry each other). Premarital sex is today most frequently heard to describe sexual relationships between teenagers and young adults who have no intention of marrying each other.

F

FALLOPIAN TUBE. The tube or duct that extends from near each OVARY to the UTERUS. After an OVUM has been produced by the ovary, the FIMBRIA and the tiny cilia of the tube wave it into the entrance and transport it toward the uterus. If on the way the ovum meets a SPERM, FERTILIZATION takes place and it begins its cell division and continues its trip down the tube, dividing into more and more cells as it goes. The tubes are from 4 to 8 inches long. At the uterine end, the passage is between $\frac{1}{16}$ and $\frac{1}{8}$ inch in diameter, about twenty times larger than an unfertilized ovum, so that it allows the already larger fertilized ovum (or ZYGOTE) to pass through into the uterus where it can IMPLANT. See Figure 6, p. 42.

FAMILY. Most commonly, parents and their children. However, the definition of family can be broadened to include people of several generations related by ties of blood (or ADOPTION), including parents, children, aunts, uncles, grandparents, cousins, and so forth. Because of many new patterns of living developing today, any couple or group of people, of either sex, who have decided to live together and to care for each other on a permanent or long-term basis needs also to be considered a family in the broader sense of the term.

FAMILY PLANNING. Another term for BIRTH CONTROL or CONTRACEPTION. It consists of planning by a couple for the number of children they wish to have and for how far apart they should be spaced.

FANTASY. In sexual terms, fantasy means imagining scenes and events, usually SEXUAL and romantic, that rarely are actually carried out. Most people's sexual lives involve a lot of fantasy, though many feel needlessly guilty about it, for fantasies or dreams cannot be controlled and therefore we are not responsible for these. Rather it is our actions for which we are responsible and which we need to learn to manage. For most people, an active sexual fantasy life is a harmless, indeed beneficial, way of enriching their sexual satisfaction.

FELLATIO. Taking the PENIS into the mouth to give sexual satisfaction, one sort of ORAL SEX. It is common practice for both HETEROSEXUAL and male HOMOSEXUAL couples. See also CUNNILINGUS; ORAL-GENITAL SEX.

FEMININITY. The quality of being "feminine," as distinguished from "masculine," the characteristics of either of which vary with each society. Whether or not there are special universal characteristics to femininity or MASCULINITY—and if there are, the extent to which these are inborn or learned—is a matter of discussion and controversy today. See also EFFEMINACY; FEMINISM; GENDER ROLE; MASCULINITY; SEXISM.

FEMINISM. Advocacy of legal, social, political, economic, and sexual rights of women to be equal to those of men. A feminist is a person, male or female, who advocates feminism. Another term for feminism is "women's liberation" or "women's lib." The term most acceptable to most women is "the feminist movement."

FERTILE PERIOD. The days during a woman's MENSTRUAL CYCLE when she can become PREGNANT. See NATURAL FAMILY PLANNING.

FERTILITY. The state of being fertile, that is, capable of CONCEPTION. The opposite state is INFERTILITY or STERILITY.

FERTILITY AWARENESS. A term used especially by people involved in NATURAL FAMILY PLANNING. It refers to a woman's awareness that she is about to OVULATE or has ovulated.

FERTILITY RATE. The number of PREGNANCIES per year per thousand women of childbearing age. Of 1,000 such women who are having SEXUAL INTERCOURSE regularly and do absolutely nothing to prevent pregnancy, approximately 800 will be pregnant by the end of a year.

FERTILITY TESTING. Various tests made to determine whether a man is capable of producing sufficient healthy SPERM to IMPREGNATE, or whether a woman is producing an OVUM every month so she can be impregnated.

FERTILIZATION. The moment of union of OVUM and SPERM which results in CONCEPTION.

FETISHISM. A VARIANT sexual activity which has fixated sexual response by a male on some object or part of the body as necessary to reach sexual satisfaction or ORGASM. Objects commonly so used are a foot or a shoe or rubber boot, female underwear, or a lock of hair.

FETUS. The unborn young from the beginning of the third month after CONCEPTION until birth. Before the third month, it is called an EMBRYO.

FIMBRIA. The fingerlike fringes at the ends of the FALLOPIAN TUBES nearest the OVARIES. After OVULATION the fimbria wave the OVUM into the tube for its journey to the UTERUS. See Figure 6, p. 42. See also FALLOPIAN TUBE.

FOAM. See SPERMICIDE.

FOLLICLE. See CORPUS LUTEUM; GRAAFIAN FOLLICLE.

FOREPLAY. The beginning stages of SEXUAL INTERCOURSE during which the partners kiss, caress, and stimulate each other before the PENIS enters the VAGINA, in other words, SEX PLAY before INTERCOURSE. One problem with such sex play may be that one partner interprets it as a preliminary to intercourse, which he or she expects will occur, while the other may think that it is merely touching and caressing for their own sake and not really foreplay at all. Another even more serious problem is the failure of one partner, usually the male, to understand the importance of foreplay before sexual intercourse begins, in order that both partners may be ready—that is, the woman aroused, the vagina LUBRICATED, the penis ERECT. See also SEX PLAY.

FORESKIN. The skin covering the tip of the PENIS, which is drawn back when the penis undergoes ERECTION. Another term for foreskin is *prepuce.*

FORNICATION. SEXUAL INTERCOURSE between two unmarried people. Fornication is still a crime in some states in the United States, although it is rarely prosecuted. It is not legally the same as ADULTERY.

FOSTER PARENTS. People who provide a home and care for a child whose needs cannot be met by its own family. In most states, foster parents must be licensed and satisfy state agencies that they will meet the state's standards for a good home. Usually the state pays all or part of the added cost involved in foster child care. Often foster children are returned to their own parents when conditions improve. Foster children do not have the same legal rights as adopted children. *See also* ADOPTION.

FREE LOVE. A now outdated term still used by some to refer to a sexual relationship between two people not married to each other and of which the person using the term disapproves. This term is too vague to be useful. Free love should not be confused with freedom *in* love or with the freedom (as well as the responsibilities and exchanges) with which many people today enter into a long-term, loving, committed relationship or a MARRIAGE. *See also* ADULTERY; COHABITATION.

FRENCH KISS. A KISS involving the use of the tongue within another's mouth for erotic pleasure. Although it is called "French," it is not now, nor was it ever, limited to France. In some societies people consider even an ordinary kiss to be an impropriety. *See also* KISSING.

FREUD, SIGMUND (1856–1939). The Austrian neurologist who developed the theory and practice of psychoanalysis and was one of the first widely known professionals to recognize the all-pervading influence of human sexuality on our lives and behavior, especially that of infant and childhood sexuality. Many people mistakenly equate Freud and sex, as if he had somehow invented it. What he did was to make us more aware of it and help us to understand its power, and its pervasiveness of all human life processes, of which we are often not aware. Later physicians, psychiatrists, psychologists, and scientists have developed Freud's theories, which are far from being universally accepted at present.

FRIGIDITY. A term formerly applied to the state of being unresponsive, indifferent, or cold with respect to sexual activity and especially SEXUAL INTERCOURSE; also, the state of being unable to experience sexual pleasure and ORGASM. The term has been applied primarily to women rather than to men, although there undoubtedly are some "frigid" men. Several different kinds of sexual DYSFUNCTIONS have been lumped under the term *frigidity*, but the term is now not considered scientifically useful. The preferred term is *pre-orgasmic,* meaning that the woman about whom it is being used has not yet learned how to be sexually responsive enough to experience orgasm. The possibility of learning how to reach orgasm is considered to be always there at no matter what age.

FROTTAGE. Sexually stimulating oneself from rubbing the GENITALS against something, or especially, someone. Much frottage occurs on crowded public buses and subway cars. The term comes from the French word *frotter* (to rub). The person (almost always male) who performs frottage is called a *frotteur.*

G

GAY. An informal but widely accepted term meaning HOMOSEXUAL, whether male or female. *Gay* is the term preferred by most homosexuals themselves. Used as a noun, as "He is a gay," or adjective, "She is gay." *See also* HOMOSEXUAL; LESBIAN.

GAY LIBERATION MOVEMENT. A movement, participated in by HETERO-SEXUALS as well as HOMOSEXUALS, promoting equal rights for homosexuals in all matters, legal, social, political, economic, and sexual. It is made up of a number of organizations such as the Gay Activist Alliance and the Gay Liberation Front, as well as by two older organizations, the Daughters of Bilitis and the Mattachine Society. Gay liberation is especially concerned for equal rights in employment, including the teaching and religious professions, and in private sexual expression.

GENDER. The overall term used for whether a person is male or female.

GENDER IDENTITY. The awareness a person has of being either male or female. A person's gender identity is established by how he or she is treated from the moment of birth, usually by three years at the latest. Once established, it can be destructive to the personality structure thereafter to try to alter it. *See also* TRANSSEXUAL.

GENDER ROLE. The types of behavior that a given society expects and tends to assign differently to males and females. Gender role is the public expression of GENDER IDENTITY. Traditionally, boys have been supposed to show their "MASCULINITY" by being aggressive, active, brave, and not crying, while girls were expected to show their "FEMININITY" by being passive, pleasing to others, dainty, and emotional. These behavior stereotypes are rapidly losing their strength in many segments of our society, but they still influence our behavior, for better or worse, according to the very different convictions that people still hold. *See also* SEX ROLE; SEXUAL STEREOTYPES.

GENES. Genes, the basic units of HEREDITY, are made up of DNA and are carried by the CHROMOSOMES. People's genes, which come from both their parents in the moment of FERTILIZATION, determine their inborn characteristics, which are then acted upon by environmental influences after birth. *See also* DNA; FERTILIZATION.

GENETIC COUNSELING. COUNSELING with prospective parents regarding possible hereditary diseases or conditions that may afflict a child they might CONCEIVE or have already conceived. The purpose of such counseling is to give the parents the information to help them determine whether or not to risk CONCEPTION or, if PREGNANCY has already begun, whether the FETUS is abnormal and whether or not to carry it to term if it is. There are some kinds of mental and physical defects which, if carried by one or both parents, may result in a badly defective or deformed child. *See also* ABORTION; AMNIOCENTESIS.

GENITALS. Also *genitalia.* The external SEX ORGANS. See Figure 2, p. 36 and Figure 8, p. 44.

GESTATION. The period between FERTILIZATION and birth, on the average 266 days, or about 8½ to 9 months. Since fertilization comes about two weeks after the previous MENSTRUAL FLOW begins, a woman can expect her baby about nine months after her last flow—8½ months plus two weeks.

GERMAN MEASLES. *See* RUBELLA.

GLAND. An organ that produces a secretion. Glands of internal secretion (ENDOCRINE GLANDS) have no duct but secrete directly into the bloodstream. The glands that relate to REPRODUCTION and sex and are ductless are the PITUITARY, the OVARIES, and the TESTICLES. Other sex-related glands, like the PROSTATE, COWPER'S and BARTHOLIN'S GLANDS, have ducts.

GLANS. The smooth, rounded, cone-shaped head of the PENIS. When an unCIRCUMCISED penis is limp, the glans is covered by the FORESKIN. When the penis enlarges in ERECTION, the glans is always exposed.

GONADOTROPINS. HORMONES that stimulate the OVARIES and TESTICLES in various ways. The PITUITARY GLAND produces several gonadotropins. So does the PLACENTA during PREGNANCY.

GONADS. The sex GLANDS: OVARIES in the female, TESTICLES in the male. *See also* GLAND.

GONORRHEA. Also called *clap, strain, dose, drip.* A sexually transmitted disease (*see* VENEREAL DISEASES). *Cause: gonococcus* (pl. *gonococci*) bacterium, a microscopic, double coffee-bean-shaped germ. *Symptoms:* in men, painful urination and milky, puslike discharge from the PENIS, but sometimes no symptoms; in women, usually no noticeable symptoms unless the infection spreads to the URETHRA. Therefore, it is extremely important that an infected person inform his or her sexual partner(s) so that they can be treated and not unknowingly spread the disease to still others. *Time from contact to first symptoms:* Two to ten days, sometimes as long as thirty days. *Method of diagnosis:* for men and women, examination, smear, and culture.* *Complications:* in

*Culture: a sample put onto a special gel surface called an *agar plate,* where the germs, if any, are allowed to grow for a day or two until there are enough to be looked at under a microscope and identified.

women, PELVIC inflammatory disease, a painful infection of the pelvic organs, often causing fever; STERILITY from scar tissue that closes the FALLOPIAN TUBES (about 50,000 women a year are rendered sterile from gonococcal infection of their tubes); sterility in men, caused by scar tissue blockage of the VAS DEFERENS; arthritis, which may be crippling if the disease is not treated promptly; blindness in babies whose mothers have gonorrhea at the time of delivery and whose eyes are not medicated. A present-day problem concerning gonorrhea is that new strains of *gonococci* are appearing which are resistant to penicillin and therefore may be very expensive or even impossible to cure. Gonorrhea can be spread both HETEROSEXUALLY and HOMOSEXUALLY by ANAL and VAGINAL INTERCOURSE and by FELLATIO, but rarely by KISSING or CUNNILINGUS.

GRAAFIAN FOLLICLE. A small sac at or near the surface of the OVARY which forms around (usually) one maturing OVUM during each MENSTRUAL CYCLE and then slowly swells and bursts open to discharge the ovum in the process called OVULATION. After ovulation, the follicle develops special cells (CORPUS LUTEUM) that secrete the HORMONE PROGESTERONE, which is necessary to maintain the PREGNANCY if one occurs. *See also* CORPUS LUTEUM; OVULATION.

GRANULOMA INGUINALE. Also called *Donovan's disease* after the physician who discovered the cause. A sexually transmitted disease (*see* VENEREAL DISEASES), which appears mainly in the tropics and is not common in the continental United States. *Cause:* rodlike bacteria called "Donovan bodies." *Symptoms:* usually painless, beefy-red GENITAL ulcers, which spread slowly, ooze, and have a foul odor. *Time from contact to first symptoms:* one to ten weeks. *Method of diagnosis:* examination, smear. *Complications:* scarring and destruction of tissues; can cause swelling of the genitals that can be mistaken for cancer.

GROIN. The frontal area of the body where the ABDOMEN joins the thighs. Contains LYMPH GLANDS and important blood vessels.

GROUP SEX. The engagement of several people, of one or both sexes, in a variety of sexual activities together. It can be, but is not always, an ORGY. *See also* ORGY.

GYNECOLOGIST. A physician especially qualified to treat the female REPRODUCTIVE organs. Derives in part from the Greek word *gynē* (female, woman). *See also* OBSTETRICIAN.

GYNECOMASTIA. Temporary enlargement of the BREASTS in about 80 percent of boys during PUBERTY. Harmless and soon disappears.

H

HANDICAPPED PERSONS AND SEX. *See* DISABILITIES AND SEX.

HEART TROUBLE AND SEX. Many people, knowing that breathing and heart rates show a marked increase during SEXUAL INTERCOURSE, believe that a heart attack should be followed by extreme caution in resuming sexual activity. A person should consult with the doctor as he or she resumes regular activities after a heart attack, but most physicians today are aware of the great psychological importance of sexual activity and feel confident in saying that, if the patient can walk up a flight of stairs without stress, then it is safe to resume his or her sex life. At first the partner of the heart attack victim may assume a more active role in SEX PLAY and intercourse until the patient feels secure and comfortable about his or her accustomed sexual preferences.

HEAT. The periodic and well-defined times during the life of a female animal when she is OVULATING and when COPULATION will almost certainly result in PREGNANCY. When the female is "in heat," she gives forth certain scents (*see* PHEROMONES) and signs, which stimulate the male and cause him to become sexually aroused and desirous of mating—that is, he "ruts" or becomes "rutty." In most mammals, only when she is in heat will the female be willing to copulate, and only then is the male responsive. In human females, there is no such thing as heat and little obvious connection between their desire for SEXUAL INTERCOURSE and the time they may become pregnant. In the human male, there is no season for being "rutty." Thus, in sex, animals are governed by their seasons and driven by their instincts, whereas human beings have the capacity to make choices and decisions about their sexual lives.

HEREDITY. The parental characteristics that are passed on to an individual, via the CHROMOSOMES of the father's SPERM and the mother's OVUM. Two factors determine the life of an individual: HEREDITY (inborn characteristics) and environment (what happens to him or her after CONCEPTION). In studying the life of an individual or a group, it is usually impossible to identify completely the comparative influences of heredity and environment (often called nature and nurture). *See also* CHROMOSOMES; DNA; GENES; GENETIC COUNSELING.

HERMAPHRODITE. An individual born with incomplete SEX ORGANS, partly male and partly female. Most plants and some lower animals are true hermaphrodites—that is, can reproduce by themselves—but there are probably no true hermaphrodites among human beings. Much more common, but still appearing in only about one in every thousand infants born, are babies born with TESTICLES in the ABDOMEN but whose external GENITALS appear somewhat female, or whose GONADS are OVARIES but whose external genitals look somewhat like a PENIS and testicles. People with such a disorder are called *pseudohermaphrodites,* and since their genetic GENDER is difficult to determine, they may be assigned at birth and brought up as members of the wrong sex. HORMONAL therapy and/or surgery can sometimes be helpful. Hermaphrodites should not be confused with TRANSSEXUALS.

HERPES PROGENITALIS. Also called *herpes, herpes 2, genital herpes.* A sexually transmitted disease (*see* VENEREAL DISEASES), often mistaken for SYPHILIS. Appears mainly in the tropics but is becoming more common in the continental United States. *Cause:* herpes 2 virus. *Symptoms:* swollen, tender, very painful sores on GENITALS, sores somewhat like fever blisters or cold sores on the lips, but caused by a different virus. *Time from contact to first symptoms:* about one week. *Method of diagnosis:* examination, smear, culture. *Complications:* in some cases destroys genital tissue, causing damage and scarring; some research suggests that it is important in the development of cancer of the CERVIX; very dangerous to newborn babies, in whom it can cause damage to the central nervous system (encephalitis) and sometimes death.

HETEROSEXUAL. Sexually attracted to the other sex, or a person so attracted. The opposite of HOMOSEXUAL. The prefix *hetero-* is from the Greek meaning "different" or "the other of two."

HETEROSEXUAL-HOMOSEXUAL BEHAVIOR RATING SCALE. A scale developed by the researcher Alfred KINSEY with seven categories, labeled 0 to 6 to denote the degree of HETEROSEXUALITY or HOMOSEXUALITY in people interviewed by him and his colleagues. People in category 0 are exclusively heterosexual, those in category 6 exclusively homosexual. People in categories 1 and 5 are predominantly heterosexual (1) or homosexual (5), while those in categories 2 and 4 show a clear preference for heterosexual (2) or homosexual (4) activity. Those in category 3 have more or less equal heterosexual and homosexual interests. By and large, the researchers found that people's sexual behavior and interests stayed within these divisions with fair consistency during their lives, with a far higher proportion of the population at the heterosexual end of the scale than the homosexual.

HOMOPHILE. A HOMOSEXUAL, that is, a person who is attracted to others of the same sex. Derives from the Greek *homos* (the same) and *-philos* (dear or beloved). *See also* HOMOSEXUALITY.

HOMOPHOBIA. A recently coined word to describe the condition of being afraid of or despising HOMOSEXUALITY and homosexuals. A person suffering from this condition is *homophobic.* Comes from the Greek word *phob* (fearing).

HOMOSEXUAL. Sexually attracted to people of the same sex, or a person so attracted. The opposite of HETEROSEXUAL. The prefix *homo-* comes from the Greek *homos* (the same), *not* from the Latin *homo* (man). *See also* GAY; HETEROSEXUAL-HOMOSEXUAL BEHAVIOR RATING SCALE; LESBIAN.

HONEYMOON. The period immediately following a wedding, when the newly married couple usually takes a vacation or trip before establishing their home.

HORMONE. One of a number of chemical substances produced by the ENDO-CRINE GLANDS, which have specific effects on various organs of the body. Three hormones especially important in relation to sex and REPRODUCTION are ESTROGEN and PROGESTERONE in the female, and TESTOSTERONE in the male.

HORMONE THERAPY. The treatment of any disorder by use of synthetic or natural HORMONES. Perhaps the most common type is insulin therapy for diabetes. Sex hormone THERAPY is not as specific or well-developed, but it can be useful at times, especially in reducing the symptoms of MENOPAUSE and occasionally some symptoms of aging in women.

HOT FLASHES OR FLUSHES. The best-known (and most disliked) symptom of MENOPAUSE. Consists of feelings of sudden, intense heat accompanied by more or less heavy perspiration. Caused by a quick change in the diameter of the surface blood vessels, resulting in a more rapid and larger flow of blood through the skin. The change in the blood vessels is the result of the drop in ESTROGEN production that comes with menopause. These flashes last from a few seconds to a few minutes.

HOT LINE. A telephone service available to people in need of emergency help, especially when they may wish the request to be kept confidential. In many large communities there are hot lines for VENEREAL DISEASE (VD) information (*see* Sources of Help, p. 315) and for RAPE, MARRIAGE, and sex COUNSELING.

HYMEN. The membrane (a very thin layer of tissue) that partially closes the entrance to the VAGINA in most females who have not had SEXUAL INTER-COURSE or used TAMPONS. It is also called the *maidenhead,* since its absence was traditionally considered by many—often wrongly—to be the sign that a female was not a "maiden," that is, an unmarried VIRGIN. When a woman willingly has sexual intercourse for the first time, the hymen seldom "tears" but is stretched or forced open farther by the entrance of the PENIS. In the flush of sexual excitement, this opening up is hardly felt, and the amount of bleeding is slight or none. A greater problem with first sexual intercourse can be the muscular tension that can cause the initial penetration to be painful and perhaps frightening, unless gentleness and consideration are used by the male. Many women, in preparation for first intercourse, use their fingers gently and gradually over a previous period of time to expand the hymeneal opening; the use of tampons also tends to enlarge the opening in the hymen. Many women have naturally large openings in their hymens, and some have no hymen at all. In a few cases, when the hymen is unusually tough and the opening or openings in it very small, a doctor may cut it surgically, a simple procedure. See Figures 8 and 9, pp. 44 and 45. *See also* DEFLORATION; SEXUAL INTERCOURSE.

HYSTERECTOMY. The surgical removal of the UTERUS for medical reasons such as fibroid tumors, cancer of the CERVIX, or uncontrollable bleeding. The OVARIES are generally not removed unless they too are diseased, and thus the secretion of female sex HORMONES remains unchanged. Hysterectomy was once a principal method of female STERILIZATION, but today, if the uterus is healthy, TUBAL LIGATION is considered preferable. Nevertheless, about one third of all women in the United States have had a hysterectomy by age sixty-five.

I

ILLEGITIMATE CHILD. A child born to an unwed mother. Traditionally in our society such children have been looked down on, even though the children had nothing whatever to do with the conditions of their CONCEPTION and birth. In recent years, with the increasing amount of NONMARITAL SEX, the number of babies born out of wedlock has greatly increased, and social attitudes and actions both toward the children and toward their mothers have become much less punitive. Today the term preferably used as more accurate is "out-of-wedlock child."

IMPLANTATION. The settling into the UTERINE ENDOMETRIUM of the FERTILIZED OVUM. If all goes normally, the implanted fertilized ovum will grow to a full-term baby.

IMPOTENCE. A sexual DYSFUNCTION among men characterized by the inability to achieve and maintain an ERECTION sufficiently or long enough to have SEXUAL INTERCOURSE or to EJACULATE. Most men have occasional episodes or periods of impotence (secondary impotence), while some others are impotent all their lives (primary impotence). The various causes of impotence, far more often psychological than physical, are often treatable, and the condition can often be cured—or it may cure itself with a change of conditions or attitudes. As a man grows older, if he expects to become impotent he probably will, but some men retain potency well into their seventies and eighties.

IMPREGNATE. To make a female PREGNANT. The ability to impregnate is unique to males; to be impregnated is unique to females.

INCEST. Sexual relations (usually but not always HETEROSEXUAL) between close relatives, for example, between mother and son, father and daughter, brother and sister, uncle/aunt and niece/nephew, or cousin and cousin. The TABOO against incest is found in almost all societies. Yet in the United States recent research is revealing that incest is very much more common than most people realize.

INCUBATOR. A small heated, enclosed, boxlike bed in which a PREMATURE baby is kept warm, protected, and fed until it is ready for life outside.

INFANTILE SEXUALITY. A universal characteristic of infants and very young children, demonstrated by their SENSUAL pleasure in being touched, caressed, and held and their pleasure in touching and caressing themselves, especially their GENITALS. Although many people deny or attempt to suppress the sexuality of children, and of course have no memory of their own sexuality as infants, we can say that the period of infancy is one of the most sensual of our whole lives, even though it does not involve SEXUAL INTERCOURSE.

INFERTILITY. The inability of a female to become PREGNANT or, in about 40 percent of infertile couples, of a male to IMPREGNATE. Between 10 and 15 percent of U.S. couples have difficulties in achieving pregnancy. The causes of infertility (also called STERILITY) are often multiple and complex, but in many cases can be dealt with successfully. *See also* STERILITY.

INTERCOURSE. *See* SEXUAL INTERCOURSE. (Note that the simple term *intercourse* can be applied to any social interchange between persons, including conversation.)

IUD. The initials stand for intrauterine device, a plastic or metal object to be placed in the UTERUS by a specially trained person to prevent PREGNANCY, probably by interfering with IMPLANTATION of the FERTILIZED OVUM in the ENDOMETRIUM. One of the major forms of CONCEPTION control.

J

JEALOUSY. A state of resentment, uneasiness, suspicion, and discomfort felt toward another person who may be seen as a rival for the attention and affections of the person feeling jealous. For example, a husband may (quite against his will) feel jealous of the new baby in the house because of the love and attention it receives from his wife, or a wife might feel jealous of her husband's business friends and acquaintances who seem to be taking his attention away from her. We have observed that in the sexual and affectional aspects of most people's lives, jealousies are likely to arise from time to time. Probably the best way to deal with it is for the jealous person to express his or her feelings rather than to stifle them, and thus give the partner a chance to understand, to explain, to put things into perspective, and, if necessary, to change his or her behavior in order to ease the harmful feelings. The jealous person should also be helped to become aware that feelings of possessing the other person are what underlie jealousy. People do need to share parts of their lives and feelings with others, and it would be an unhealthily narrow marriage or friendship that required a total monopoly of one partner by the other. However, researchers are finding that comparatively few marriages (perhaps 10 percent) are able to withstand the strains of sexual sharing with others outside the marriage. *See also* OPEN MARRIAGE.

JELLY. *See* SPERMICIDE.

K

KINSEY, ALFRED C. (1894–1956). The American entomologist and biologist who became aware of how little was known about human sexual behavior and, with a team of researchers, succeeded in collecting sex histories from more than 18,000 volunteer men and women across the United States. The results were published in two major volumes, *Sexual Behavior in the Human Male* (1948) and *Sexual Behavior in the Human Female* (1953). These studies proved revolutionary, for it was the first time such complete information on human sexual behavior had been collected from so many varied individuals and reported in such a careful, objective manner. The studies revealed that many kinds of sexual activities previously assumed to be quite rare and "immoral" were in fact engaged in by relatively large segments of the general population of the United States. The Kinsey reports also had the eventual effect of opening up the way to the present-day broad research on many aspects of human sexuality.

KISSING. The act of touching, pressing, or joining lips as an expression of greeting, affection, love, good fellowship, reverence, and so forth, or of touching with one's lips and/or mouth any other part of another's body or any object. Kisses can range from the most unEROTIC, quick peck of a grandchild on a grandparent's cheek, through the formal and old-fashioned kiss that a gentleman might bestow on a lady's hand on a social occasion, to a highly erotic, lengthy, and intimate contact of lips, mouth, and tongue with any part of another's body. The amount of kissing, and its significance, sexual and otherwise, differ greatly from social class to social class, culture to culture, generation to generation. *See also* FRENCH KISS; ORAL-GENITAL SEX.

KOTEX. *See* SANITARY NAPKIN.

L

LABIA. A term referring to the lips of the female GENITALS. The *labia majora* are the hairy outer, larger lips; the *labia minora* are the smaller, inner pair. All these are parts of the VULVA. The word is the same as the Latin word *labia* (lips).

LABOR. In childbirth, the contractions of the muscles of the UTERUS that first dilate the CERVIX then, with the help of the ABDOMINAL muscles, push the baby through the cervix and on down the BIRTH CANAL into the world. The average length of labor, counting from the first contractions is, for a first-time mother between nine and eleven hours, and for mothers who have previously borne a child around six hours. The labor of childbirth is divided into three stages: Stage 1: from the beginning of regular contractions until the cervix is completely dilated; Stage 2: from the end of Stage 1 until the baby is born; Stage 3: the period during which the uterus continues to contract in order to expel the PLACENTA and other tissues. The discomfort or pain of labor is caused almost entirely by the very hard work done by the uterine muscles rather than by friction or stretching. The pain is felt less if the mother is relaxed and feels in control of the situation, and if she understands the process of childbirth and what to expect.

LACK OF DESIRE. *See* SEXUAL DESIRE.

LACTATION. The secretion of milk by the GLANDS in a mother's BREASTS. *See also* NURSING.

LAMAZE METHOD. A type of NATURAL CHILDBIRTH that originated in Russia but was popularized by the French doctor Fernand Lamaze. The prospective mother must undergo a considerable period of training during the PREGNANCY to learn how to control and manage her contractions, how to relax between them, and how to push with them at the right moments. This makes possible an almost painless experience without drugs to kill or reduce the pain. As often as possible, the father is also trained to cooperate with the mother and give her support, especially during the actual DELIVERY.

LAPAROSCOPY. A method of seeing inside a woman's ABDOMEN with a miniature telescope provided with a light (called a *laparoscope*). It is used for diagnostic purposes and also for doing a TUBAL LIGATION. The laparoscope is inserted into the woman's abdomen by means of a small incision, usually in her NAVEL so that the scar will not show. Sometimes the incision is made for the same purposes through the upper end of the VAGINA. In this case, there is no visible scar and the term is *culdoscopy*.

LATENCY PERIOD. The period between the end of active expression of infantile sexuality and the beginning of PUBERTY, roughly between around age four and the early teens when, according to FREUD's theory, a person's sexuality and sexual feelings and interests become "latent," that is dormant or tranquil. For years, people have believed that the sexual interests of children in kindergarten and elementary school largely disappeared. The facts are that children during this period, although they usually no longer so obviously engage in the actively SENSUAL body enjoyment of infancy, and have not yet reached the time when the physical and psychological changes of puberty and ADOLESCENCE occur, are still very much interested in sexual questions, do engage in SEX PLAY, and in general are continuing their psychosexual development. They have, however, learned that the grown-up world does not approve of children's sexuality, and so they hide it. There is general agreement among psychological researchers and theorists today that the latency period described by Freud simply does not exist.

LESBIAN. A female HOMOSEXUAL. The name comes from that of the Greek island of Lesbos where, in ancient times, many of the inhabitants were women who enjoyed a homosexual way of life together, among them Sappho, the Greek poetess (ca. 620–ca. 565 B.C.).

LIBIDO. Sex drive. A psychoanalytic term referring mainly to the instincts that urge the individual to seek to be satisfied by sexual pleasure. The term was invented by Sigmund FREUD and derives from the Latin word for desire, lust, willfulness.

LICE. *See* CRAB LICE.

LOVE. An emotion far too complicated and varied to be defined or explained in an entry of a short encyclopedia. Love is not simply sex, nor is sex simply love. However, the two are often—but certainly not always—closely related. It may be enlightening to note the forms of love that were distinguished by the ancient Greeks: *eros:* sexual love, including the urge toward good human relationships; *philia:* brotherly love, the love between friends; and *agape* (ah-GAH-pay): universal, selfless love.

LOVER. One who loves in an EROTIC way. Used especially to refer to a person who sexually loves another person to whom he or she is not married. However, married people certainly can be lovers too. The term is used to describe HOMOSEXUAL as well as HETEROSEXUAL relationships.

LUBRICANTS. Substances that cause slipperiness and reduce friction. For pleasant, satisfying SEXUAL INTERCOURSE, lubrication of the entrance and walls of the VAGINA is important. If a man inserts his PENIS into a woman's vagina before she is sexually aroused so that her vagina has become moist and slippery, the intercourse, especially at the start, may be uncomfortable for her and difficult for both. If time is taken so that the woman becomes sexually aroused through FOREPLAY, the vaginal walls will have "sweated" mucus and the LABIA and area around the CLITORIS also will have been lubricated. Many sexual partners will be helped by applying *lubricating jelly* (a common brand is "K-Y") or CONTRACEPTIVE cream or jelly before they start intercourse. Saliva is also useful. Petroleum jelly works but should not be used with a CONDOM or DIAPHRAGM since it causes deterioration of the rubber.

LUBRICATION. *See* LUBRICANTS.

LYMPHOGRANULOMA VENEREUM. Also called *LGV, Frei's disease,* or *tropical bubo.* A sexually transmitted disease (*see* VENEREAL DISEASES). Appears mainly in the tropics and is not yet common in the continental United States. *Cause:* a viruslike organism. *Symptoms:* initially, a single painless sore on the GENITALS, which is usually missed by the patient; thereafter, the patient notices swelling and aching in the GROIN, as the lymph nodes enlarge; there is fever, headache, generalized achiness, and loss of appetite; a large lymph node may break open and drain pus. *Time from contact to first symptoms:* three days to three weeks; average ten days. *Method of diagnosis:* examination, blood test. *Complications:* causes lymph nodes to break down and drain; the resultant scarring can cause narrowing of the RECTAL opening, making it more difficult to move the bowels, especially in women and in HOMOSEXUAL men who take part in ANAL INTERCOURSE.

M

MAIDENHEAD. An old-fashioned term for the HYMEN.

MAKING OUT. A term used today—especially by young, unmarried people —to refer to physical sexual contact beyond hand-holding and light KISSING. May include anything from NECKING to PETTING, may also refers to actual SEXUAL INTERCOURSE. Making out can be unwise and irresponsible when it leads to the risk of unwanted PREGNANCY.

MALE CHAUVINISM. A state of mind in some men that involves an unreasoning belief in the superiority of males over females and of the rights of males over those of females. A term of disapproval used against such men, especially by FEMINISTS, is "male chauvinist pig." Some males who have been brought up or choose to treat women with a special sort of politeness and respect and who believe that "the weaker sex" enjoys such chivalrous treatment are chagrined to have such a label applied to them, especially since even "liberated" women often enjoy being treated chivalrously, provided their basic needs and desires as equal human beings are respected. *See also* DOUBLE STANDARD.

MARIJUANA. Dried cannabis leaves that are crushed, smoked, and inhaled in a pipe or as cigarettes. Also called *pot* or *dope*. There is no evidence that smoking marijuana increases SEXUAL DESIRE, SEX DRIVE, or performance, but many people report that it lessens anxiety and reduces inhibitions and therefore increases the sense of pleasure in sexual activity and may cause the experience of ORGASM to be perceived as lasting longer than it really does. It is known that heavy users of marijuana may become temporarily IMPOTENT. The danger with any inhibition-reducing drug—including alcohol—is that it will put a person into a state in which he or she might do something that, in a nondrugged state, he or she would not do and can later regret having done.

MARRIAGE. A legal and often religious contract entered into by a man and a woman to live together as husband and wife. It is a complicated and persistent social institution and—despite reports to the contrary—still very popular.

MARRIAGE COUNSELING. *See* COUNSELING. (It is important to distinguish between marriage counseling, which should involve the entire range of the relationship of husband and wife, and SEX THERAPY, in which the emphasis is specifically on sexual DYSFUNCTIONS and satisfactions.)

MASCULINITY. The quality of being masculine, especially as distinguished from FEMININITY, the characteristics of either of which vary with each society. No one can say for certain to what extent the characteristics we label masculine are inborn and to what extent they are learned. *See also* GENDER ROLE; SEXISM.

MASOCHISM. A form of VARIANT SEXUAL BEHAVIOR in which a person receives primary sexual satisfaction from having pain inflicted on him or her. The word derives from the name of Leopold Ivan Sacher-Masoch (1836–95), an Austrian novelist who described it. Masochism is not illegal in any state. *See also* SADO-MASOCHISM.

MASTECTOMY. The surgical removal of a BREAST or both breasts of a woman who suffers from cancer of the breast, the most common form of cancer in women. A mastectomy can be a very difficult psychological experience for a woman who fears not only that her cancer may recur but also that she may lose her sexual attractiveness, an especially common fear in our strongly breast-oriented society. After mastectomy a woman needs careful follow-up to identify and deal with as early as possible any recurrence of the cancer.

Just as important, she will also need counseling and support from such sources as organized groups of women who have been through the same experience. She and her mate may also welcome COUNSELING now available about the psychological and sexual aspects of the mastectomy experience.

MASTURBATION. Stimulation or SELF-PLEASURING of one's own SEX OR-GANS, usually to experience ORGASM. Stimulation of each other's sex organs (mutual masturbation) usually forms a part of SEX PLAY.

MENARCHE. The first MENSTRUATION in the human female, an indication that a girl may now be OVULATING and is becoming capable of producing a child. Some sexually active girls become PREGNANT even before menarche; others do not ovulate until a year or so after the first menstruation. Menarche is considered to be the beginning of a girl's ADOLESCENCE. An equivalent stage in a boy's development is the first time he EJACULATES during ORGASM, usually during a "WET DREAM" or MASTURBATION. By contrast, menarche is unrelated to the girl's sexual responsiveness.

MENOPAUSE. The period, usually between ages forty-five and fifty-five, when a woman ceases to MENSTRUATE. Although she can no longer become PREGNANT after menopause, it does not mean the end of, or even reduction in, her SEXUAL DESIRE and enjoyment of sexual activity but often quite the opposite. See also AGING AND SEX; CHANGE OF LIFE; CLIMACTERIC.

MENSTRUAL CYCLE. The more-or-less regular female FERTILITY cycle. It begins with Day 1 of one MENSTRUAL PERIOD, is followed in about two weeks by OVULATION, and continues for another two weeks until Day 1 of the following menstrual period. On the average, women's menstrual cycles last about 28 to 30 days but can vary from 21 to 35 or 40 days, or even longer.

MENSTRUAL FLOW. See MENSTRUATION.

MENSTRUAL PAD. See SANITARY NAPKIN.

MENSTRUAL PERIOD. See MENSTRUATION.

MENSTRUATION. The monthly discharge of the UTERINE lining (the EN-DOMETRIUM), the flow being composed of minute blood vessels and tissue that have been built up during the preceding two weeks (approximately) in anticipation of a possible PREGNANCY. Menstruation takes place if no FER-TILIZED EGG has been IMPLANTED in the endometrium, that is, if there is no pregnancy. The *menstrual period* lasts from three to six days, during which a woman may say she is "having her period." If a woman's period does not occur within two weeks of the time she usually expects it, she should see a doctor to determine the cause. It may mean that she is PREGNANT, although there can be other reasons.

MIDWIFE. A person, not a physician, who is trained to assist women in childbirth. These days, midwives are usually nurses (male as well as female) who have received special training and who work under the general supervision of a doctor. In former times, or in less-developed societies, midwives might simply be women who gathered experience and expertise in helping in childbirth. The practice of midwives is called midwifery.

MISCARRIAGE. A SPONTANEOUS ABORTION, when the EMBRYO or FETUS is expelled. Between 10 and 15 percent of PREGNANCIES end in spontaneous abortion, most before the end of the third month of pregnancy. Frequently, a miscarried fetus is found to have been defective in some way. Most women who have had miscarriages will probably have an undiminished chance of carrying their next pregnancy to full term.

"MISSIONARY POSITION." Probably the position most commonly used in SEXUAL INTERCOURSE throughout the world. The couple lies face-to-face, the man on top. The name is said to have been given by Polynesians in the South Pacific, who, because they preferred other positions, found this missionary-approved way strange and unacceptable.

MISTRESS. A fairly old-fashioned term for a woman who provides sexual and other companionship to a man—not her husband—over an extended period of time in return for his providing continuing financial support, usually including a place to live. The relationships between men and their mistresses can range from those based mainly on the exchange of sex for money and support, to those that involve a deep and long-standing exchange of affection, understanding, and even commitment. Other old-fashioned terms are "paramour" and "kept woman."

MITTELSCHMERZ. The German word for "pain in the middle," used to describe the slight twinge or even cramping pain in the lower ABDOMEN that some women feel around the middle of the MENSTRUAL CYCLE, within a day or so of the presumed time they OVULATE. It cannot be counted on in calculating the so-called SAFE PERIOD.

MODESTY. In the sexual sense, modesty means the state of mind or belief that one should not expose one's body to others. The most important consideration about modesty is not whether it is bad or good but rather that those people who have deep feelings of sexual modesty should have their feelings respected. Many young people, as they approach PUBERTY, desire to have their modesty and privacy protected in a way that was not important to them earlier, and may not be of importance to them when they become fully mature.

MOLESTER. SEE CHILD MOLESTER.

MONILIAL VAGINITIS. Also called *monilia, candida, yeast infection, fungus, vaginal thrush.* It is sometimes transmitted sexually but usually not, because the fungus causing it is normally carried on most people's skin, in the hair, and sometimes in the mouth. It also commonly inhabits normal women's VAGINAS without causing any symptoms. When conditions inside the vagina change (because of PREGNANCY; taking an ORAL CONTRACEPTIVE, or antibiotics—especially penicillin and tetracycline; or too much DOUCHING), the fungus multiplies very rapidly and causes the symptoms. Thus, it is transmitted both sexually and nonsexually. *Symptoms:* thick, cheeselike vaginal discharge; severe GENITAL itching; SKIN IRRITATION. *Time from contact to first symptoms:* varies, since in most cases there is no moment of contact but only a change in conditions which causes the rapid multiplication of the fungus. *Method of diagnosis:* examination; microscopic identification; culture. *Complications:* difficult to get rid of; can cause mouth and throat infections (thrush) in newborn infants. *See also* SEXUALLY TRANSMITTED DISEASES.

"MORNING-AFTER" PILL. A pill containing a heavy dose of a synthetic ESTROGEN, which can usually prevent PREGNANCY if taken within 72 hours after SEXUAL INTERCOURSE, preferably within 24 hours. In many women it has the side effects of nausea and vomiting. (Because of its bad aftereffects, the estrogen DES is no longer used for this purpose.)

MORNING SICKNESS. A feeling of nausea and aversion to food or even the odors of food that many women experience during the first six to eight weeks of PREGNANCY. It is felt most commonly upon awakening but may occur at other times of the day. Sometimes vomiting is involved, and if this is severe and frequent, prompt treatment is necessary.

MULTIPLE BIRTHS. The most common multiple births are twins, two babies CONCEIVED, GESTATED, and born at the same time. *Fraternal twins* are the products of two EGGS FERTILIZED by two SPERM, and so are no more alike than any other brother or sister would be, except they are of the same age. Fraternal twins may not resemble each other at all, may be of the same sex or different sexes, and there are always two PLACENTAS and AMNIOTIC SACS. *Identical twins* are the products of a single egg which, after being fertilized, has split into two cell masses, each of which develops separately. These are therefore always of the same sex, being the results of fertilization of one egg by one sperm, and they usually are so alike in appearance that often they are hard to tell apart. They also share a single placenta and sac. Other multiple births—triplets, quadruplets, and quintuplets—are quite rare, and the babies may be identical, fraternal, or any combination of both.

N

NARCISSISM. Sexual excitement from admiring one's own body; also, excessive self-love. The word comes from the name of Narcissus, a beautiful youth in Greek mythology who saw his own reflection in a pool of clear water, fell in love with it, wasted away, and was changed into a flower, narcissus. The term can be applied to anyone who excessively admires himself or herself, even if not sexually.

NATURAL CHILDBIRTH. A term coined by the British physician Grantly Dick-Read in the early 1930s. Dr. Dick-Read developed a method of preparing women for childbirth based on his observation that the pain of giving birth is related to the fears the mother feels and the tension arising from them. The natural childbirth method educates and trains expectant mothers to break the cycle of fear, tension, and pain—all this without the use of painkillers—by teaching her to understand the process of childbirth and to work along with it by relaxation methods so that they may actually enjoy the experience. The method is best described in Dr. Dick-Read's book *Childbirth Without Fear* (1942). *See also* LAMAZE METHOD.

NATURAL FAMILY PLANNING. A system of FAMILY PLANNING based on sexual ABSTINENCE during the portion of a woman's MENSTRUAL CYCLE when she is presumed to be FERTILE. It involves teaching a woman to use various physical signs, such as body temperature and consistency of CERVICAL mucus, to indicate when she is about to OVULATE, so that she can avoid SEXUAL INTERCOURSE during the calculated fertile days. Former terms such as the RHYTHM METHOD or the CALENDAR METHOD are no longer appropriate, since natural family planning techniques have recently become more sophisticated and effective than these. Natural family planning is not, however, as effective as some medical CONTRACEPTIVE methods.

NATURAL/UNNATURAL. *Natural* means according to nature, the way "Nature" intended things to be and to be done, assuming that nature can be considered to have intentions and assuming that we can understand or prove these "intentions." The term *unnatural* is used by many people, and in some legal language, to refer to sexual activities that are disapproved of by the users of the word, such as ORAL-GENITAL SEX, ANAL INTERCOURSE, and HOMOSEXUALITY. The label is not scientifically useful, since the activities it labels do occur also "in nature." The word *natural* also refers to a method of childbirth (NATURAL CHILDBIRTH) and of family planning (NATURAL FAMILY PLANNING). *See also* ABNORMAL; NORMAL.

NAVEL. The roundish depression on the ABDOMEN where the UMBILICAL CORD entered the body of the FETUS until it was cut off just after birth. It is also called the *umbilicus* and, less formally, the *belly button.*

NECKING. The lighter forms of PETTING and MAKING OUT, involving such activities as arms around neck and waist, sitting close, and simple KISSING.

NECROPHILIA. A very rare and clearly pathological form of sexual behavior by which sexual pleasure is obtained from corpses. The term comes from the Greek words *nekros* (corpse) and *-philos* (loving).

NIPPLE. The tip of the BREAST, to which the milk ducts carry the milk manufactured by the breast for the baby to suck. For many women the nipples are also important as EROGENOUS ZONES and they become ERECT during sexual arousal. (Men's nipples may also become erect during sexual arousal, and some men experience sexual pleasure when their nipples are stimulated.)

NOCTURNAL EMISSION. The involuntary EJACULATION of SEMEN during sleep, often called a *wet dream.* In many boys, it signifies that PUBERTY has arrived, although more often a boy's first ejaculation of semen occurs during MASTURBATION.

NONMARITAL SEX. SEXUAL INTERCOURSE unrelated to MARRIAGE. *See* EXTRAMARITAL SEX.

NONSPECIFIC URETHRITIS or NONGONOCOCCAL URETHRITIS. Also called *NSU* or *NGU. Painful inflammation of the* URETHRA. *Cause:* doctors are not sure exactly what causes it—perhaps several kinds of bacteria, which is why it is called *nonspecific;* it can often appear without sexual contact, so it is not, strictly speaking, a SEXUALLY TRANSMITTED DISEASE; but it can also follow sexual activity, perhaps from mechanical irritation. *Symptoms:* in women, there may be no symptoms or there may be a slight burning or bleeding on urination; in men, most often a discharge from the PENIS and slight burning on urination; the symptoms are usually milder than those of GONORRHEA. *Time from contact to first symptoms:* overnight (in the case of mechanical irritation) to three weeks. *Method of diagnosis:* smear and culture to make sure the condition is not gonorrhea. *Complications:* an uncomfortable disease but not dangerous; the disease has a high frequency of recurrence, even without SEXUAL INTERCOURSE.

NORMAL. A term often too loosely used, even in science. The dictionary defines it as "corresponding to the median or average of a large group in types, appearance, achievement, function, development, etc." It should be made clear that the term used in this way by scientists is simply a statistical description and does not imply that "normal" is the same as "good" or "desirable." *See also* ABNORMAL; NATURAL/UNNATURAL.

NUDITY. The state of being without clothing or covering; naked; bare. The feelings, traditions, and TABOOS relating to nudity vary greatly from culture to culture, group to group, generation to generation, family to family, and individual to individual—and also from time to time. Our feeling is that nudity should not be forced on anyone who feels uncomfortable with it or whose sense of MODESTY it offends. However, within families in which it does not go contrary to the in-family customs and beliefs, it can provide an easy, comfortable means of education in what the human body looks like and how it acts. As children reach PUBERTY, they often develop a strong desire for privacy and don't want to be seen nude or to see members of their families nude. This desire should be respected.

NURSING. The feeding of an infant at the BREAST. Bottles for the artificial feeding of infants are often called nursing bottles. Breast-feeding is being more and more recognized as better than bottle-feeding for two reasons: (1) physically, breast-fed infants tend to develop better, and (2) psychologically, the bond between mother and baby that is so important to both tends to be established more strongly and faster than it is with artificial feeding. This is not to say, however, that most bottle-fed babies do not thrive, for they do, and the mother-baby bond can be established if the baby is held closely while it nurses from the bottle.

NYMPHOMANIA. This term is no longer used by informed people. It was formerly used to describe a supposed condition of insatiable SEXUAL DESIRE in women, which is now known not to exist. (The same is true for SATYRIASIS.) The word *nymphomania* comes from *nymph,* a lesser goddess of Greek and Roman mythology, one of a band of beautiful and sexually attractive females, and *mania,* meaning excessive excitement and craziness, from the Greek word for madness of mind.

O

OB/GYN. Short for a physician who is an OBSTETRICIAN and a GYNECOLOGIST, or for the field of medicine that combines these two specialities.

OBSCENITY. Material, language, or behavior which is socially or legally defined as *obscene,* that is, indecent, disgusting, repulsive, lewd, causing (or intending to cause) sexual excitement or lust in a manner or place that is objectionable. What one person finds obscene, of course, another may find unobjectionable and pleasure-giving, and it is unlikely that there will ever be general agreement on just what is and is not obscene. There are those, for example, who find the tasteless depiction of violence on TV and in literature more obscene than tasteless EXPLICIT SEXUAL MATERIALS. The word obscenity probably derives from the two Latin words *ob* (toward) and *caenum* (filth). *See also* MODESTY; PORNOGRAPHY.

OBSTETRICIAN. A physician who specializes in *obstetrics,* the care of women during PREGNANCY, childbirth, and immediately after childbirth. *See also* GYNECOLOGIST.

OEDIPUS COMPLEX. FREUD used this term to describe the unresolved desire of a very small boy for sexual gratification through his mother. Its opposite is the ELECTRA COMPLEX, the desire of a nursery-school-age girl for her father. Usually by age three or four, children outgrow their natural Oedipal feelings. Only when they continue into later years are these feelings considered a "complex"—a combination of emotional feelings, compulsive but often unconscious, that may drive the person into difficulties in life adjustment. The name comes from the ancient Greek king, Oedipus, who killed a man he did not know was his father, married a woman he did not know was his mother, and blinded himself and was exiled when this was discovered. *See* INCEST.

ONANISM. An old-fashioned term for MASTURBATION. The word comes from the name of Onan, an Old Testament biblical figure who "spilled his seed on the ground" rather than IMPREGNATE his dead brother's widow (as Jewish law then required) so that the brother's name might be carried on.

OPEN MARRIAGE. A MARRIAGE in which both partners willingly agree that each is free to have intimate friendships with others, usually including SEXUAL INTERCOURSE. Most marriages enjoy a degree of non-sexual "openness," but THERAPISTS for the most part agree that only a small percentage can survive full sexual openness.

ORAL CONTRACEPTIVE. A BIRTH CONTROL method taken by mouth—"THE PILL."

ORAL-GENITAL SEX. Sexual activity involving contact between the mouth and the GENITALS. Attitudes toward oral-genital sex range from the many HETEROSEXUAL or HOMOSEXUAL couples who practice it as a major source of sexual pleasure, to those who consider it "unnatural" or repulsive. In some states it is illegal. *See* CUNNILINGUS; FELLATIO.

ORAL SEX; ORALISM. *See* ORAL-GENITAL SEX.

ORGASM. The peak or CLIMAX of excitement during sexual activity. Although, in males, EJACULATION and orgasm usually occur simultaneously, some male adults and boys who have just reached PUBERTY, may experience orgasm without ejaculation. The idea, originated by FREUD, that females have two types of orgasm, clitoral and vaginal, has been shown by scientific research to be false. The complex group of physical responses that constitute orgasm in the human female is the same whether produced by stimulation of the CLITORIS, the VAGINA, the BREASTS, the ears, or other EROGENOUS ZONES, or by FANTASIES. Similarly, orgasms have been shown to be the same in HOMOSEXUALS and HETEROSEXUALS.

ORGY. Wild, passionate, abandoned revelry and pursuit of pleasure, usually sexual pleasure, by a number of people together. *See also* GROUP SEX.

ORIENTATION. *See* SEXUAL ORIENTATION.

ORIFICE. A hole or opening, of which the human body has several, any of which (except probably the nostrils) can be considered to be EROGENOUS, by some people at some times.

OVARY. One of the pair of female SEX GLANDS in which OVA are matured and from which usually one ovum is ovulated once a month. The ovaries also produce the sex HORMONES (ESTROGEN and PROGESTERONE) important in the development of sexual maturity in women, for regulation of the MENSTRUAL CYCLE, and for achievement and maintainance of PREGNANCY.

OVULATION. The release, about once a month, of an OVUM from an OVARY. After ovulation, the ovum is carried into the FALLOPIAN TUBE, in which it may or may not be FERTILIZED by a SPERM.

OVUM (plural, ova). The egg—the female REPRODUCTIVE cell. A newborn female baby contains in her two OVARIES about 400,000 immature ova, some 400 to 500 of which will mature and be OVULATED during her reproductive lifetime, beginning with MENARCHE and ending with MENOPAUSE.

P

PANDERER. A person who supplies customers for PROSTITUTES or prostitutes for customers; more generally, a person who profits from weaknesses and vices in others. *See also* PIMP.

PAP TEST. Also called *Pap smear test.* Taking a sample of mucus from the opening of the CERVIX by means of a cotton swab or wooden applicator and smearing the fluid on a glass slide, where it may be examined under a microscope for evidence of disease, most often for cancer cells. Women should have a Pap test at least once a year as a part of their physical checkup. It is named after its inventor, George Papanicolaou, a Greek-born American doctor.

PARTHENOGENESIS. A form of REPRODUCTION during which the female OVUM is caused to develop without contact with SPERM. It is the only method of reproduction among certain insects and other lower animals, plants, and, under some circumstances, frogs, but has never been known in human beings.

PATHOLOGICAL. Having to do with illness and disease, whether physical or mental.

PEDERASTY. A term meaning "love of boys" or, often, ANAL INTERCOURSE between a man and a boy. A pederast is one whose sexual satisfaction comes from sexual activity with boys. The word comes from the Greek *pais-* (boy) and *erastes* (lover). PEDOPHILIA has a different meaning.

PEDOPHILIA. A SEXUAL VARIANCE in which an adult desires or engages in sexual activity with a minor of either sex. The word derives from the Greek words *paedo-* (child) and *-philos* (loving).

PEEPING TOM. A person who obtains sexual gratification by watching the NUDITY (as when undressing for bed) or the sexual activities of others who do not realize they are being watched. Of course, many people are turned on by seeing pictures of such activities, but only when they go to some length to obtain such pleasure by secretly observing live people can they be called Peeping Toms. Peeping Toms are harmless, though they may be a nuisance. The name comes from the name of Tom the Tailor, who peeped out from behind the shutters when the nude Lady Godiva rode down the street of Coventry, as told in *Godiva, a Tale of Coventry*, a poem by Alfred Tennyson. *See also* VOYEURISM.

PELVIS. In the human body, the basin-shaped circle of bones at the bottom part of the trunk. It supports the spinal column and rests on the leg bones. At its center front is the *pubis*, from which come the words *pubic* and *puberty*. The area enclosed by the pelvis is called the *pelvic area* and in both sexes contains the urinary BLADDER and in the female the organs of REPRODUCTION.

PENICILLIN. A powerful antibiotic (germ-killing drug) widely used in treating VENEREAL and many other diseases. It was discovered almost by accident in 1928 by Alexander Fleming, a British bacteriologist.

PENILE. Having to do with the PENIS, as, for example, in the phrase "penile-vaginal penetration," meaning the entrance of a penis into a VAGINA.

PENIS. The principal male SEX ORGAN. See Figure 4, p. 38. *See also* ERECTION; PHALLUS.

PENIS CAPTIVUS. A PENIS "captured" or "trapped" in a VAGINA. There are many wild tales about this, but the fact is that it never occurs in human beings. However, it does commonly happen among dogs, for the penis of a male dog contains a bone that allows it to enter the vagina of a female dog before true erection occurs. When erection does occur, a swelling forms at the base of the dog's penis that may cause the penis to be trapped in the vagina, which has become swollen and tight from sexual excitement. Hence, the post-copulatory yelps and barks of dogs in heat and in rut. It sounds and appears to be very uncomfortable for the dogs, but it does ensure that EJACULATION occurs inside the vagina.

PENIS ENVY. The reaction of some little girls to the discovery that boys have penises and they do not. According to FREUD, this is a common psychological condition in little girls, one that is almost always outgrown. In fact, it is as futile for a girl to envy a boy his penis as for a boy to envy a girl her VAGINA and UTERUS, which enable her to GESTATE and bear a baby. Parents can be most helpful in these matters by calmly explaining that boys have penises and girls have vaginas and uteruses and that's a good way for things to be— otherwise there would be no babies.

PERINEUM. The area between the legs that extends from the VAGINA to the ANUS in a female, and from the SCROTUM to the anus in a male.

PERIOD. A word frequently used to refer to MENSTRUATION, as in "having her period" or "her period did not come."

PERVERSION. A term loosely applied to sexual behavior that the user of the term does not approve of. A person engaging in a "perversion" is called a *pervert,* but a more scientific (and less judgmental) term for sexual behavior that is different from the usual is SEXUAL VARIANCE. *See also* ABNORMAL.

PETTING. Sexual activity that includes caressing the most sensitive parts of the body, such as the BREASTS or GENITALS, and deep KISSING, the kind of lovemaking that tends to make a couple ready for SEXUAL INTERCOURSE. *See also* FOREPLAY; MAKING OUT.

PHALLUS. PENIS, usually in ERECTION. The word *phallic* is the adjective meaning "pertaining to a penis." The phallus has been the subject or theme of much art and of some religious ceremonies. The word derives from the Greek *phallos* (penis).

PHEROMONES. Substances that have an odor and are secreted by the bodies of many species of animals and insects, the smell of which produces or affects sexual behavior in other members of the species. They are especially important in the sexual stimulation of one animal or insect by another of the opposite sex. Anyone who has observed dogs, cats, or farm animals has seen the strong effects of pheromones (*see* HEAT). The sense of smell has a strong effect on human sexual behavior—pleasant odors and perfumes turn many people on; foul odors turn most people off. Scientists are not sure whether there are specific human pheromones, and since we have evolved into much less scent-guided creatures than our animal ancestors were and most other animals still are, even if pheromones exist in humans they probably do not play a major part in affecting our sexual behavior. However, the whole field of the "chemistry" of sexual attraction needs much more research before we can be sure how important pheromones are in our lives.

PHIMOSIS. A condition in which the FORESKIN is so tight that it cannot be pulled back over the head of the PENIS. The condition can be corrected by stretching or by CIRCUMCISION.

PILL, THE. A type of BIRTH CONTROL medication taken by mouth and containing synthetic HORMONES that prevent a woman from OVULATING. The pill is available only by doctor's prescription, and the directions for its use must be followed exactly. In general, a woman takes a pill a day for three weeks and then stops for a week. Taking one or a few pills is useless, and if a woman forgets her pill for a day or two, she may become PREGNANT unless she uses another means of birth control or abstains from SEXUAL INTERCOURSE during that MENSTRUAL CYCLE. Especially during the first few months of using the pill, a woman should consult with her doctor about any side effects she may experience. Correctly used, the pill is a highly effective means of CONTRACEPTION.

PIMP. A "business manager" of one or more PROSTITUTES who usually collects all or most of their proceeds but pays their expenses. *See also* PANDERER.

PIMPLES. *See* ACNE.

PINCH TECHNIQUE. *See* SQUEEZE TECHNIQUE.

PITUITARY GLAND. The master GLAND or "time clock" that largely governs the functioning of the other glands of internal secretion, including the sex glands. The pituitary thus determines the timing and sequence of body growth and changes occuring during PUBERTY and ADOLESCENCE; it controls FERTILITY, PREGNANCY, LACTATION, and other body processes. It is located at the base of the brain.

PLACENTA. The thick disk-shaped collection of blood vessels and tissues growing on the inner wall of the UTERUS, through which oxygen, nourishment, and waste products (but not the blood itself) are exchanged between the mother and the baby developing within her. The placenta is connected to the baby by the UMBILICAL CORD, which contains blood vessels leading from the baby to the placenta and others leading from it back to the baby. The exchanged materials pass through the placental blood vessels and filter through their thin walls. Very soon after the baby is born, the placenta and the sac that surrounded the baby are expelled from the uterus during the third stage of LABOR. This AFTERBIRTH is then discarded.

PLANNED PARENTHOOD. An organization in the United States, whose full name today is Planned Parenthood–World Population (PP-WP), which has Planned Parenthood affiliates in most cities of the United States. Throughout the world, national independent family planning organizations, both private and governmental, form the International Planned Parenthood Federation

(IPPF). All these groups are concerned with the two problems of unwanted pregnancies and overpopulation, both in families and in countries. They provide CONTRACEPTIVE advice and materials; ABORTION COUNSELING and, in many cases, abortion services; and information concerning population questions. Although in the United States, young people who use Planned Parenthood services are strongly encouraged to discuss their problems, feelings, and plans with their parents, the family-planning organizations do not require this, and information obtained and given, and services provided, are kept confidential. Basically, the organization urges couples to space the births of their children and to have only the number of children that they want and can care for. Many Planned Parenthood centers also provide INFERTILITY services to couples who want children but have been unable to CONCEIVE them. Planned Parenthood is supported by private donations and foundation and government grants. People who want to be in touch with a Planned Parenthood center can usually find an address and telephone number in their telephone directory.

PLATONIC LOVE. An intimate companionship (or sometimes MARRIAGE) between any two people—man and woman, woman and woman, man and man—based on common ideas, ideals, and needs but without any physical sexual element; a spiritual relationship. If one says about two people, "Their relationship is platonic," one means that sexual interest and activity are not a part of it. The phrase comes from the name of Plato, a Greek philosopher (427–347 B.C.), who idealized this kind of relationship.

PLEASURING. Activities other than SEXUAL INTERCOURSE that give EROTIC pleasure. Although pleasuring is usually an important preliminary to sexual intercourse (*see* FOREPLAY), it can also be very often just for physical pleasure, comfort, and intimacy that are ends in themselves rather than being specifically intended to lead to intercourse. *See also* MASTURBATION; SELF-PLEASURING.

POLYANDRY. An established MARRIAGE between one woman and two or more men. The word derives from the Greek term *poly-* (many) and *andros* (male). *See also* POLYGAMY; POLYGYNY.

POLYGAMY. Having several SPOUSES—usually referring to wives, although in some cultures it might mean two or more husbands for one wife. From the Greek *poly-* (many) and *gamia* (marrying). *See also* POLYANDRY; POLYGYNY.

POLYGYNY. An established MARRIAGE between a man and two or more women. From the Greek term *poly-* (many) and *gynē* (woman). *See also* POLYANDRY; POLYGAMY.

PORNOGRAPHY. For this word there are almost as many definitions as there are people, and attempts at definitive interpretations even by the United

States Supreme Court have not ended the confusion. If universally accepted, a useful definition might be: the presentation or production of visual and audiovisual materials specifically intended to be sexually arousing (in art, literature, motion pictures, music, etc.), and sold commercially for this exact purpose. The various laws and regulations in the states relating to pornography are not helpful. One person's "pornography" may be another's great art or literature, or vice versa. The word derives from the Greek words *porne* (PROSTITUTE) and *graphos* (drawn or written). Because "I can't define it but I know it when I see it" appears to be a prevailing criterion, a preferable and more scientific term (because it is descriptive rather than judgmental) is EXPLICIT SEXUAL MATERIAL. *See also* EROTIC.

POSTPARTUM DEPRESSION. The feelings of fatigue, sadness, and being generally let down, rejected, or neglected that occur in many women during the postpartum period, that is, the few days or weeks just after childbirth. Well over half of all women experience such feelings during the first few weeks after DELIVERY. Other terms for the phenomenon are *postpartum blues* or *baby blues*. Fortunately the condition almost always soon passes. If it does not, or if the feelings are severe, the mother should seek COUNSELING. Certainly she will be helped by extra love, help, and attention from her husband and perhaps her own mother, mother-in-law, or other relatives and close friends.

POT. *See* MARIJUANA.

POTENCY. In the field of sexuality, a term that refers to the ability of a male to achieve and maintain an ERECTION and to EJACULATE—that is, to perform SEXUAL INTERCOURSE. Its opposite is IMPOTENCY.

POX. *See* SYPHILIS.

PREGNANCY. The time during which an EMBRYO or FETUS is developing in the UTERUS. It ends in childbirth, MISCARRIAGE, or ABORTION. The usual, "full-term," pregnancy lasts for a period of approximately 266 days, during which the woman is termed *pregnant*. Many women have been pregnant several times in their lives without ever having been aware of it, for research has shown that a FERTILIZED OVUM has perhaps a 30 percent chance of not even IMPLANTING, or else of implanting imperfectly or of being imperfect itself. In these cases the body usually rids itself of the pregnancy very early, appearing as a usual or perhaps only slightly delayed MENSTRUAL PERIOD.

PREMARITAL COUNSELING. Talking with a trained professional about a forthcoming MARRIAGE. Such COUNSELING can be very useful to a couple in helping them to get to know each other better and more openly, to communicate with each other, and to be sure that they are ready and well prepared for marriage and are entering it with realistic expectations. *See also* COUNSELING.

PREMARITAL SEX. Strictly speaking, the term means SEXUAL INTERCOURSE between two people who intend to be married, but today it is loosely used to refer to sexual intercourse between two unmarried people who may have no intention of marrying, especially teenagers. It should be distinguished from EXTRAMARITAL SEX, in which at least one of the partners is married to someone other than the partner. *See also* ADULTERY.

PREMATURE BIRTH. The birth of a baby weighing less than five pounds, eight ounces (2,500 grams). The smaller the baby, the lower its chances of survival as a normal person, but modern medical science is steadily increasing the chances. A premature baby is usually cared for at first in an INCUBATOR. *See also* VIABILITY.

PREMATURE EJACULATION. A sexual DYSFUNCTION in which a man consistently EJACULATES before or immediately after his PENIS enters his partner's VAGINA and thus before she has had a chance to be sufficiently aroused to achieve ORGASM. With proper THERAPY, almost all men so afflicted can learn to prevent it. *See also* SQUEEZE TECHNIQUE; STOP-START METHOD.

PRE-ORGASMIC. The preferred term for *frigid*. *See* FRIGIDITY.

PROGESTERONE. The female "PREGNANCY" HORMONE produced by the CORPUS LUTEUM. Its two primary functions are to govern the preparation of the UTERUS to receive the FERTILIZED OVUM, and to maintain the pregnancy so that it will go to term successfully. It also helps prepare the BREASTS to produce milk.

PROMISCUITY. The activity of engaging in SEXUAL INTERCOURSE with a number of different partners on a more-or-less casual basis. As with the term PORNOGRAPHY, however, different people attach different meanings and value judgments to the word. To some, having had sexual intercourse with two people implies promiscuity. Dr. Alfred KINSEY's favorite definition of a promiscuous person was "someone who has had sexual intercourse with one more person than the one applying the term." True promiscuity, however, is not recognized except as a medical diagnosis—that is, as a form of compulsive sexual behavior originating from complex social causes, many of them deriving from infancy and childhood. Such truly promiscuous people are known to derive little or no sexual satisfaction from their sexual adventures.

PROSTAGLANDINS. HORMONES secreted by many organs of the body, including the PROSTATE GLAND, and therefore contained in SEMEN. It has long been known that human semen injected into the UTERUS causes vigorous contractions of the uterine muscles, and now synthetic prostaglandins are used as a method of inducing ABORTION, usually after the first TRIMESTER of PREGNANCY.

PROSTATE GLAND. The chestnut-shaped GLAND that surrounds the male URETHRA just below the BLADDER and that produces certain HORMONES and helps to manufacture SEMEN. The muscles of and around the gland are the principal ones that force the semen through the urethra and out of the erect PENIS during EJACULATION. Cancer of the prostate is the most common form of cancer in men and often requires the removal of all or part of the gland. Also, with age, the prostate may simply enlarge and tend to block the passage of urine. This condition also requires surgery. A "prostate operation" may but usually does not mean the end of a man's capacity to perform sexually and to enjoy sex. It may, however, result in "reverse ejaculation," whereby the semen is forced up into the bladder instead of down through the urethra. This is nothing to worry about, and the pleasurable sensations of orgasm do not change. Reverse ejaculation does mean, however, that the man can no longer IMPREGNATE a woman.

PROSTATE OPERATION. *See* PROSTATE GLAND.

PROSTITUTE. A person, male or female, who exchanges sexual services for money.

PUBERTY. The period during which a boy or girl enters adolescence. More specifically, the beginning of puberty is marked by the first EJACULATION of SEMEN for the boy, and the first MENSTRUATION for the girl. Children arrive at puberty according to a definite but highly individualized schedule of physical events that it is helpful for them to understand in advance. The fact that a boy or girl has reached puberty does not mean that he or she is an adult or ready for the responsibilities of parenthood but only that the boy is now capable of IMPREGNATING a girl and the girl of becoming PREGNANT.

PUBIC HAIR. The hair, at first downy but then darker, curlier, and coarser, that appears just above the PENIS in a boy and above and on the upper part of the VULVA in a girl. The arrival of pubic hair is a signal of the onset of PUBERTY.

Q

QUEEN. A slang term for a male HOMOSEXUAL who willingly plays the female role in a GAY relationship. It is important to know that male/female role-playing is much less common among homosexuals today than it was a few years ago, when gay people tended to live out the stereotyped expectations that society forced upon them. *See also* HOMOSEXUAL.

R

RAPE. Forcible SEXUAL INTERCOURSE with a person against the person's will. *See also* STATUTORY RAPE.

RECTUM. The lower end of the large intestine. Its opening is called the ANUS. See Figure 8, p. 44.

REFRACTORY PERIOD. A period shortly after ORGASM in most men and some women in which further sexual response is not possible. After EJACU-LATION, a man's PENIS soon becomes limp, and he is temporarily unable to have another ERECTION or ejaculation. The period may last anywhere from a few minutes to several days, depending upon the man's age, state of health, and the degree of subsequent sexual stimulation. A woman's refractory period may last from a few seconds or minutes to several days, depending more on her previously established sexual response level than on her age, although as with men its duration does increase with age.

REPRODUCTION. The process of generating or reproducing its own kind by any species of life, encompassing various processes that are specifically characteristic of each species, whether in plants, animals, or humans.

REPRODUCTIVE SYSTEM. The male and female organs directly involved in REPRODUCTION. This system is not the same as the SEXUAL RESPONSE SYSTEM, although closely related to it. For example, the CLITORIS is an important part of the sexual response system but has no function in the reproductive system. (See the diagrams of the two systems in Figures 6 and 8, pp. 42 and 44.)

RHYTHM METHOD. A method of BIRTH CONTROL which relies on the fact that there is a rhythm or regularity in a woman's MENSTRUAL CYCLE and that by careful recording of the events of her cycle she may be able to predict when she will OVULATE and then abstain from SEXUAL INTERCOURSE around that time. The term is not much used today, since more sophisticated methods of FERTILITY AWARENESS have been developed by specialists in NATURAL FAMILY PLANNING. *See also* CALENDAR METHOD.

RIGHT TO LIFE. A term used to cover the ideas and organizations supporting the concept that the FERTILIZED OVUM from the moment of fertilization is a person and has an absolute right to be born. Regardless of the circumstances into which a baby may be born, Right-to-life people oppose ABORTION and state that the EMBRYO and, later, the FETUS, are human life, developing babies, harmless and sacred, with as much right to live as any human being, and that we have no more right to "kill" them for our "social convenience" than to "kill" any person for such reasons. Right-to-life organizations counsel couples on NATURAL FAMILY PLANNING methods and oppose artificial and chemical methods of CONTRACEPTION.

RUBBER. An informal word for CONDOM.

RUBELLA. The scientific term for *German measles,* a disease which, if the mother contracts it during the first three months of her PREGNANCY, may cause serious birth defects in the baby.

S

SADISM. A SEXUAL VARIANCE in which a person receives sexual pleasure through inflicting pain upon another person. A person who practices sadism is called a *sadist.* The word comes from the name of the French Marquis de Sade (1740–1814), whose novels described such sexual activity. Sadism is illegal in most states. *See also* MASOCHISM; SADO-MASOCHISM.

SADO-MASOCHISM. A term describing the sexual relationship between a SADIST and a MASOCHIST. It is interesting that it is the masochist (the person who gets pleasure from receiving pain) who probably controls such a relationship, since the sadist (the inflictor of pain) wants the relationship to continue and therefore must be careful not to inflict such excessive pain that the masochist might withdraw from the relationship.

SAFE PERIOD. The time during a woman's MENSTRUAL CYCLE during which it might be "safe" to have SEXUAL INTERCOURSE, that is, the days when she is least likely to become PREGNANT. Without expert instruction, it is difficult for women to identify this safe period, since most women have irregular cycles and thus are not able to predict exactly when they will OVULATE or even to know when they have ovulated. *See also* NATURAL FAMILY PLANNING.

SAFETY (or SAFE). Informal word for CONDOM.

SALINE ABORTION. The method of induced ABORTION that involves injecting a solution of salt into the AMNIOTIC FLUID surrounding the FETUS. The salt solution kills the fetus and causes LABOR contractions, during which it is expelled as in childbirth. The method is used after the first three months of PREGNANCY and may lead to some complications. *See also* ABORTION; CURETTAGE.

SALTING OUT. A term commonly used to refer to SALINE ABORTION.

SALTPETER. The drug potassium nitrate, commonly but incorrectly thought to reduce SEXUAL DESIRE in men. All it does is increase the flow of urine. It has no effect on sexual POTENCY or interest.

SANGER, MARGARET (1883–1966). One of the early American leaders in the BIRTH CONTROL movement and founder of the American Birth Control League that later became the Planned Parenthood Federation of America. She believed that the poor especially needed to control the sizes of their families, so that they could have happier, healthier lives and better sexual relationships between the parents. She worked not only in the United States but also in India.

SANITARY NAPKIN. A disposable pad or napkin used to absorb the MEN-STRUAL FLOW. It is made of cellulose or other absorbent material in a gauze covering and can be held in place along the opening of the VAGINA by an elastic panty, belt, or adhesive backing that clings to the panty. *See also* TAMPON.

SATYRIASIS. A sexual disorder involving such excessive and extreme SEXUAL DESIRE in a man that the pursuit of sexual satisfaction dominates his life to a degree that is harmful to himself and usually to others. The word comes from the *satyrs* of Greek mythology, who were supposed to be part human and part animal and to have SEX DRIVES that could never be satisfied. Comparable to NYMPHOMANIA in women, but both terms are unacceptable in modern medicine. *See also* PROMISCUITY.

SCROTUM. The pouch of loose, wrinkled skin suspended below the base of the PENIS. This sac contains the two TESTICLES, the two EPIDIDYMIDES, and the beginning of the two VASA DEFERENTIA. See Figure 2, p. 36.

SECONDARY SEX CHARACTERISTICS. The physical sex characteristics (other than the main REPRODUCTIVE organs) that develop during PUBERTY, such as PUBIC HAIR, underarm and facial hair, BREASTS, deepening of the voice (especially in the male), and changing body shape.

SEDUCTION. The act of persuading or inducing a person into sexual activity without the use of force. Seduction can be harmful when a person is lured into sex against his or her better judgment and contrary to his or her welfare. In a well-established relationship such as MARRIAGE, however, it can be a great pleasure for either partner to be "seduced" by the other into mutually pleasurable and acceptable sexual activity.

SELF-PLEASURING. MASTURBATION, or the caressing of one's own body for physical pleasure and release of tension.

SEMEN. The mixture of SPERM (manufactured by the TESTICLES and stored in the VAS DEFERENS) and SEMINAL FLUID (secreted mainly by the PROS-TATE GLAND), which is EJACULATED from the PENIS during ORGASM. The function of the seminal fluid is to keep the sperm in lively and healthy condition and transport them safely into the VAGINA. Semen comes from the

Latin word for seed, but neither it nor the sperm are true seeds in the agricultural sense.

SEMINAL FLUID. A fluid that is secreted mainly by the PROSTATE GLAND during EJACULATION and that mixes with SPERM to form SEMEN.

SEMINAL VESICLES. Two small pouches at the back of the PROSTATE GLAND, behind the BLADDER, each attached to a VAS DEFERENS. At the time of EJACULATION, these vesicles discharge a special fluid that constitutes a part of SEMEN and enlivens the SPERM. See Figure 2, p. 36.

SENSUAL. Interested in and seeking bodily pleasure, but especially sexual pleasure; or, interested in arousing such interest and seeking it in others. *See also* LIBIDO; SEXUAL DESIRE.

SENSUOUS. Enjoying all bodily sensations that involve the five senses.

SEX. A word with a number of meanings, some of which are: GENDER, that is, male or female; SEXUAL INTERCOURSE, as in "having sex"; the sexual attraction felt by one person for another; or to arouse sexually, as to "sex up" a person. *See also* SEXUALITY.

SEX AND AGING. *See* AGING AND SEX.

SEX-CHANGE OPERATION. A surgical operation performed on a male or female diagnosed as TRANSSEXUAL, that physically changes him or her as nearly as possible into a member of the other sex. The surgery supplies a structural PENIS to a female or a VAGINA to a male and removes the unwanted sex GLANDS (TESTICLES or OVARIES). For the rest of the person's life, he or she must receive maintenance dosages of the HORMONES of the other sex into which the transformation has been made. Such surgery is performed only on people who have for years been convinced that they were members of the other sex imprisoned, as it were, in a body that as a consequence was for them of the wrong sex. Sex-change surgery is performed by ethical and competent surgeons only after several years of the most careful study and treatment, including hormonal treatment preceding the surgery and the requirement that the person desiring the change must for at least a year successfully live the life of the desired sex. After this, careful study and certification by a qualified psychotherapist is required as indication for operation. Of course, people who have had a sex-change operation can never IMPREGNATE or become PREGNANT. However, some can and do marry and live sexually satisfying lives. TRANSSEXUALISM is unrelated to HOMOSEXUALITY. *See also* TRANSSEXUAL.

SEX DRIVE. *See* LIBIDO; SEXUAL DESIRE.

SEX GLANDS. *See* GONADS.

SEX HORMONES. Chemicals secreted by the SEX GLANDS directly into the bloodstream which affect the characteristics and behavior of males and females. ANDROGEN is the principal male sex hormone and ESTROGEN the principal female sex hormone.

SEXISM. Discrimination against a person because of his or her GENDER. Usually sexism arises from a prejudice against women or a belief, often even by women themselves, that only certain kinds of jobs, activities, behavior, household duties, and recreation are suitable for women, who are, according to the sexist (a person who practices sexism), "the weaker sex." However, sexism is damaging to both men and women insofar as it forces people of either sex into roles and behavior that are not comfortable for them but which they perform because they feel society expects it of them. On the other hand, many people of both sexes feel comfortable and fulfilled in their sex-prescribed roles and do not perceive themselves as damaged by sexism. *See also* FEMINISM; MALE CHAUVINISM; SEX ROLES; SEXUAL STEREOTYPES.

SEX ORGANS. The external and internal organs that distinguish males and females from each other.

SEX PLAY. A term with several quite different meanings, among which are: the activities that precede SEXUAL INTERCOURSE, also called FOREPLAY; the more or less sexually arousing activities involved in NECKING and PETTING, whether or not they are intended to lead to intercourse; the lighthearted, somewhat sexual fooling around that two people may engage in, in a recreational sense; the sexual playing of children as they "rehearse" and learn the roles and activities through which they will later express their sexuality as adults; the activities involved in "playing with oneself," or MASTURBATION.

SEX ROLE. The group of behaviors and activities that people assume to be appropriate to their GENDER, whether male or female. *See also* SEXISM; SEXUAL STEREOTYPES.

SEX THERAPY. Psychological, physical, and perhaps medical treatment with the aim of enabling a person to overcome a sexual DYSFUNCTION. (*See* COUNSELING for the distinction between THERAPY and counseling.) Sex therapy must almost always be carried out with the two people involved.

SEXUAL. Having to do with sex in any sense.

SEXUAL DESIRE. A strong feeling of wanting and needing sexual activity and/or ORGASM. Also called *sex drive.* Its opposite is lack of desire, a complaint of many men and women today. Especially in recent years, rightly or wrongly, our society has promoted the idea that a person must be sexually very active in order to have a good life. It can be a problem if one member of a couple believes this and the other does not, or if one member of a couple feels much less desire for sexual activity than the other member. COUNSELING and SEX THERAPY can in some cases help couples deal with such problems. They can also help couples realize that there are many other rewarding experiences in life and that the desire for sexual activity and the capacity to "perform" sexually may be accepted at a lower level, or even as unnecessary. Many couples consider themselves very happily married even though they do not experience a strong sexual desire or engage in frequent sexual activity, or even any at all. *See also* LIBIDO.

SEXUAL DEVIANCY. *See* DEVIATION.

SEXUAL DREAMS. *See* DREAMS.

SEXUAL IDENTITY. The conviction a person has of being a male or a female. *See also* GENDER IDENTITY.

SEXUAL INTERCOURSE. Principally, the sexual union of male and female in which the PENIS enters the VAGINA. Usually, but not invariably, the male EJACULATES and often the female has an ORGASM. On occasion, the partners reach their CLIMAXES simultaneously. There are many varieties of and positions for sexual intercourse, according to the preferences of the partners. Other terms for sexual intercourse are *coitus* and *sexual relations. See also* ANAL INTERCOURSE; HYMEN; STAGES OF SEXUAL RESPONSE.

SEXUALITY. The quality or condition of being a sexual person and of expressing one's sexual nature in a variety of ways; the part of our lives that has to do with our being male or female.

SEXUALIZATION. The process—especially during infancy, childhood, and adolescence but also during any other period of life—through which we develop our SEXUALITY, or sexual natures. The three primary elements of this process are the development of our GENDER IDENTITY, of concepts of our appropriate GENDER ROLE, and of the capacity for sexual pleasure and response.

SEXUALLY TRANSMITTED DISEASES (STDs). *See* VENEREAL DISEASES.

SEXUAL ORIENTATION. The state of being sexually attracted to and interested in members of the other sex or of the same sex or of either sex. A person's sexual orientation can thus be HETEROSEXUAL, HOMOSEXUAL, or BISEXUAL. It is quite firmly established during the first few years of life and not likely to change.

SEXUAL RELATIONS. *See* SEXUAL INTERCOURSE.

SEXUAL RESPONSE CYCLE. *See* STAGES OF SEXUAL RESPONSE.

SEXUAL REVOLUTION. The supposed radical change in sexual behavior that many people think has occurred in recent years. The word *revolution* is not a good one because, correctly defined, it means a sudden overturn of the established order, and there have been no sudden, nearly universal changes in sexual behavior in our culture over a period of some years. Rather, there have been periods of more or less rapid *evolution*. Without doubt, the sexual behavior of the young today is quite different from that of their parents and grandparents at the same ages, involving more freedom of sexual activity, larger amounts of activity started earlier, and especially a vastly increased ease in talking about it all. Perhaps one of the most revolutionary changes, one that started a few years ago and continues apace, is the increased conviction of such professionals as doctors, nurses, counselors, teachers, public health workers, and social workers that they have a responsibility to become properly informed about human sexuality and to take it into account on behalf of the people they serve. The state of California now has a law requiring all health workers to have training in the human sexuality field. The clergy too, because of their great involvement in the mental and social health of people, increasingly include themselves in professional activities in the field of human sexuality.

SEXUAL STEREOTYPES. A stereotype is an oversimplified concept of something that is really quite complex and differentiated. Sexual stereotypes are those that represent a simple, often traditional, idea of what it is to be a human male or female: males are strong, brave, unemotional, reasoning, etc.; females are weak, in need of protection, emotional, illogical, etc. Without doubt, there are some important inherited and many cultural differences between males and females in all societies, and these should be studied and understood, but they are not simple, and there is a much broader range of differences and potential differences between boys and girls and men and women, as well as more similarities, than used to be commonly thought. *See also* FEMINISM; SEX ROLES; SEXISM.

SEXUAL RESPONSE SYSTEM. The parts of the human body involved in the expression and enjoyment of SEXUALITY and EROTIC feelings. Functioning from before birth, the sexual response system should be distinguished from the REPRODUCTIVE SYSTEM, to which it is closely related but not identical and which does not begin functioning until PUBERTY. (See Figures 2, 6, and 8, pp. 36, 42 and 44.) *See also* REPRODUCTIVE SYSTEM; STAGES OF SEXUAL RESPONSE.

SEXUAL TENSION. The feeling of unease and desire for sexual activity that seeks ORGASM for relief.

SEXUAL VARIANCE. *See* VARIANT SEXUAL BEHAVIOR.

SISSY. A young boy who acts in an EFFEMINATE manner and seems not to be interested in the rough and noisy behavior that "all-American boys" are supposed to display. The opposite of sissy is TOMBOY, although the word *sissy* has such overtones of fright and timidity that it is much more of a put-down term than is tomboy. There is no reliable evidence to indicate that effeminate-acting boys must inevitably be HOMOSEXUAL, despite a wide-spread belief and fear to the contrary. But if a boy's family is concerned about sissiness, professional help should be consulted.

SITUATION ETHICS. An approach to deciding what are right and wrong ways to behave that does not refer to fixed rules but instead takes into account all the consequences of a possible action, consequences to self and others, consequences present and future. On the basis of these consequences (the situation) a decision is reached as to what to do or not do. It is sometimes called "the new morality." Situation ethics is risky in that people may be so greatly influenced by their immediate self-interest or desire for self-gratification that they may come up with a rationalized decision that could prove to be unwise. But living by fixed rules is also risky, since the rules may have been established at a time when circumstances were quite different from the present ones and therefore may not apply well and helpfully today. Whether a person makes decisions on the basis of situation ethics or fixed rules, the fact is that life is full of risks and possibilities for doing harm or good.

SIXTY-NINE. A slang term describing the positions taken by two people simultaneously engaging in ORAL SEX with each other, which positions somewhat resemble the number 69.

SMEGMA. The cheeselike, unpleasant-smelling substance that accumulates under the FORESKIN of an unCIRCUMCISED PENIS or under the hood of a CLITORIS that has not been regularly cleansed. Children should be taught early to pull back the foreskin or the hood and with their fingers wash the area gently but thoroughly with soap and water. This will remove smegma quite easily.

SODOMY. This word has been used biblically and legally to label as "unnatural," repulsive, or wrong various forms of sexual activity that the person doing the labeling doesn't approve of. In the United States, there are three types of sexual behavior legally defined as sodomy: sex with an animal (BESTIALITY), ANAL INTERCOURSE, and FELLATIO. HOMOSEXUALS are more likely than other people to be prosecuted under sodomy laws, although such prosecution is becoming less and less common when the activity is engaged in by mutually consenting adults. The name comes from that of

Sodom, an ancient city which, according to the biblical book Genesis, was destroyed by God along with the city of Gomorrah because of the wickednesses of the inhabitants of the two cities.

SOFT CHANCRE. *See* CHANCROID.

SPANISH FLY. A powder called cantharides made from dried blister beetles found in southern Europe, especially Spain. When taken internally, it has an irritating effect on the URINARY TRACT and so is supposed to act as an APHRODISIAC, stimulating SEXUAL DESIRE and increasing sexual feeling. It can produce dangerous illness and death and should never be used.

SPERM. The male REPRODUCTIVE cell manufactured by the TESTICLES and EJACULATED in the SEMEN. Its function is to FERTILIZE the female OVUM, thus causing PREGNANCY. The plural is either sperm or sperms; the scientific term is *spermatozoon* (singular), *spermatozoa* (plural).

SPERMATOGENESIS. The process by which TESTICLES generate or form SPERM.

SPERM BANK. A place for storing SPERM that have been flash-frozen in a glycerine solution for later use for ARTIFICIAL INSEMINATION. Sperm are also being stored in sperm banks as FERTILITY insurance by men who have VASECTOMIES but who may change their minds about desiring a child in the future. Donor sperm are also stored for later insemination of women who wish to have children but whose husbands are unable to produce enough sperm to make them PREGNANT. Sperm stored for as long as five years provide a 50 percent chance of pregnancy, although the longer the sperm are stored, the smaller the chance of their being effective.

SPERM COUNT. The number of sperm contained in an EJACULATION of SEMEN, usually measured as the number of SPERM in a cubic centimeter of semen. A normal sperm count is 35 million per cubic centimeter or higher, or 150 to 600 million in the teaspoonful or so of semen usually ejaculated. A man's sperm count is always determined when he and his wife have been unable to CONCEIVE children, and is one of the number of tests done to discover why a couple is INFERTILE. *See also* INFERTILITY.

SPERMICIDE. Any substance that, when injected or placed into the VAGINA before SEXUAL INTERCOURSE, will serve to destroy the SPERM EJACULATED in intercourse. Spermicidal creams, foams, and jellies are commonly used as CONTRACEPTIVES. They can be purchased at drugstores without a doctor's prescription, are easy to use, and are very effective if the male also uses a CONDOM or the female a DIAPHRAGM. Used alone, they are not very effective, but they are more effective than using no contraceptive at all.

SPONTANEOUS ABORTION. *See* ABORTION.

SPOUSE. A married partner—husband or wife. The word derives from the Latin *spons* (pledged).

SQUEEZE TECHNIQUE. A method used for curing PREMATURE EJACULATION. It involves training exercise and practice in which the man's sex partner first stimulates ERECTION, then squeezes the head of his PENIS quite hard with her thumb and two fingers when he signals that he has arrived at the point just before EJACULATION is inevitable. The technique is highly effective when used as treatment, but it is complicated and subtle to learn, and couples should not try it without the guidance of an accredited SEX THERAPIST.

STAGES OF SEXUAL RESPONSE. The generalized patterns of sexual response observed and recorded by sex researchers Masters and Johnson. In brief, the stages, which constitute what Masters and Johnson call the *sexual response cycle,* are these: (1) excitement, during which sexual feeling and great interest are aroused, the man has an ERECTION, the woman's VAGINA becomes LUBRICATED and aroused, and various other complex but definite body changes occur; (2) plateau, during which the man's erection increases in size, the woman's body maintains and increases the physical changes observed in the excitement stage, and both man and woman (although quite likely not at the same time) maintain a high degree of sexual feeling; (3) ORGASM, the period of CLIMAX and EJACULATION in a man, lasting only a few seconds, and the not necessarily simultaneous period in a woman, when she has one, or perhaps two or several, orgasms; (4) resolution, the period of declining sexual excitement, when the man quite quickly loses his erection and returns to a calm and relaxed state, and the woman, perhaps much more slowly than the man and possibly after having been reexcited one or more times, finally relaxes and feels satisfied. After the resolution stage, a man and most women go through a REFRACTORY PERIOD, during which for variable periods of time both are incapable of further stimulation. There is no such period in some women, who may be capable of almost immediate reexcitement. It is important to understand that these four stages are generalized descriptions and that they differ in length and intensity from one individual to another. They are not clearly demarcated one from another, and it is quite possible for one member of a couple to proceed through the stages at a rate quite different from that of the other member. However, the sequence of the stages is always the same. *See also* SEXUAL INTERCOURSE.

STATUTORY RAPE. Any act of SEXUAL INTERCOURSE with a female under the "age of consent," whether voluntary or involuntary on her part. The age varies from state to state, the most common being from sixteen to eighteen, but in some states as low as ten and as high as twenty-one. *See also* RAPE.

STD. The initials stand for the term *sexually transmitted disease*. *See* VENEREAL DISEASES.

STEREOTYPES. *See* SEX ROLES; SEXUAL STEREOTYPES

STERILITY. The state of being unable to IMPREGNATE (on the part of a man) or to become PREGNANT (on the part of a woman)—that is, the inability to CONCEIVE. The state of sterility of a couple is due about half the time to a difficulty in the woman's generative apparatus and half the time to a difficulty in the man's. *See* INFERTILITY.

STERILIZATION. Any procedure or event that renders an individual incapable of producing offspring. The most common procedures are VASECTOMY for men and the TUBAL LIGATION for women. The most common sterilizing disease among women is GONORRHEA, which may infect and then permanently block the FALLOPIAN TUBES with scar tissue. In males, the most common disease causing INFERTILITY is mumps.

STILLBIRTH. The birth of a dead child. A stillbirth differs from a MISCARRIAGE in that in a stillbirth the dead FETUS is beyond the sixth month of PREGNANCY and fully recognizable as a dead baby, whereas most miscarriages occur much earlier in pregnancy. The causes of many stillbirths are not known.

STOP-START TECHNIQUE. A term for one of two successful methods to cure PREMATURE EJACULATION. As the man feels himself approaching the moment of inevitable ejaculation, he must stop all stimulation, whether by himself or his partner. Once the moment has passed, he can begin again. As taught by a SEX THERAPIST, with practice he can learn to gain good control of the timing of his EJACULATION. The advantage of this over the other method is that it can be learned and practiced by the man alone during masturbation. *See* SQUEEZE TECHNIQUE.

STRAIGHT. An informal term meaning HETEROSEXUAL in orientation, as distinguished from GAY or HOMOSEXUAL.

SUBLIMATION. A term loosely used to refer to efforts to redirect the SEX DRIVE into nonsexual channels, like strenuous work, sports, or very strong alternative interests. Some people seem to succeed quite well in "sublimating," even to the point of effective elimination of their conscious drive to sexual activity.

SUCTION METHOD OF ABORTION. *See* VACUUM ASPIRATION.

SURROGATE. In general, a person appointed to act for another person. In the field of SEX THERAPY, to be a sex surrogate means to serve professionally as a partner in the sex therapy desired; it is looked upon by some as being a new profession. A sex therapist trains and supervises the surrogate's work with the patient, who is usually a male with no partner to work with him in therapy to overcome a sexual difficulty, such as PREMATURE EJACULATION. The therapist refers the surrogate to the patient, who pays her fee. It is a business relationship, not a personal or social one. In many cases the use of surrogates in this manner has been very successful. However, this is obviously a controversial subject on which many people, including sex therapists, have mixed or strongly negative feelings. Because of this, most sex therapists do not at present routinely use surrogates.

SWINGING. A life-style involving the sexual exchange of partners between two or more married couples; also called *mate-swapping.* The custom is not very common in the United States and involves many difficulties and risks— in addition to being illegal, although it is rarely prosecuted. However, there are some couples who enjoy it and defend the practice. A person who practices swinging is called a *swinger.* Wife-swapping (a term that implies that a wife is a piece of property to be swapped) is not uncommon in some tribes of Eskimos, among whom the custom is to offer one's wife to a guest as a gesture of hospitality. This is entirely different from swinging.

SYMPTO-THERMIC METHOD. A method of BIRTH CONTROL in which a woman learns to recognize the symptoms of OVULATION and also to predict it by keeping a record of her temperature. *See also* NATURAL FAMILY PLAN-NING.

SYPHILIS. Also called *syph, pox, lues, bad blood.* One of the sexually transmitted VENEREAL DISEASES (STDs). *Cause:* spirochete bacterium called *Treponema pallidum* (meaning pale, twisted thread, shaped like a corkscrew). *Symptoms:* Symptoms come in three stages: In Stage 1 there are chancres (pronounced *shankers*), usually one or sometimes more painless, round, hard ulcers or "sores," which disappear after three to six weeks. They appear usually on the GENITALS but occasionally on the mouth or BREASTS; in some cases they cause swelling of the lymph nodes in the GROIN. The chancres are very infectious. Stage 2 comes usually a month to six months after the first stage has disappeared, but may overlap it; it commonly lasts for from six weeks to six months. The most common symptoms are like those of flu—fatigue, aching joints and muscles, fever. Other Stage 2 symptoms are (a) a rash of brownish-red, flat pimples, which are painless and appear most often on the palms of the hands or the soles of the feet (this rash is infectious if it touches a cut or scrape or mucous membrane of another person); (b) swollen lymph nodes; and (c) hair falling out in patches. The "Latent Period," after the Stage 2 symptoms are gone and before Stage 3 has set in, is when the disease enters a "quiet" stage; the patient is infected but not infectious, and the spirochetes are traveling thoughout the body, entering and beginning to damage various organs. This period may last from one to twenty years. At Stage 3, the disease is called *late syphilis* or *tertiary syphilis,* when the effects of the damage being done by the spirochetes become evident and when the organs of the body reveal that they have become seriously damaged. Here the symptoms vary according to the organs affected (heart, brain, etc.). *Time from contact to Stage 1 symptoms:* ten to ninety days; average three weeks. *Method of diagnosis:* blood test; smear from chancre; examination. *Complications:* if syphilis is treated and cured during Stage 1 or 2, there are no complications. If it is allowed to enter the Latent Period and then Stage 3, the complications are very serious: brain damage (sometimes resulting in insanity), heart and blood-vessel disease, kidney disease, and possible death from any of these. Infants infected during PREGNANCY suffer various kinds of serious damage and disfigurement and may be born dead. For this reason, the law requires that couples have a blood test for syphilis before marriage, and pregnant women must be tested as soon as they become pregnant, so that if the test is positive, treatment during the pregnancy can result in a nonsyphilitic baby.

T

TABOO (or TABU). Something forbidden by social custom or religious belief. INCEST is a taboo in almost every society and social class. PREMARITAL or NONMARITAL SEX, male EFFEMINACY, or female mannishness might be taboo among certain groups and entirely acceptable among others. A number of slang words that refer to sex are presently taboo on radio and television, though used far more liberally in literature, magazines, and the press.

TAMPON. A small roll of absorbent material that is inserted into the VAGINA to absorb the MENSTRUAL FLOW. Tampons come in different sizes and absorbencies. *See also* HYMEN; SANITARY NAPKIN.

TESTICLES (or TESTES). The singular is *testicle* or *testis.* These are the two male SEX GLANDS, oval-shaped and each about 1½ inches long in a grown man, that are carried in the SCROTUM suspended between the legs. These glands manufacture SPERM, the male REPRODUCTIVE cells. In most men, one testis hangs lower than the other. See Figure 2, p. 36. *See also* EPIDIDYMIS; SCROTUM; UNDESCENDED TESTICLES.

TESTOSTERONE. The primary male sex HORMONE (or ANDROGEN) manufactured by the TESTICLES. Not only is it the inducer and maintainer of the male SECONDARY SEX CHARACTERISTICS, but it is also responsible for the SEX DRIVE (LIBIDO) in males—and in females too, for in the female the adrenal GLANDS always manufacture a certain amount of testosterone.

TEST-TUBE BABIES. Babies who start their lives in a test tube. If a woman's FALLOPIAN TUBES are blocked and she wishes to have a child, it is now possible to take a mature OVUM from her OVARY and mix it in a test tube with SPERM from her husband. When the ovum is thus FERTILIZED, it can be placed in the woman's UTERUS, where it may become IMPLANTED and grow normally. The procedure is complicated, and the first known success was in England in 1978.

THERAPY. The treatment of disease or DYSFUNCTION. *See also* COUNSELING; SEX THERAPY.

TOMBOY. A young girl with boyish ways. Probably most tomboys are girls who find the limits of behavior that society has set for girls too restricting of their freedom and who simply revolt against these limits and behave the way they want to rather than "the way nice little girls should." The opposite of "tomboy" is SISSY, but this word expresses a more critical attitude about boys than tomboy does about girls.

TRANSSEXUAL. A person who feels that he or she is a member of the other sex, imprisoned in the body he or she was born in. Many such persons earnestly seek to have their bodily sex changed by surgery and HORMONES. *See also* SEX-CHANGE OPERATIONS.

TRANSVESTITE. A person, almost always a male, who has a strong desire or compulsion to dress in the clothing of the other sex—that is, to engage in *cross-dressing.* Often a male transvestite depends upon cross-dressing to be able to perform sexually and to achieve sexual satisfaction. Not all wives wish to cooperate with this desire. The root of the word is the Latin *vest* (garment), which combines with the prefix *trans-* (across).

TRICHOMONAS VAGINALIS. Also called *trichomoniasis, trich, TV.* It can be a sexually transmitted VENEREAL DISEASE. *Cause:* a protozoan (microscopic, single-cell organism, like an amoeba). *Symptoms:* copious grayish, foul-smelling discharge from the VAGINA; intense itching, burning, and redness of GENITALS and thighs; painful SEXUAL INTERCOURSE. Men often have no symptoms, carrying the disease without knowing it. *Time from contact to first symptoms:* one to four weeks. *Method of diagnosis:* microscopic examination and identification of the organism in discharge. *Complications:* GLAND infections in females; increased risk of cancer of the CERVIX; possibility of considerable discomfort after the woman has given birth. Fortunately there is now a specific cure but, as with SYPHILIS and GONORRHEA, reinfection is always possible.

TRIMESTER. In PREGNANCY, one of the three approximately three-month time divisions. The first trimester includes approximately the first twelve weeks after CONCEPTION; the second, the second twelve; and the third trimester the final weeks, at the end of which the child is born.

TRIPLETS. *See* MULTIPLE BIRTHS.

TUBAL LIGATION. The method of female STERILIZATION in which a surgeon ties and cuts a woman's FALLOPIAN TUBES so that OVA cannot pass down the tubes or SPERM pass up. A more modern and frequent procedure involves electrically cauterizing (searing closed with heat) rather than tying the tubes. The word comes from the Latin *ligare* (to tie). *See also* LAPAROSCOPY.

TUBAL PREGNANCY. *See* ECTOPIC PREGNANCY.

TUBES. *See* FALLOPIAN TUBE.

TWINS. *See* MULTIPLE BIRTHS.

U

UMBILICAL CORD. A ropelike cord, filled with blood vessels, that runs from the baby's ABDOMEN to connect the developing baby to the PLACENTA. By means of the umbilical cord the baby is supplied with nourishment and oxygen from the mother and the baby's circulatory system passes waste materials into the mother's circulatory system. The baby and mother have separate blood systems and do not exchange blood. What happens is that in the placenta, where a multitude of tiny blood vessels lie next to each other, nutriments and oxygen from the mother and waste materials from the baby can filter through their thin walls. The NAVEL marks the spot where a person's umbilical cord was attached.

UNDESCENDED TESTICLES. TESTICLES that have failed to descend into the SCROTUM as they should before birth. Normally, very early in PREGNANCY the SEX GLANDS of both male and female are located high up in the ABDOMINAL cavity of the EMBRYO and then in the FETUS. By about the tenth week of pregnancy they shift down to the upper edge of what will be the PELVIS. In a female, the OVARIES remain at about that level, but in a male, starting about the third month, the testicles begin to descend toward the scrotum, a process usually completed by the fourth or fifth month of pregnancy. However, one baby boy out of fifty is born with one or both testicles undescended. In most such boys the descent subsequently takes place before puberty. If it does not, HORMONAL and perhaps surgical treatment are necessary. If the testicles remain within the abdomen, not only will the temperature be too high to permit the making of sperm, but there is also a possibility of cancer development in the GLAND.

UNISEX. A recently coined word denoting the state of affairs in which it is difficult to distinguish by clothing or hair length to which GENDER a person belongs. Some people, especially older ones, are worried that unisex dressing and hair may be the result of, or result in, confusion of GENDER IDENTITY or GENDER ROLE. However, the young apparently have no difficulty making the distinction, and unisex (or androgynous) clothing and hairdos are, on occasion and among some groups, quite fashionable.

UNNATURAL. A term that is never used by scientists but that, when applied to sexual behavior by lawyers, legislators, reporters, or the public usually refers to activities the user of the term does not approve of (or does not understand). *See also* NATURAL/UNNATURAL; SODOMY.

URETHRA. The tube through which urine is discharged from the BLADDER. In the female the urethra is very short, and urine exits from an opening (the urethral orifice, or meatus) located between the CLITORIS and the VAGINA; in the male, the urethra extends from the bladder to the tip of the PENIS. SEMEN is EJACULATED through the male's urethra, but never at the same time as urine. See Figures 2 and 8, pp. 36 and 44.

URINARY TRACT. In both male and female this consists of the kidneys, ureters (tubes between kidneys and BLADDER), bladder, and URETHRA.

UROLOGIST. A physician who specializes in the treatment of diseases and problems of the URINARY TRACTS of males and females, and of the GENITAL tracts of males. Some but not all urologists are trained as sexologists.

UTERINE. Of or relating to the UTERUS.

UTERUS. Also called *womb.* The organ of the female located in the PELVIS between the OVARIES, in which the FERTILIZED OVUM is IMPLANTED and GESTATES until ready to be born, and from which, if there is no fertilized ovum, the MENSTRUAL FLUID is discarded. The uterus is shaped like an upside-down pear and is about 3 inches long in a mature female who has not had children. It is tremendously stretchable, so that it can contain a fully developed FETUS, and it is made up of very powerful muscles, which push the baby out through the BIRTH CANAL when the time comes. *See also* ENDOMETRIUM.

V

VACUUM ASPIRATION (or VACUUM CURETTAGE). Today this is the most common and best method of performing ABORTIONS, but it is possible only during the first TRIMESTER of PREGNANCY. A small plastic tube is inserted through the cervical canal (*see* CERVIX) into the UTERUS and attached to an aspirator—a suction machine. Through holes in the tube, the EMBRYO and other products of CONCEPTION are vacuumed out of the uterus. The procedure is simple, relatively painless, and brief, and it can be done on an outpatient basis.

VAGINA. The soft, muscular, usually collapsed tube, about 3 or 4 inches in length, that provides a passageway between the UTERUS and the outside of a woman's body. It is the passageway, or BIRTH CANAL, through which babies are born and the MENSTRUAL FLUID flows. It is also the passageway into which the PENIS fits during SEXUAL INTERCOURSE and into which SPERM are EJACULATED. See Figure 6, p. 42.

VAGINISMUS. A condition in which the muscles surrounding the VAGINA go into such powerful, uncontrollable contraction that it is difficult or impossible for the PENIS to enter during SEXUAL INTERCOURSE. *See also* DYS-PAREUNIA.

VARIANT SEXUAL BEHAVIOR (or SEXUAL VARIANCE). The preferred term for sexual behavior that is not engaged in by most people. The term *variant* is simply descriptive, whereas terms like "perverted," "unnatural," or "abnormal" are judgmental.

VAS DEFERENS (plural, VASA DEFERENTIA). The two ducts that convey SPERM from the TESTICLES and store them. Each vas is about 18 inches long. See Figure 2, p. 36.

VASECTOMY. A relatively simple surgical procedure for STERILIZING a male by tying, cutting, and removing a portion of each of the two VASA DEFER-ENTIA, thus preventing passage of SPERM to mingle with the SEMINAL FLUID. Vasectomy is a method of CONTRACEPTION, in most cases irreversible.

VD. *See* VENEREAL DISEASE.

VENEREAL DISEASE. Also referred to as *VD*. Any of a number of diseases passed from person to person by close body contact, especially SEXUAL INTERCOURSE. The two best-known and most dangerous venereal diseases are GONORRHEA and SYPHILIS, but there are many others whose names and descriptions are given in this Encyclopedia. They are: CHANCROID, CRAB LICE, GRANULOMA INGUINALE, HERPES PROGENITALIS, LYMPHO-GRANULOMA VENEREUM, NONSPECIFIC or NONGONOCOCCAL URETHRI-TIS, TRICHOMONAS VAGINALIS, and VENEREAL WARTS. The term *venereal* comes from Venus, the name of the Roman goddess of love. Today's more scientific term for venereal diseases is *sexually transmitted diseases (STDs)*.

VENEREAL WARTS. Can be a sexually transmitted disease (*see* VENEREAL DISEASES). *Cause:* a virus. *Symptoms:* small warts, pinkish-red and soft, or yellowish-gray and hard, in the GENITAL area that itch and become irritated. *Time from contact to first symptoms:* up to two months. *Method of diagnosis:* examination. *Complications:* can spread enough to block VAGINAL opening; highly contagious.

VIABILITY. The state of being viable, that is, capable of living and developing normally, as a newborn infant. By the sixth or seventh months of PREG-NANCY, a FETUS has matured enough so that it would have some slight chance to live if born PREMATURELY. Some people believe that an ABOR-TION is morally acceptable up until a fetus is viable, but not afterward. This seems a shaky basis for argument, since medical science has steadily reduced the age of viability as techniques for caring for premature babies have improved and, it must be recognized, a baby born full-term, that is, after nine months of GESTATION, is still very far from being able to live independently, needing for a number of years the help of a complex support system called a mother, or a mother substitute.

VIBRATOR. An electric machine that vibrates, or causes the hand that holds it to vibrate. When such vibrations are applied to the area in and around the CLITORIS or, with a PENIS-shaped soft rubber vibrator, to the clitoral area and outer end of the VAGINA, they cause many of the women who use them (or whose sexual partners cooperate in using them) to experience an intense ORGASM or series of orgasms. Vibrators have been notable in helping women experience orgasm for the first time in their lives, even as late as at forty years of age. A vibrator also helps a women analyze what it is that causes her to orgasm, so that she can then communicate this information to her sexual partner. In this way it can serve as a bridge to orgasm in SEXUAL INTERCOURSE. On the other hand, it can cause her to become so dependent upon it that she actually becomes less capable of orgasm with a partner when she is without it.

VICTORIAN ATTITUDES. Attitudes toward sexuality said to be characteristic of Western culture during the age of Queen Victoria of Great Britain, who ruled from 1837 to 1901. The stereotype of a Victorian is a person who believes that sex is nasty; that nice people don't talk about it; that only "bad" women really enjoy sex, whereas "nice" women endure it and must be careful not to move or become excited in bed; and that women endure sex only out of a necessity to please their husbands and to beget children. Of course, many people living in the age of Victoria did not hold the Victorian attitudes, whereas, for better or worse, many people today are still committed to them without realizing how destructive they have been in many cases to the sexual and marital happiness of many people.

VIRGIN. A term used for a person, female or male, who has not had SEXUAL INTERCOURSE. In some societies—for example, Islamic ones—virginity in a female is essential if she is to find a good husband. In our society, there are many young people, both females and males, and more of their parents, who consider premarital CHASTITY important. The word *virginity* is used to describe the state of being a virgin. *See also* DOUBLE STANDARD; HYMEN.

VOICE CHANGE. *See* CHANGE OF VOICE.

VOYEURISM. A SEXUAL VARIANCE in which a person, almost always a male, derives sexual pleasure from observing, usually from a hiding place, the sexual activities of others or even their simple undressing. *See also* PEEPING TOM.

VULVA. The external female SEX ORGANS, including the LABIA, the CLITORIS, and the VAGINAL opening.

W

WARTS. *See* VENEREAL WARTS.

WET DREAM. *See* NOCTURNAL EMISSION.

WHORE. An old-fashioned word for PROSTITUTE. A whorehouse is a house of prostitution, or BROTHEL.

WIFE-SWAPPING. *See* SWINGING.

WITHDRAWAL. A method of CONTRACEPTION in which the male withdraws his PENIS from the woman's VAGINA just before EJACULATION. Also known as *coitus interruptus*. Withdrawal is not an effective method of contraception, because a man's penis often releases SEMEN containing SPERM even before ejaculation and because many men find it difficult to withdraw at the height of sexual excitement. However, it is better than using no method at all.

WOMB. *See* UTERUS.

WOMEN'S LIBERATION. *See* FEMINISM.

Y

YEAST INFECTION. *See* MONILIAL VAGINITIS.

Z

ZOOPHILIA. A SEXUAL VARIANCE, quite rare in our society, involving sexual contact with animals. *See also* BESTIALITY.

ZYGOTE. Scientific term for the single cell that results from union of SPERM and OVUM at the instant of FERTILIZATION. The zygote immediately begins to grow by cell division as it proceeds down the FALLOPIAN TUBE toward the UTERUS.

Other Family Reading About Sexuality

We believe that it is helpful to read widely about sex and sexuality. Every author phrases things differently, opinions may vary, and from such differences comes the discrimination by which one learns to make one's own choices and decisions.

Most of the best books published in this important field are reviewed for the Sex Information and Education Council of the U.S. by experts in various specialties. Every other year two lists are published in the *SIECUS Report*—one for professionals, the other for nonprofessionals—which include recent books as well as the most important titles from previous lists.

We are grateful to SIECUS for permission to reprint here its list for nonprofessionals from the *SIECUS Report* for September 1980.

Human Sexuality: Books for Everyone

This reading list is selective, but it includes titles for all age groups and special interests. It will be useful not only for parents and young people, but also for their teachers, counselors, clergy, and youth leaders.

Books on sexuality continue to be published, and many hours have been devoted to sifting the good from the not-so-good, the helpful from the exploitive, the serious from the titillating, the factually accurate from the inaccurate. These titles represent a variety of viewpoints at different levels of sophistication. Since individuals of the same age vary greatly in maturity, it is important for a family bookshelf to include a wide variety to cover the needs of different age groups in their rapid periods of development.

SIECUS does not sell any of these books. If your local bookstore cannot get them for you, write directly to the publishers whose addresses are listed at the end.

Young Children

DID THE SUN SHINE BEFORE YOU WERE BORN? *Sol and Judith Gordon, illustrated by Vivien Cohen.* A book which parents can read with their children, ages 3–6. In addition to answering the question "Where do babies come from?" clearly and directly, it deals with other aspects of how different kinds of families live and grow. *Ed-U Press, 1977.*

GIRLS ARE GIRLS AND BOYS ARE BOYS—SO WHAT'S THE DIFFERENCE? *Sol Gordon.* A nonsexist, liberating sex education book for children. *Ed-U Press, 1979.*

HOW BABIES ARE MADE. *Andrew C. Andry and Steve Schepp.* The story of reproduction in plants, animals, and humans told through the use of color photographs of paper sculptures. Factually accurate and simple enough to be understood by the youngest group. *Time-Life Books, 1974.*

HOW WAS I BORN? *Lennart Nilsson.* To be read by parents with their children. Tells the story of reproduction and birth using a combination of the famous Nilsson photographs of fetal development with warm family scenes and other illustrations. *Delacorte Press, 1975.*

WHAT IS A GIRL? WHAT IS A BOY? *Stephanie Waxman.* A simply written, nonsexist message for young children: names, hair lengths, interests, clothing, and emotions do not identify a person as a boy or a girl—only a person's genitals can do that. *Peace Press, 1976.*

"WHERE DID I COME FROM?" *Peter Mayle.* The facts of life without any nonsense, with illustrations. In its 11th printing. *Lyle Stuart, Inc., 1973.*

X: A FABULOUS CHILD'S STORY. *Lois Gould.* Entertaining, imaginatively presented story about gender identity. Fun for the whole family. *Daughters Publishing Company.*

Preteens

GROWING UP—'SPECIALLY FOR PRE-TEENS AND YOUNG TEENS. *Marilyn Lyman, illustrated by Helen Kahn.* Fourteen illustrated pages on menstruation, wet dreams, masturbation, and how babies get started. *Planned Parenthood Center of Syracuse, Inc., 1973.*

LOVE AND SEX AND GROWING UP. *Eric W. Johnson and Corrine B. Johnson.* Covers a broad range of topics to help preadolescents think about what being a man or a woman means in today's world. *Bantam Books, Inc., 1979.*

PERIOD. *JoAnn Gardner-Loulan, Bonnie Lopez, and Marcia Quackenbush.* Reassuring, cleverly illustrated book about menstruation, explaining why *all* girls are normal, at the same time that everyone is special. Includes personal narratives. *New Glide Publications, 1979.*

"WHAT'S HAPPENING TO ME?" *Peter Mayle.* A clear, concise, straightforward guide to puberty for preadolescent children. *Lyle Stuart, Inc., 1975.*

Early Teens

BOYS AND SEX. GIRLS AND SEX. *Wardell B. Pomeroy.* These classic sexual guides for teenage boys and girls are now being updated. *Delacorte Press. Revised editions in press for Spring 1981.*

CHANGES: YOU AND YOUR BODY. *CHOICE.* Easy-to-read booklet, prepared for and by teenagers, about puberty. *CHOICE, 1978.*

FACTS ABOUT SEX FOR TODAY'S YOUTH. Revised Edition. *Sol Gordon.* A short, direct approach in explaining anatomy, reproduction, love, and sex problems. Includes slang terms when giving definitions, and a section answering the ten most common questions children ask. Well illustrated. *Ed-U Press, 1979.*

FACTS ABOUT VD FOR TODAY'S YOUTH. Revised Edition. *Sol Gordon.* Up-to-date, accurate information written in clear and simple language. Stresses prevention. *Ed-U Press, 1979.*

LEARNING ABOUT SEX: A CONTEMPORARY GUIDE FOR YOUNG ADULTS. *Gary F. Kelly.* Without neglecting basic factual information, focuses on attitudes and the process of sexual decision making. *Barron's Educational Series, Inc., 1977.*

LOVE AND SEX IN PLAIN LANGUAGE. Revised Edition. *Eric W. Johnson.* Provides basic information on sexuality, and emphasizes that sexuality should always be seen in the context of one's total personality and expressed in responsible, respectful interpersonal relationships. *Bantam Books, Inc., 1979.*

THE PROBLEM WITH PUBERTY. *Sheri S. Tepper.* For boys, explaining emotional and physical changes taking place in puberty, and discussing problems of peer pressure. *Rocky Mountain Planned Parenthood, Inc., 1976.*

SEX: TELLING IT STRAIGHT. *Eric W. Johnson.* A simple but honest treatment of those topics in human sexuality of greatest concern to adolescents. Written for teenage slow readers, especially those within a ghetto environment, and presents positive views on sex without preaching or moralizing. *Lippincott and Crowell, 1979.*

SEX WITH LOVE: A GUIDE FOR YOUNG PEOPLE. *Eleanor Hamilton.* Includes discussion of the rituals of early dating and filling the body's need for affection and sexual expression. *Beacon Press, 1978.*

TEEN QUESTIONS ABOUT SEX—AND ANSWERS. *Marilyn Lyman, illustrated by Helen Kahn.* Thirty pages on: What is sex? Is sex before marriage OK? Whose values should I choose? *Planned Parenthood Center of Syracuse, Inc., 1973.*

WHAT TEENS WANT TO KNOW BUT DON'T KNOW HOW TO ASK. A concise pamphlet which answers the questions most adolescents ask about sex. *Planned Parenthood Federation of America, Inc., 1976.*

Later Teens

AM I PARENT MATERIAL? *Carole Baker.* Pamphlet listing thoughtful questions about an important decision. Available in Spanish. *National Alliance for Optional Parenthood, 1977.*

BREAKING THE SEX ROLE BARRIER. *Robert H. Loeb.* Guides the teenage reader through a structured exploration of the forces that program male and female behavior, and the myths and misconceptions involved. *Franklin Watts, Inc., 1977.*

COMMONSENSE SEX. *Ronald M. Mazur.* Based on the premise that sex is a positive aspect of human personality, and concludes with a suggestion of a liberal religious framework for decision making. *Beacon Press, 1973.*

CONCEPTION, BIRTH AND CONTRACEPTION: A VISUAL PRESENTATION. Second Edition. *Robert J. Demarest and John J. Sciarra.* A fine, concise pictorial presentation of human reproduction. Text is simply stated, expanding upon the illustrations. *McGraw-Hill Book Company, 1976.*

THE FACTS OF LOVE: LIVING, LOVING AND GROWING UP. *Alex Comfort and Jane Comfort.* A dynamic book about sexuality, ideal as a catalyst for conversations with young people. *Crown Publishers, 1979.*

GROWING UP SEXUAL. *Eleanor Morrison, Kay Starks, Cynda Hyndman, and Nina Ronzio.* Unique view of patterns of human sexual development based on anonymous autobiographical papers by students in a college human sexuality course. *D. Van Nostrand Company, 1980.*

PARENTING: A GUIDE FOR YOUNG PEOPLE. *Sol Gordon and Mina Wollin.* A thoroughly modern exposition to prepare potential parents for mature parenting roles. *William H. Sadlier, Inc., 1975.*

SEX AND BIRTH CONTROL: A GUIDE FOR THE YOUNG. Revised Edition. *E. James Lieberman and Ellen Peck.* Written to encourage sensible and responsible use of birth control, and to encourage young people to develop principles and values by which they will live their sexual lives. *Harper & Row, Publishers, in press for Spring 1981.*

SEXUALITY . . . DECISIONS, ATTITUDES, RELATIONSHIPS. *Katherine Whitlock, ed.* Booklet about how to clarify feelings about sexuality and relationships. *Planned Parenthood of Southeastern Pennsylvania, 1979.*

THE TEENAGE BODY BOOK. *Kathy McCoy and Charles Wibbelsman.* A thoughtfully written, reassuring resource for adolescents, dealing with their various psychological and physiological concerns. *Pocket Books, 1979.*

A WAY OF LOVE, A WAY OF LIFE: A YOUNG PERSON'S INTRODUCTION TO WHAT IT MEANS TO BE GAY. *Frances Hanckel and John Cunningham.* A unique, sensitive book written by people who are having the experience for people who want to understand it. *Lothrop, Lee and Shepard Books (William Morrow), 1979.*

WHAT IS A MAN? WHAT IS A WOMAN? *Morton Hunt.* Focus on sex roles and behavior for adolescents concerned with their sexual identities. *Farrar, Straus, and Giroux, 1979.*

WHY AM I SO MISERABLE IF THESE ARE THE BEST YEARS OF MY LIFE? Revised Edition. *Andrea Boroff Eagan.* Encourages young women to be self-determining. Includes factual information on physiology, menstruation, venereal disease, and birth control. *Avon Books, 1979.*

Adults

ESPECIALLY FOR MEN

GOOD SEX: A HEALTHY MAN'S GUIDE TO SEXUAL FULFILLMENT. *Gary F. Kelly.* Insightful and sensitive self-help book for men who want more total sexual fulfillment. *Harcourt Brace Jovanovich, 1979.*

THE JOY OF GAY SEX. *Charles Silverstein and Edmund White.* A-Z format. An introduction to the techniques of gay sex, including advice on various emotional components. *Crown Publishers, 1977.*

MALE "MENOPAUSE"—CRISIS IN THE MIDDLE YEARS. Useful pamphlet on the subject. *Public Affairs Committee, Inc.*

MALE SEXUALITY. *Bernie Zilbergeld.* For the man who wants to get more in touch with his own sexuality, or for any woman who wants to understand more fully the potentials of male sexuality. *Little, Brown and Co., 1978.*

MAN'S BODY: AN OWNER'S MANUAL. *The Diagram Group.* Clear answers to questions about how the male body functions, from infancy to old age. Bantam Books, 1976.

MEN'S BODIES, MEN'S SELVES. *Sam Julty.* A comprehensive collection of thoughts and information relating to men and masculinity in contemporary society. *Delta (Dell), 1979.*

THE VIEW FROM OUR SIDE: SEX AND BIRTH CONTROL FOR MEN. *Tom Zorabedian.* Well-written, intelligent booklet on the male role in sexual relationships. *Emory University—Grady Memorial Hospital Family Planning Program, 1975.*

WOMEN: A BOOK FOR MEN. *James Wagenvoord and Peyton Bailey, eds.* With its companion book, MEN: A BOOK FOR WOMEN, recommended for joint reading by heterosexual couples needing or wanting to deepen their understanding of one another as sexual persons. *Avon Books, 1979.*

ESPECIALLY FOR WOMEN

BECOMING ORGASMIC: A SEXUAL GROWTH PROGRAM FOR WOMEN. *Julia Heiman, Leslie LoPiccolo, and Joseph LoPiccolo.* A detailed growth program for women who feel they have problems in experiencing orgasm. Also includes a section relating to male partners. The emphasis is on orgasm as a part, rather than the only or primary goal, of sexuality and sexual experience. *Prentice-Hall, 1976.*

FOR YOURSELF: THE FULFILLMENT OF FEMALE SEXUALITY. *Lonnie Garfield Barbach.* Discusses sources of confusion about female sexuality, describes female sexual physiology, and suggests specific exercises women can do at home to increase their body awareness and orgasmic response. *Doubleday and Co., 1975.*

THE HITE REPORT. *Shere Hite.* Based on responses to in-depth questionnaires returned by some 3,000 women. A provocative and revealing study which examines the subject of female sexuality from the inside. Makes extensive use of direct quotes to illustrate the various topics. *Macmillan, Inc., 1976.*

THE JOY OF LESBIAN SEX. *Emily L. Sisley and Bertha Harris.* A-Z format. First major sex manual for lesbians, discussing their needs and concerns. *Crown Publishers, 1977.*

MEN: A BOOK FOR WOMEN. *James Wagenvoord and Peyton Bailey, eds.* With its companion book, WOMEN: A BOOK FOR MEN, recommended for joint reading by heterosexual couples needing or wanting to deepen their understanding of one another as sexual persons. *Avon Books, 1978.*

THE MENOPAUSE BOOK. *Louisa Rose, ed.* A carefully documented, highly readable compilation of information aimed at dispelling myths surrounding sexuality and aging. Raises some important issues concerning men and women in the middle period. *Hawthorn Books, 1977.*

MY MOTHER/MYSELF. *Nancy Friday.* An intensely personal and yet universally appealing approach to the mother-daughter relationship, focusing on the repressions and denials involved in the daughter's journey toward sexual womanhood. *Dell Publishing Co., 1977.*

OUR BODIES, OURSELVES. Revised Edition. *Boston Women's Collective.* Written by women, for women, to help them know themselves and their bodies better. Covers sexuality, contraception, women and health care, sexual physiology, and reproduction. *Simon and Schuster, 1976.*

OUR RIGHT TO LOVE: A LESBIAN RESOURCE BOOK *Ginny Vida, ed.* Sensitively chosen, remarkable collection of essays written by and for lesbians about their needs and values. *Prentice-Hall, 1978.*

WOMAN'S BODY: AN OWNER'S MANUAL. *The Diagram Group.* Well-illustrated guide with clear, straightforward information for women of all ages. *Bantam Books, 1977.*

WOMEN: MENOPAUSE AND MIDDLE AGE. *Vidal S. Clay.* A moving, compassionate book which contributes to a positive recognition of the right of postmenopausal women to a full sexual life. Includes a useful annotated bibliography and several self-study exercises. *Know, Inc., 1977.*

YOUR MENOPAUSE. Useful discussion of the subject. *Public Affairs Committee, Inc.*

General

ABORTION TO ZOOPHILIA: A SOURCEBOOK OF SEXUAL FACTS. *Anne Mandetta and Patricia Gustaveson.* A clear, sensible, information-packed book of sexual facts, conveniently presented and well backed with references. Contains a 520-item index. *Carolina Population Center, 1976.*

SEXUAL ADJUSTMENT IN MARRIAGE. CHANGING VIEWS OF HOMOSEXUAL-ITY. Written in nontechnical language, Public Affairs pamphlets are known for covering their subject matter in a concise, effective manner. *Public Affairs Committee, Inc.*

THE FAMILY BOOK ABOUT SEXUALITY. *Mary S. Calderone and Eric W. Johnson.* A creative, comprehensive approach to a family's understanding of the sexuality and sexual concerns of all of its members. Includes encyclopedic glossary of terms. *Harper & Row Publishers, in press for Spring 1981.*

THE JOY OF SEX: A GOURMET GUIDE TO LOVE-MAKING. *Alex Comfort.* A finely illustrated, civilized, and explicit guide to lovemaking. *Simon and Schuster, 1974.*

LEARNING TO LOVE: HOW TO MAKE BAD SEX GOOD AND GOOD SEX BETTER. *Paul Brown and Carolyn Faulder.* A subtle and valuable combination of sexual information, clearly described exercises, case histories, and permission-giving attitudes. *Universe Books, 1978.*

MAKING LOVE DURING PREGNANCY. *Elisabeth Bing and Libby Coleman.* Frank, firsthand description of pregnancy experiences. Discusses fears and misconceptions of future parents. *Bantam Books, 1977.*

MORE JOY. *Alex Comfort.* A sequel to *The Joy of Sex,* emphasizing the role of sex in improving relationships and personal growth. Includes sections on sex and aging and sex and the handicapped. Also discusses unconventional sex styles such as group sex. *Simon and Schuster, 1975.*

THE NEW INTIMACY. *Ronald Mazur.* A good discussion of some of the real issues involved in such alternative lifestyles as open marriage. Topics include the double standard, possessiveness and jealousy, divorce and separation. *Beacon Press, 1974.*

QUESTIONS AND ANSWERS ABOUT LOVE AND SEX. *Mary S. Calderone and the Editors of* Bride's *magazine.* Excellent practical guide and reference source which encourages the development of healthy sexual attitudes in marital relationships. *St. Martin's Press, 1979.*

SAR GUIDE FOR A BETTER SEX LIFE. *National Sex Forum.* A provocative manual for persons interested in examining their sexual attitudes and practices in order to enrich their experiences and stimulate new perspectives. *Multi-Media Resource Center, 1977.*

THE SEX BOOK: A MODERN PICTORIAL ENCYCLOPEDIA. *Martin Goldstein, Erwin J. Haeberle, and Will McBride.* Reference work viewing human sexuality as natural and beautiful. Deals with every aspect of sexual function. *Bantam Books, 1971.*

SEX FACTS. *Marilyn Lyman, illustrated by Helen Kahn.* A simply written booklet for *all* ages—anyone over 12. Discusses sex and sexuality, birth control, orgasm, sex problems, and much more. *Planned Parenthood of Syracuse, Inc., 1977.*

SEX TALK. *Myron Brenton.* Recognizing the need for clear communication about sex between man and woman, parent and child, suggests how such communication can be achieved. *Stein and Day, 1977.*

SEXUAL AWARENESS: A PRACTICAL BOOK. *Barry W. McCarthy, Mary Ryan, and Fred A. Johnson.* Suggests exercises to enhance sexual enjoyment and comfort, including ways to increase vaginal feeling and response, and improve arousal and ejaculatory control in men. *Boyd and Fraser, 1975.*

SEXUAL MYTHS AND FALLACIES. *James Leslie McCary.* Seventy sexual myths explored in the light of the best information available. *Schocken Books, 1973.*

SOME THINGS ABOUT SEX FOR BOTH MEN AND WOMEN. *Nancy G. Varner and Malcolm G. Freeman.* Simplified explanations of sexual intercourse, masturbation, birth control, etc. An excellent resource for limited readers of all ages. *Emory University, Grady Memorial Hospital Family Planning Program, 1976.*

UNDERSTANDING GAY RELATIVES AND FRIENDS. *Clinton R. Jones.* Sensitive, useful book by an Episcopal priest with insightful psychological and theological reflections on the interpersonal relations of gay people and their families and friends. *Seabury Press, 1978.*

Especially for Parents

A FAMILY MATTER: A PARENTS' GUIDE TO HOMOSEXUALITY. *Charles Silverstein.* Written for parents with a homosexual child, examining the realities of the situation, and suggesting how to turn the experience into a positive relationship. *McGraw-Hill, 1977.*

THE FLIGHT OF THE STORK. *Anne C. Bernstein.* A book for parents, using theories from Piaget and Kohlberg, illustrating how to explain reproduction in terms of children's understanding at various age levels. *Delacorte Press, 1978.*

HOW TO TELL YOUR CHILD ABOUT SEX.

SCHOOLS AND PARENTS—PARTNERS IN SEX EDUCATION.

SEX EDUCATION: THE PARENTS' ROLE.

TALKING TO PRETEENAGERS ABOUT SEX. Well-written pamphlets designed to give advice and accurate information to parents. *Public Affairs Committee, Inc.*

NOT MY DAUGHTER: FACING UP TO ADOLESCENT PREGNANCY. *Katherine B. Oettinger with Elizabeth Monney.* Helpful for parents and for those seeking perspectives on the problem in their search for preventive measures. Stresses need for early communication between adults and teens. *Prentice-Hall, 1979.*

NOW THAT YOU KNOW: WHAT EVERY PARENT SHOULD KNOW ABOUT HOMOSEXUALITY. *Betty Fairchild and Nancy Hayward.* Informative, sensitively written guide for parents of homosexuals. Highly recommended. *Harcourt Brace Jovanovich, 1979.*

RIGHT FROM THE START. *Selma Greenberg.* Recommended for parents who want to help children of either sex build on their own particular strengths. Redefines motherhood, fatherhood, and family power relationships, and demonstrates how differential treatment of boys and girls hinders their development. *Houghton Mifflin, 1979.*

THE ROOTS OF LOVE: HELPING YOUR CHILD LEARN TO LOVE IN THE FIRST THREE YEARS OF LIFE. *Helene S. Arnstein.* Shows how physical, mental, and motor development in the young child relate to concurrent emotional development. Suggests methods for parents to use in helping their infants' growing ability to love and form human attachments. *Bobbs-Merrill, 1975.*

SEX AND THE SINGLE PARENT. *Jane Adams.* Realistic portrait of intellectual and emotional struggles. Recommended for practitioners dealing with single-parent families, as well as for the members of single-parent families themselves, including adolescents. *Coward, McCann and Geoghegan, 1978.*

SEX EDUCATION AT HOME: A GUIDE FOR PARENTS. *Marilyn Lyman.* This pamphlet presents an excellent and easy-to-read basic approach to the topic. *Planned Parenthood Center of Syracuse, Inc., 1974.*

SEX EDUCATION FOR TODAY'S CHILD: A GUIDE FOR MODERN PARENTS. *Arlene S. Uslander, Caroline Weiss, and Judith Telman.* Provides model answers to typical questions asked by children concerning sex. *Association Press/Follett, 1977.*

YOUR CHILD AND SEX: A GUIDE FOR PARENTS. *Wardell Pomeroy.* Gives parents a better understanding of their own sexuality, both in their marriage relationship and in their relationships with their children. Also deals with ways and means of talking about sex to children at various age levels, from the very young to postadolescents. *Delacorte Press, 1976.*

Sexuality and the Later Years

THE FIRES OF AUTUMN: SEXUAL ACTIVITY IN THE MIDDLE AND LATER YEARS. *Peter A. Dickinson.* Encyclopedic and wide open on the topic of sexuality and aging. Written in a witty and humorous style. *Sterling Publishing, 1977.*

GOOD SEX AFTER FIFTY. *Ruth K. Witkin and Robert J. Nissen.* Compact, well-written booklet designed to encourage middle-aged and older people to maintain their sexual life. *Regency Press, 1980.*

SEX AFTER SIXTY-FIVE. Useful pamphlet for older people about sexual concerns. *Public Affairs Committee, Inc.*

SEX AFTER SIXTY. *Robert N. Butler and Myrna I. Lewis.* Practical book giving older people guidance in enjoying—to whatever degree, and in whatever way, they wish—the satisfactions of physical sex and pleasurable sensuality. *Harper & Row, 1976.*

SEXUALITY AND AGING. *Mona Wasow.* Sensitively written booklet for older people, maintaining that sex should be a pleasure, not a chore. *Family Life Publications, 1976.*

SOUND SEX AND THE AGING HEART. *Lee D. Scheingold and Nathaniel N. Wagner.* Discusses sex in the middle and later years, with special reference to cardiac problems. *Human Sciences Press, 1974.*

Special Concerns: or Disability

FEMALE SEXUALITY FOLLOWING SPINAL CORD INJURY. *Elle F. Becker.* Offers an opportunity to understand the struggle of a quadriplegic or paraplegic woman in a world that represses and defies her sexual expression and identity, and to learn what disabled people look to from the professional community, and from their families and friends. *Cheever Publishing, 1978.*

LIVING FULLY: A GUIDE FOR YOUNG PEOPLE WITH A HANDICAP, THEIR PARENTS, THEIR TEACHERS, AND PROFESSIONALS. *Sol Gordon, Charles Weening, Betty Lou Kratoville, and Doug Biklen.* Designed to help integrate a disabled person into all aspects of society. *Ed-U Press, 1975.*

LOVE, SEX, AND BIRTH CONTROL FOR MENTALLY RETARDED: A GUIDE FOR PARENTS. *Winifred Kempton, Medora Bass, and Sol Gordon.* Thoughtful guide for parents of mentally handicapped, covering sex education and sexual responsibility. Available in Spanish. *Planned Parenthood of Southeastern Pennsylvania, 1973.*

THE SENSUOUS WHEELER: SEXUAL ADJUSTMENT FOR THE SPINAL CORD INJURED. *Barry J. Rabin.* Informal, positive treatment of the subject, stressing the sharing of sexual responsibilities and vulnerabilities. *Multi-Media Resource Center, 1980.*

SEX EDUCATION FOR DISABLED PERSONS. Useful guide outlining sexual concerns of the disabled. *Public Affairs Committee, Inc.*

SEXUAL OPTIONS FOR PARAPLEGICS AND QUADRIPLEGICS. *Thomas O. Mooney, Theodore M. Cole, and Richard A. Chilgren.* Because the senior author is a near quadriplegic himself, a personalized style of writing results that, with the explicit illustrations, provides an excellent self-help, teaching, or counseling resource. *Little, Brown, 1975.*

TOWARD INTIMACY: FAMILY PLANNING AND SEXUALITY CONCERNS OF PHYSICALLY DISABLED WOMEN. *The Task Force on the Concerns of Physically Disabled Women.* Booklet discussing various relationships within a disabled woman's life, to promote communication and understanding. *Human Sciences Press, 1978.*

Publishers and Distributors

ASSOCIATION PRESS/FOLLETT CORPORATION
1010 W. Washington Blvd.,
Chicago, IL 60607

AVON BOOKS
959 Eighth Avenue,
New York, NY 10019

Bantam Books, Inc.
666 Fifth Avenue
New York, NY 10019

Barron's Educational Series Inc.
113 Crossways Park Drive
Woodbury, NY 11797

Beacon Press
25 Beacon Street
Boston, MA 02108

The Bobbs-Merrill Co., Inc.
4300 West 62nd Street
Indianapolis, IN 46206

Boyd & Fraser Publishing Company
3627 Sacramento Street
San Francisco, CA 94118

Carolina Population Center
University Square
Chapel Hill, NC 27514

Cheever Publishing Company
P.O. Box 700
Bloomington, IL 61701

CHOICE
1501 Cherry Street
Philadelphia, PA 19102

Coward, McCann & Geoghegan, Inc.
200 Madison Avenue
New York, NY 10016

Crown Publishers, Inc.
1 Park Avenue
New York, NY 10016

Daughters Publishing Co., Inc.
Ms590, Box 42999
Houston, TX 77042

Dell Publishing Co., Inc. (Delacorte Press; Delta Books)
1 Dag Hammarskjold Plaza
New York, NY 10017

Doubleday & Co., Inc.
501 Franklin Avenue
Garden City, NY 11530

Ed-U Press
P.O. Box 583
Fayetteville, NY 13066

Emory University Grady Memorial Hospital
Family Planning Program
80 Butler Street SE
Atlanta, GA 30303

Family Life Publications, Inc.
219 Henderson Street
P.O. Box 427
Saluda, NC 28773

Farrar, Straus & Giroux, Inc.
19 Union Square West
New York, NY 10003

Harcourt Brace Jovanovich, Inc.
757 Third Avenue
New York, NY 10017

Harper & Row, Publishers, Inc.
10 East 53rd Street
New York, NY 10022

Hawthorn Books, Inc.
260 Madison Avenue
New York, NY 10016

Houghton Mifflin Company
1 Beacon Street
Boston, MA 02107

Human Sciences Press
72 Fifth Avenue
New York, NY 10011

Know, Inc.
Box 86031
Pittsburgh, PA 15221

Lippincott & Crowell, Publishers
See Harper & Row, Publishers, Inc.

Little, Brown & Company
34 Beacon Street
Boston, MA 02106

Lothrop, Lee & Shepard Company
See William Morrow & Co., Inc.

Macmillan, Inc.
855 Third Avenue
New York, NY 10022

McGraw-Hill Book Company
1221 Avenue of the Americas
New York, NY 10020

William Morrow & Co., Inc.
105 Madison Avenue
New York, NY 10016

Multi Media Resource Center
1525 Franklin Street
San Francisco, CA 94109

National Alliance for Optional Parenthood
2010 Massachusetts Avenue NW
Washington, DC 20036

New Glide Publications
330 Ellis Street
San Francisco, CA 94102

Peace Press
3828 Willat Avenue
Culver City, CA 90230

Planned Parenthood Federation of America, Inc.
Publications Section
810 Seventh Avenue
New York, NY 10019

Planned Parenthood Center of Syracuse, Inc.
1120 East Genesee Street
Syracuse, NY 13210

Planned Parenthood of Southeastern Pennsylvania
1220 Sansom Street
Philadelphia, PA 19107

Pocket Books
See Simon & Schuster, Inc.

Prentice-Hall, Inc.
Englewood Cliffs, NJ 07632

Public Affairs Committee, Inc.
381 Park Avenue South
New York, NY 10016

Regency Press
32 Ridge Drive
Port Washington, NY 11050

Rocky Mountain Planned Parenthood, Inc.
1852 Vine Street
Denver, CO 80206

William H. Sadlier, Inc.
11 Park Place
New York, NY 10007

St. Martin's Press, Inc.
175 Fifth Avenue
New York, NY 10010

Schocken Books, Inc.
200 Madison Avenue
New York, NY 10016

The Seabury Press, Inc.
815 Second Avenue
New York, NY 10017

Simon & Schuster, Inc.
1230 Avenue of the Americas
New York, NY 10020

Stein & Day Publishers
Scarborough House
Briarcliff Manor, NY 10510

Sterling Publishing Co., Inc.
2 Park Avenue
New York, NY 10016

Lyle Stuart, Inc.
120 Enterprise Avenue
Secaucus, NJ 07094

Time-Life Books
777 Duke Street
Alexandria, VA 22314

Universe Books
381 Park Avenue South
New York, NY 10016

D. Van Nostrand Company
Van Nostrand Reinhold Company
135 West 50th Street
New York, NY 10020

Franklin Watts, Inc.
730 Fifth Avenue
New York, NY 10019

Sources of Help

Sometimes when people have personal problems, especially those relating to an aspect of sexuality, they feel desperately that there really is no one to turn to for help. That might have been so twenty years ago, but it is no longer true today, even though perhaps in some of the less populated areas of the country it still might be true. Nevertheless, the saying that "help is just a phone call away" is really so. With perseverance, what might seem like a fairly long series of telephone calls, each one leading to another, will usually pay off. What is important is to find a way of judging how responsible is the source of that help. So think first of asking someone you trust—your doctor, religious adviser, a friend. There's nothing shameful today about seeking help for personal problems, including sexual ones.

Today also, in contrast to ten years ago, medical schools and hospitals are beginning to accept their responsibility as sources of help for many community problems, as are the public health departments of cities and states. So keep on looking for what you need, asking plenty of questions and making sure that what you are getting is on the up-and-up and can really be helpful to you.

It is worthwhile, though, at the same time to use the pages of your telephone book, whether the white or the yellow, to track down local addresses where active services are provided for special needs. For instance, in the white pages of the Manhattan telephone book alone there is one reference to a crisis intervention center; two for rape counseling, including a rape hot line; two for birth control; one for sterilization; and eleven for abortion information, including two 800 hot-line numbers. And in the yellow pages, under Counseling, appears the following item:

Counseling—Personal & Family
See "Clergy," "Clinic," "Marriage & Family Counselors,"
"Medical Groups," "Physicians & Surgeons (M.D.),"
"Psychologists," "Social Svce. Organizations"

There are many, many adolescent and teenage counseling centers in the United States. These are generally connected with the pediatric or psychiatric departments of a local hospital or medical school, or with a Planned Parenthood organization, so that they can be easily located in the local telephone book and called for details. Counseling about sexual problems is most usually included in the work of such centers.

Although reading about human sexuality in its many aspects can be immensely helpful, because it allows time for thought and for confronting oneself with attitudes and beliefs that perhaps need refurbishing or replacement, there are inevitably certain times when only direct one-to-one consultation will do. Rather than list the manifold organizations that, whether tangentially or directly, might supply such help, we have elected to list below only certain national organizations to which readers can write to find out where, in their own localities, they may obtain direct assistance.

National Organizations

General Counseling Services

FAMILY SERVICE ASSOCIATION
44 East 23 Street, New York, NY 10010   (212) 674-6100
Over 300 agencies in the United States are affiliated with the Family Service Association of America, and where you live may be the site of one of them. Look in the telephone book under the following headings: Family Service Association, Council for Community Services, County Department of Health, Counseling Clinic, Mental Health Clinic, United Fund. If the agency you reach in your community is unable to help you with your specific problem, write to the New York office.

Birth Control, Contraception, Family Planning

HUMAN LIFE AND NATURAL PLANNING FOUNDATION OF AMERICA
205 South Patrick Street, Alexandria VA   (703) 836-3377

PLANNED PARENTHOOD FEDERATION OF AMERICA, INC.
810 Seventh Avenue, New York, NY 10019   (212) 541-7800
If you cannot find a listing under Planned Parenthood in your telephone book, this national organization will send you the name and address of its affiliate nearest to you. You should remember that young people under the age of 18 have been given the legal right to obtain contraceptive information independently of their parents.

Breast-Feeding

LALECHE LEAGUE INTERNATIONAL
9616 Minneapolis Avenue, Franklin Park, IL 60131   (312) 455-7730

Childbirth

Look in the telephone book white pages of the city, county, or state where you live under Department of Public Health, and ask for information on prenatal care or childbirth classes.

MATERNITY CENTER ASSOCIATION
48 East 92 Street, New York, NY 10028   (212) 369-7300
Will send you information about childbirth education.

Disability

SEX AND DISABILITY PROJECT
1828 L Street NW, Washington, DC 20036   (202) 676-6377
The Sex and Disabiliy Project produces a handbook that includes a list of nationwide resources for sexual health care for people with disabilities.

Gay Services

There are many of these in the United States, including hot lines and counseling centers. For immediate information you might look in your own telephone book under gay, homosexual, or lesbian. You might get the information you need from the Gay Switchboard in Philadelphia (215) 928-1919, or write to any of the following:

GAY COMMUNITY SERVICES CENTER
1213 North Highland, Hollywood, CA 90028   (213) 437-4621

HOMOSEXUAL COMMUNITY COUNSELING CENTER
30 East 60 Street, New York, NY 10021   (212) 688-0628

GAY INFORMATION CENTER
5020 Cathedral Avenue NW, Washington, DC 20008   (202) 363-3381

Genetic Counseling

THE NATIONAL GENETICS FOUNDATION
555 West 57 Street, New York, NY 10019   (212) 586-5800

Marriage and Family Counseling

AMERICAN ASSOCIATION OF MARRIAGE AND FAMILY COUNSELORS &
THERAPISTS
924 West 9 Street, Upland, CA 91786   (714) 981-0888
Can refer you to accredited members of the organization in your area.

COUPLE TO COUPLE LEAGUE
P.O. Box 11084, Cincinnati, Ohio 45211   (513) 661-7612

Parenthood or Nonparenthood

NATIONAL ALLIANCE FOR OPTIONAL PARENTHOOD
2010 Massachusetts Avenue NW, Washington, DC 20036
(202) 296-7474
This organization recognizes that many people will decide not to become
parents, either temporarily or permanently. It has free literature that may
help you arrive at a decision that will fit your life plan.

Sex Education, Sex Therapy

AMERICAN ASSOCIATION OF SEX EDUCATORS, COUNSELORS & THERAPISTS
Suite 2700, One East Wacker Drive, Chicago, IL 60601
(312) 222-1600
Maintains a listing of sex educators and therapists accredited by the organization in the United States.

Sterilization

ASSOCIATION FOR VOLUNTARY STERILIZATION
708 Third Avenue, New York, NY 10017   (212) 573-8350
For information on sterilization for men or women and the names of physicians in your area who perform this procedure.

Hot Lines

In the last five years several hundred crisis hot lines have been established. The people who serve these hot lines are for the most part trained especially to refer you for specific help that you might need. Quite a number of these have been for the use of teens exclusively, whatever their problems may be.

Abortion

ABORTION AND BIRTH CONTROL CENTER (PA)
(800) 523-5101 (toll free)

ABORTION COUNSELING, INFORMATION & REFERRAL SERVICES
(212) 873-6650

ABORTION INFORMATION SERVICE
(800) 321-0575 (toll free)

Alternatives to Abortion

FLORENCE CRITTENTON ASSOCIATION
67 Irving Place, New York, NY 10011   (212) 254-7410
May be listed in your telephone book and can help you with discussions of the alternatives to abortion. If you do not find such a listing, write to the one in New York City.

Birthright

Check white pages for local listing.

Marriage

SAVE A MARRIAGE INC.
41 Central Park West, New York, NY 10023   (212) 799-0101
Trained marriage counselors can refer you for help in a crisis.

Rape

If you are raped or are unwillingly involved in a sexual relationship with someone whom you feel is taking advantage of you, check your local pages under Rape Crisis Center, or Rape Crisis Hot Line, or Children's Protective Services, or call (212) 777-4000.

Runaways

NATIONAL RUNAWAY SWITCHBOARD
(800) 621-4000; in Illinois, (800) 972-6004 (toll free)
This is a special service for young people who have run away from home, and for their parents. This number can refer you to a source of help in your community or wherever you are.

Sex

COMMUNITY SEX INFORMATION INC.
380 Second Avenue, New York, NY 10010   (212) 982-0052
Highly trained professional volunteers answer your questions week nights, 6 P.M. to 8 P.M.

Venereal Disease

VD NATIONAL HOT LINE
(800) 227-8922 outside California (toll free), 11:30 A.M. to 1:30 A.M. (Eastern Time); (800) 982-5883 in California (toll free), 8:00 A.M. to 8:00 P.M. weekdays, 10:00 A.M. to 6:00 P.M. weekends (Pacific Time).
It provides counseling and referral service over the telephone at no charge.

General Index

coils, IUD, 88
coitus, *see* sexual intercourse
coitus interruptus, 85
Cole, Theodore, 159
colostrum, 72
"coming," *see* ejaculation
communication:
  advice and, 146–147
  children's initiative in, 147–148
  intimacy and, 31–32
  opportunities for, 143–145, 146–147,
    150, 151, 153–154
  about sex, in family, 143–148
  in sexual relationships, 29
  slang and, 152–153, 172–173
conception, 76–77
  process of, 33–34
  sexual development and, 3
  see also pregnancy
condoms (rubbers), 82, 83–85
Constitution, U.S., 103, 179–180
contraception (birth control), 80–106
  abortion as, 99–106
  advice on, 82, 94–97
  combining methods of, 85–86
  comparison of methods of, 93–94, 95
  consistency of use, 86
  as couple's decision, 82
  failure of, 97
  legal status of, 96
  methods not recommended at all, 93
  methods not requiring doctor's help,
    83–86
  methods requiring doctor's help, 86–93
  wrong information as problem in, 94
Copper 7, IUD, 88
Copper T, IUD, 87
copulation, 54
counseling:
  on birth control, 82, 94–97, 101–102
  on family sexual problems, 138
  marriage, 125, 130–131
  on physical conditions affecting sexual
    life, 121
  for rape victims, 191–192
  for sexual dysfunctions, 31
  sources of help and, 28, 66, 101, 130,
    191–192, 201–205, 315–320
Cowper's glands, 36
creams, spermicidal, 82, 85
culdoscopy, 92
cultural differences, 12, 172, 177
  see also society

death of partner, as crisis, 122–123
decision-making, sexual activity and, 108,
  222–225
  ethical and moral principles in, 223–225

decision-making (*cont'd*)
  family planning and, 108
  self-knowledge and, 222–223
diaphragms, as contraceptive, 82, 88–89
dilation and curettage (D & C) method,
  induced abortion, 100
"dirty words," 153
disabled people, 157–160
  mentally, 160
  physically, 159–160
  young, 157–159
divorce, as crisis, 122–123
douching, as ineffective contraceptive, 93
drugs:
  fertility, 73
  in menopause, 75
  during pregnancy, 58–59
  sexual problems and, 196–198
dysfunctions, sexual, *see* sexual problems
dyspareunia, 31

eggs (ova):
  birth control pill and, 86
  female reproductive cycle and, 39–41, 57
  fertilized (zygote), 41
  multiple births and, 73
  in reproductive act, 57
  X chromosome in, 3
ejaculation:
  "coming" as, 39
  premature, 30
  process of, 39
  at puberty, 14, 51
  in reproductive act, 57
Electra complex, 178
embryos, 60
endometrium, 41, 60
epididymis, 37, 38
erections, penis:
  aging and, 120–121
  of fetus, 63
  prostate surgery and, 121
estrogen, 109
  synthetic, as contraceptive, 92
  XX chromosomes and, 3–4
estrogen replacement therapy, 75
excitement stage, in response cycle, 16
exhibitionism, 174, 176

fallopian tubes, 41, 57
family, 132–154
  adolescents in, 140–143
  changing concepts of, 131, 133, 161
  choices in form of, 134–135
  communication about sex in, 143–148,
    151, 153–154
  definition and function of, 133–134
  differing attitudes and, 148

Peeping Toms, 194
penis (phallus):
  description and function of, 34–37
  erection of, 18, 63, 120–121
  of fetus, 61, 63
  orgasm and, 16
  in reproductive act, 57
"period," *see* menstruation
"perversion," as question, 112–113
pictures, nude, 153–154
Pilagá Indians, 12
pill, birth control, *see* birth control pills
pimps, 186
placenta, 60, 67
Planned Parenthood, 97, 101, 221
plateau stage, in response cycle, 16
Pomeroy, Wardell, 57
population concerns, 80–81, 106–108
  religious beliefs and, 170
pornography, 179–184
  civil rights and, 179–180, 184
  definition of, 179–180
  as "explicit sexual material," 179
  sexual arousal by, 180–181
pregnancy, 57–63
  care during, 58–59
  first trimester of, 60–61, 99–100, 102
  high-risk age-group for, 81
  length of, 59–60
  miscarriage of, 99
  second trimester of, 61, 63, 100–101,
    102
  sexual intercourse during, 58
  as shared experience, 59
  signs of, 49, 57–58
  third trimester of, 63, 102
  tribal, 88
  unplanned, choices after, 98–106
  venereal disease and, 199
premature ejaculation, 30
prenatal sexual development, 3–4, 76–77
Presidential Commission on Obscenity and
    Pornography, 184
"primal scene," 140
privacy, importance of, 23, 148–149
programming, sexual:
  after birth, 110
  before birth, 3, 73, 76, 109–110
"Pro-Life" groups, 103
prophylactics (condoms), 83–85
prostaglandins method, induced abortion,
    101
prostate gland, 39, 101
  orgasm and, 16
  surgery of, sexual vitality and, 121
prostitution, 184–189
  child, 186–187
  decline of, 187

prostitution (*cont'd*)
  forms of, 185–186
  individual's character in, 185
  legal aspects of, 184–185, 188, 189
  male, 186, 187
  venereal disease and, 188
psychoanalytic theory, 177–178
puberty:
  age differences for, 49, 51, 54
  description of, 6–7
  growth spurt at, 51, 54
  ova maturation at, 39
  reproductivity and, 3
  timetable, 49–54
pubic hair, appearance of, 51, 54
Public Health Service, U.S., venereal
    disease and, 199, 200, 202–203
punishment, sexual arousal and, 30

quadruplets, 73
quintuplets, 73

rape, 189–193
  as act of violence, 189
  child molestation vs., 173
  counseling for victims of, 191–192
  precautions against, 190–191
  rapists' character and, 190
  statutory, 193
reciprocity, intimacy and, 31–32
refractory period, in response cycle, 17
rehearsal play, in childhood, 25–26
religious beliefs:
  on abortion, 103
  birth control methods and, 91, 97
  counseling and, 97
  on homosexuality, 119
  human sexuality training and, 216
  marriage counseling and, 130
  masturbation and, 27, 170
  negative feelings about sex and, 169–172
  sexual decision-making and, 224
  values vs., 210
remarriage, children and, 137
reproductive act, 54, 57
reproductive systems, *see* sexual
    reproductive systems
reproductivity, sexualization process vs., 3
research, new findings from, 1, 4, 14, 113, 114
resolution stage, in response cycle, 17
rhythm method, of contraception, 89
"Right to Life" groups, 103
rings, IUD, 88
role models, 118
  for marriage, 125, 127–128, 130
  in media, 11
  parents as, 5–6, 11–12, 27–28, 125,
    127–128, 130, 136